BEST RADIO
PLAYS OF 1990

BEST RADIO PLAYS OF 1990

with an Introduction
by Alan Drury

The Giles Cooper Award Winners

Tony Bagley: The Machine
David Cregan: A Butler Did It
John Fletcher: Death and the Tango
Tina Pepler: Song of the Forest
Steve Walker: The Pope's Brother

METHUEN/BBC PUBLICATIONS

First published in Great Britain in 1991 by Methuen Drama,
Michelin House, 81 Fulham Road, London SW3 6RB and
distributed in the USA by HEB Inc., 361 Hanover Street,
Portsmouth, New Hampshire NH 03801 3959 and in the UK by
BBC Publications, 35 Marylebone High Street, London W1M 4AA.

A CIP catalogue record for this book
is available from the British Library

ISBN 0-413-65210-6

Typeset in Garamond by
Hewer Text Composition Services, Edinburgh
Printed in Great Britain by
St Edmundsbury Press, Bury St Edmunds, Suffolk

CONTENTS

THE GILES COOPER AWARDS: a note on the selection

Giles Cooper

As one of the most original and inventive radio playwrights of the post-war years, Giles Cooper was the author who came most clearly to mind when the BBC and Methuen were in search of a name when first setting up their jointly sponsored radio drama awards in 1978. Particularly so, as the aim of the awards is precisely to encourage original radio writing by both new and established authors – encouragement in the form of both public acclaim and of publication of their work in book form.

Eligibility

Eligible for the awards was every original radio play first broadcast by the BBC domestic service from December 1989 to December 1990 (almost 500 plays in total). Excluded from consideration were translations, adaptations and dramatised 'features'. In order to ensure that a broad range of radio playwriting was represented, the judges aimed to select plays which offered a variety of length, subject matter and technique by authors with differing experience of writing for radio.

Selection

The editors-in-charge and producers of the various drama 'slots' were each asked to put forward about five or six plays for the judges' consideration. This resulted in a 'short-list' of some 30 plays from which the final selection was made. The judges were entitled to nominate further plays for consideration provided they were eligible. Selection was made on the strength of the script rather than of the production, since it was felt that the awards were primarily for writing and that production could unduly enhance or detract from the merits of the original script.

Judges

The judges for the 1990 awards were:
Peter Davalle, radio critic for *The Times*
Alan Drury, Literary Manager, BBC Radio Drama
Michael Earley, Senior Editor, Methuen Drama
Diana Quick, actress

INTRODUCTION

It is traditional to say that radio is the purest medium for the dramatist, and on the surface it is clear to see why this is so. There are the words, the actors and the listener, and that, give or take a few sound effects, would seem to be that. One is not lumbered with a film director trying to be an auteur; whoever refers to Douglas Cleverdon's *Under Milk Wood*? Neither does one have to contend with a shamanistic stage director eager to make an interpretive statement, although the BBC did recently broadcast a production of Shakespeare's *King John* in which there was a helicopter. The attraction of radio to the playwright is the directness of its through line – from the mind of the dramatist to the mind of the listener with the fewest possible filters – and the Giles Cooper Awards, the radio play awards to be judged on scripts rather than production, celebrate this.

Of course it is not quite so simple. No medium is transparent, and the purity of radio stems from another source. When we are in the theatre, we are watching real people in the same time and place as us. They are showing us an artificial experience which has been stylised, but receiving it is nevertheless an authentic transaction between them and us. We are in the same world and the actor's reality is our reality, even if that reality is the creation of an illusion. The relationship between audience and reality in the cinema is different. Film gives us an edited reality, and our sense of it is a result of the selection and subtraction of detail. In theatre it is suggested where you look, but you don't have to. In the cinema you are given no choice in the matter. The whole process of film making, from setting up the camera angle to the final edit, is a process of excluding irrelevant detail. Whereas the reality of theatre is ultimately mutual, that of film is based on selection, reduction. The reality of radio drama, on the other hand, is based on accretion.

Radio starts from silence, to which things are added, and each layer of additions brings its own network of detail and implication, suggesting things to the listener. Film shows but radio implies, and it is the particular skill of people working in all functions in radio to give the listener enough to go on but not too much so the audience is overloaded and cannot see the wood for the trees. Film sculpts a reality from its material; radio conjures a reality from nothing and this is what gives it its particular directness, its particular sense of purity. (Television is a hybrid medium, and appears to have a hybrid aesthetic. A TV studio drama works in a different way from a TV film. There are many sophisticated arguments taking all sorts of things into account, even that there is grain in film but not in videotape, but the jury is still out.) Radio creates a world, film reveals it. Giles Cooper instinctively understood this, and a recurring theme in his radio work was the creation of worlds, both public and private.

In *Mathry Beacon* a group of people on an isolated Welsh hill-top are unaware that the Second World War has ended, and have their own alternative reality until the final inevitable collision occurs. In *Under the Loofah Tree*, as in so many Cooper pieces, we enter the private mental world of a man having a bath, and characteristically it proves extremely potent. The power of a lot of Cooper's work stems from his writing paralleling the act of listening.

The five Giles Cooper Award winning plays of 1990 all create their own distinctive worlds; indeed the selection looks as if a mythopoeic editorial decision had been taken by the judges. This was not the case, but all five plays have the power to draw you into their own universe. Whereas film and theatre are designed for the collective response of an audience, most radio plays are listened to in audiences of one or at most two, and their potency is in their ability to provoke an individual, subjective rather than aggregate response. This is not to say, however, that the natural territory of radio drama is the outer reach of solipsism. It deals with the outside world, the real worlds, the political world; but its strategies are more insidious than social realism, be it (as it was) at the Royal Court or in the 'Wednesday Play'.

Tony Bagley's *The Machine* creates an alternative Jacobean era with a mechanical, non-electrical prototype of the tape-recorder. All looks set for a period re-run of the play *Krapp's Last Tape*, but that leaves out the other side of the play; an economic and socially precise account of the protagonist's job in terms of the Poor Laws, which is sketched in with Edward Bond like flintiness. This incursion of the real world opens up the piece to basic metaphysical speculation about good, evil and the place of the soul. David Cregan, on the other hand, uses the formal freneticism of farce in *A Butler Did It* to analyse shifting social currents of the last twelve years. This is no treatise and is full of his characteristic wit, and manages to bring off at one point an elegantly Freudian nightmare which, I suspect, would only work on radio – after all, the natural place for nudity.

It is always said that radio has the best pictures, and John Fletcher's *Death and the Tango* has two of the most striking visual images I have encountered in a year of reading scripts for all media. Two ordinary Birmingham men, with only an interest in the tango to mark them out, take us on an extraordinary odyssey to the end of the world on a ship of fools and back to a transformed, transcendent Birmingham. A fair part of the power of the piece comes from the precision of the images. This is a gradually transforming world, but it is a concrete one.

Tina Pepler's *Song of the Forest* creates a very abstract world, the mind of a monkey, and it becomes clear that something else is going on, which I don't want to spoil. Again the detail with which the play's worlds are built allows the author to explore the most crucial questions about man's relationship to other animals and the natural environment. Finally, Steve Walker's *The Pope's Brother* is a baroque comedy, playing with many of the themes of *The Machine* and *Death and the Tango*, again a coincidence rather than a deliberate editorial decision. It starts in a betting shop and ends with a confrontation with a comic vision of ultimate evil, a journey that can only be taken from a recognisable world.

What of the context in which these plays are written? Previous introductions have noted the contraction of theatrical new writing in this country, and as we enter a period of renewed pressure on the public funding of theatre, in some cases terminal, things can only get worse. However, despite changes in scheduling, the amount of drama broadcast by BBC radio remains constant. It covers the whole range of drama: from thriller to intellectual experiment, from comedy to love story, from classic adaptation to soap opera. Most of the drama department's output is heard on Radios 4 and 3, and the normal lengths of plays are 30, 60, 75 and 90 minutes.

Generally, the longer plays are broadcast in the afternoon and evening. Scripts should be submitted either to individual producers in London or the regional production centres, or to the Literary Manager in London. A free booklet with further information on radio drama and some practical tips, *Writing Plays For Radio*, is available if you send a stamped addressed envelope to The Literary Manager, BBC Radio Drama, Broadcasting House, London, W1A 1AA. Radio 5 presents a range of early evening drama aimed at younger listeners, which is made entirely separately from the drama department. A look at *Radio Times* will give an up-to-date feel of the range of drama being done across all channels, but for specific details of Radio 5 contact the Editor, Drama, Radio 5 at Broadcasting House in London. BBC TV Drama have closed down their TV Drama Script Unit, and it is not clear what, if anything, will replace it.

Radio drama hardly exists outside of BBC national radio networks. Some local stations, both BBC and commercial, do a very occasional original play, but it is rare. Others have a policy of broadcasting radio versions of local theatre productions, but again they are few and far between. LBC, one of the London commercial stations, had been developing drama but have now virtually pulled out of the area, leaving their talented and ingenious independent producers stranded.

Drama is an expensive form of broadcasting compared to music, chat-shows and phone-ins, and it will be fascinating to see if the successful bidders for the new national commercial radio networks will contain drama in their proposals and, if they do, whether it survives.

Alan Drury
Literary Manager, BBC Radio Drama
April 1991

THE MACHINE

by Tony Bagley

Tony Bagley lives in Sussex and has worked variously as a transportation economist, journalist, copy editor and script reader. Apart from *The Machine*, his radio plays include *Catching Bullets*, *Life on a New Planet* and *Public Interest*. Between 1986 and 1988 he contributed scripts to *The Archers* and he has recently written some episodes for the new BBC 1 police series, *The Specials*. The BFI Production Board awarded a grant to produce his screenplay *Enemy*. A stage play, *The New Boy*, was performed in the 1983 Brighton Festival. He has just had two comedy pilot scripts commissioned by BBC Radio Light Entertainment and over the years has had copious sketch material performed on TV (*Smith & Jones*, *Spitting Image*, etc.) and on radio (*Arnold Brown*).

The Machine was first broadcast on 'Drama Now,' BBC Radio 3 on 16 October 1990. The cast was as follows:

NED PRYNNE	James Bolam
RICHARD CORNFORD	Simon Treves
TYLER	Paul Nicholson
THOMAS BLACKTIN	Stephen Sylvester
HEPPENSTAL	Anthony Donovan
A PETTY CONSTABLE	David Bannerman
A BOY	Kim Wall
A GIRL	Josephine Sinclair

Director: Alec Reid
Running time, as broadcast: 1 hour

The action takes place in southern England in 1602.

Scene 1

Interior. PRYNNE's *workroom. Day. Soft, grinding noise as* PRYNNE *turns spindle.*

PRYNNE'S VOICE (*filtered, distorted*). My name is Ned Prynne . . . (*Stops spindle.*)

PRYNNE (*disbelief*). It was me! (*Turns spindle again.*)

PRYNNE'S VOICE (*still filtered*). My name . . . (*Stops spindle.*)

PRYNNE. Not just the words . . . the voice too! (*Starts spindle.*)

PRYNNE'S VOICE (*more distortion*). . . . is Ned Prynne.

PRYNNE. My voice . . . speaking my words. Perishable words . . . gone this past hour . . . back from the dead!

PRYNNE'S VOICE. My name . . .

PRYNNE. Not just the words . . . the manner in which they are conveyed.

PRYNNE'S VOICE (*now barely audible*). . . . is Ned Prynne. . . .

PRYNNE. It's going . . . a pulse only now . . . as if trying to control its own rhythm.

PRYNNE'S VOICE. . . . and this is his machine. (*Hissing noise finally masks sound. Stops spindle.*)

PRYNNE (*disappointment*). Gone . . . the whining, wavering old woman has gone.

TYLER (*off*). I'm locking up now, Master.

PRYNNE. Practice never does justice to the notion . . . the imagination's too big for anything that follows. How could that be me? It was just the overheated imagination playing tricks.

TYLER (*approaching*). Them cells still pong to high heaven . . . and they haven't seen a guest in weeks!

PRYNNE. It's an idea without wit. Reason reverses on itself as soon as it tantalises us with its possibilities.

TYLER. Still at your bench, I see.

PRYNNE. You perceive shape to the sounds I make?

TYLER. Shape?

PRYNNE. If there's no shape, how do I claim to construct a machine that will hold sound in time? I'm unable even to reconstitute those things I can see . . . it would be simpler to restore flesh to crumbling bones.

TYLER. Is that what it does?

PRYNNE. It memorises our every utterance . . . even words that miscarry when committed to writing.

TYLER. It does all that?

PRYNNE. It means to show up the best of what we are . . . as well as the fear that cuts us off inside our own gizzards.

TYLER. It's magic, then.

PRYNNE. If it worked.

TYLER. If it's magic, it should work on its own.

PRYNNE. How should this work? Everything we hear . . . see . . . distorts. By the time my words reach you they've reformed as something else . . . as something only you understand. We're buried too deep inside our poor, blind bodies.

TYLER. Buried?

PRYNNE. The message arrives so altered from the machine, its purpose so cunningly disguised, that it threatens no more to . . . No matter – the machine miscarries and that's an end to it!

TYLER (*going*). You shouldn't stop work, though. You've given it too much time to stop now.

PRYNNE (*shouts after him*). So much time that it's ruined me for all else. (*Under his breath.*) Except hunting down masterless men . . . it doesn't ask that I disdain hunting down masterless men.

Scene 2

Exterior. Wood. Day. Trees being felled. Hammer hitting anvil. A frightened BOY *babbles tearfully, as if holding a conversation with himself.* PRYNNE *and a* PETTY CONSTABLE *close to microphone.*

BOY (*off*). I'm just a boy . . . just a boy.

CONSTABLE. Says he's just a boy.

PRYNNE. He's here on beggar's business . . . it's written all over him.

BOY. Just a boy . . .

PRYNNE. And how old do we reckon this boy to be?

CONSTABLE (*to the* BOY). Present yourself, then! Tell the bailiff what he seeks to know!

PRYNNE. So many fatherless children . . . the wood hawks 'em up like gob.

BOY. Just a boy . . . just a boy . . .

PRYNNE. You reckon he's worth the attention on my time, then?

CONSTABLE. You'll have no trouble finding him a home. He'll finance a good month's work at your bench.

PRYNNE. Less your commission.

BOY. I'm old enough to see to myself!

CONSTABLE. And the others?

PRYNNE. Too old . . . not worth bothering about.

CONSTABLE. Just him, then?

PRYNNE. Bring him here.

A scrimmage ensues as CONSTABLE *hauls the struggling* BOY *over to the Bailiff.*

BOY. No! Let go!!

CONSTABLE (*straining*). You'd better watch your shins . . . these young 'uns kick like a horse in a fret. (*To the* BOY.) Be still, damn you, or it'll be bad for you!! (*The* BOY *emits a winded howl.*) Now will you sit quiet?

PRYNNE. Closer.

BOY. Let me go, sir. I'm just a boy, sir. I hope to be married soon.

PRYNNE. No licence . . . no business to move here.

CONSTABLE. You don't want to marry while passions incense reason . . . the itch persuades too many girls to mischief round here. A young 'un like you'll be dead with the rot inside the year.

PRYNNE. We're wasting time. Confess him to be here on beggar's business. . . . Confess him to be without a licence to move here.

CONSTABLE. The Bailiff asks to see your licence, boy.

HEPPENSTAL (*approaching*). There *is* no licence, Bound Bailiff, as you well know.

PRYNNE. Then you'll loan us use of your fire for our brand.

CONSTABLE. Always found him most obliging in the past.

The PETTY CONSTABLE *removes brand from saddle-bag. Horse snorts.*

HEPPENSTAL. Boy's poor . . . as poor as I am myself. He left his parish to find work.

PRYNNE. Then the boy is no boy . . . he's a masterless man. Masterless men are prey to long and detailed self-justification.

HEPPENSTAL. Masterless he may be . . . he's no beggar, though. He seeks no help from this parish.

The brand is thrust into the fire.

PRYNNE. You profess him to be poorer than poor, but I wager his rags conceal the most fashionable of undergarments.

CONSTABLE. They're never as poor as they make out.

PRYNNE. London's own Recorder has himself made estimates of the truest poor. . . . His endeavours for last year have yielded up only eight and twenty in the entire kingdom.

CONSTABLE. It's true . . . the Sheriff showed us . . . only eight and twenty. (*Turns the brand.*)

PRYNNE. The boy surely cannot claim to be one of this eight and twenty . . . a score of these unfortunates subsist under the Recorder's own jurisdiction.

CONSTABLE (*laughs*). That leaves just eight . . . just eight!

PRYNNE. They say he's so concerned to acquaint himself with their plight that he's had their names put to rote and committed to memory.

HEPPENSTAL. You impede the Queen's business, Bound Bailiff. We've a navy to supply and keep in readiness.

PRYNNE. And you impede the Deputy Lieutenant's business. For it is his business I transact here. I'm charged in his name and by our parish to rid the forest of its beggars and masterless men. It's not in my name that I brand this boy.

HEPPENSTAL. Doubtless you'd even cause folk to be sent into slavery for lying out on common land.

PRYNNE. If they lie out suspiciously.

CONSTABLE. Brand's ready.

PRYNNE. Hold him!

BOY. No!! (*The* BOY *struggles as the* CONSTABLE *tries to hold him still.*)

HEPPENSTAL. Steady yourself, boy. The brand has taken out the eye of many a beggar in fret.

CONSTABLE. Good advice.

The BOY *cries out as* PRYNNE *brands him.*

HEPPENSTAL. Now he'll have your mark for all eternity.

PRYNNE. A precaution only . . . in case he's tempted to slip his leash before fully acquainting his new master with his skills.

HEPPENSTAL. You can't put him into service unless he refuses work. He has to refuse first.

PRYNNE. There *is* no work . . . unless you wish me to set him toiling in your place and send you off in his.

HEPPENSTAL. You offered him no work because there's no profit in it.

PRYNNE. There is no profit in burning out his eyes . . . or in hanging him as a felon without benefit of clergy. Yet these profitless things I could have done and more. Do not urge profitless acts upon me, Heppenstal, I am when it occasions attentive even to the advice of your kind.

HEPPENSTAL. You might find profit in these things, Bailiff.

PRYNNE. And allow my body to starve to feed the bad in me? For I would starve if I found no masters for stray boys such as these. I receive no wage from the Deputy Lieutenant or the Sheriff. . . . Would *you* serve a man who gave no reward for your work?

HEPPENSTAL. I have to serve the smell on the wind.

CONSTABLE. You make the smell . . . you and all your kind . . . the filth who put known beggarly boys to work for little more than a morsel of stewed rabbit.

HEPPENSTAL. He'd still stay with me if he could choose.

PRYNNE. Then we shall have to be vigilant . . . now it's clear so many beggarly boys choose to stay with you.

Scene 3

Interior. PRYNNE'*s room. Night. Commotion from the new prisoners in the outbuildings.* PRYNNE *unlocking and opening a box.*

PRYNNE. Everything's here. . . . It's all in place . . . what there is. There are precious few papers to speak of. Just three small boxes . . . evidence of a life disdainful of detail and complication. I've as good as abolished my need to be here . . . in so far as the administration of my affairs warrant . . . business that could be settled in so many hours. It amuses me that I am as unencumbered as the men in my cells.

Closes box and locks it.

Should I pleasure so in the hunt? And yet not to hunt is to be hunted.

A shriek from the cells.

Why don't they sit quiet? Soon the days'll blur into each other. The passage of time favours those who suffer. It threatens only men who are free to pleasure . . . men from whom its grace can be withdrawn.

Unlocks and opens a second box.

The doubt of every man born into indecent times . . . could I have embraced the world with the ease of the men in my cells? I'd not fret so if I disdained the voluptuous due to disinclination. Should I then have embraced it as wetly as the libertine? Would I have shown myself to be as practised? It troubles me more than fear itself. Are these just reparations to be paid in an age made unsafe by the pleasuring of other men? Or do I waste precious life on the inventions of the brain?

The commotion in the cells subsides.

Quiet again. That's the difference between us, my friends. You just give up . . . all fight deserts you. I stay scared. Well, I shall keep you going until you start hoping again. Fear won't be far behind . . . depend on it.

Closes box and locks it.

Scene 4

Interior. PRYNNE's *workroom. Day.* PRYNNE *slowly turns the spindle on his machine.*

CORNFORD. Such a smell!

PRYNNE. Sheep's gut . . . freshly cut and stretched tight across its opening.

CORNFORD. Must I stand this close?

PRYNNE. It won't pick up your sound unless you bend close.

CORNFORD. And this is the queerest paper! . . .

PRYNNE. It's been treated with wax.

CORNFORD (*most amused*). The needle . . . it seems to go up and down with my voice.

PRYNNE. It should move more levelly across the paper.

CORNFORD. Turn the spindle faster, then!

PRYNNE. The spindle draws the paper through to the other needle.

CORNFORD. So many needles . . . this is a machine for the seamstress!

PRYNNE. It instructs the second gut . . . the receiving gut.

CORNFORD. It seems to have two of everything! . . . (*A hint of friendly suspicion.*) Confess it, Ned, the spindle causes the machine to flux . . .

PRYNNE. The furrows in the paper flux the needle.

CORNFORD. To what end?

PRYNNE. If the machine's a success, you'll know soon enough. If it fails, you'll have amused yourself at my expense.

Reverses direction of spindle.

CORNFORD. You put a high price on my –

CORNFORD'S VOICE (*thin and distorted*). It seems to have two of everything! . . .

A stunned silence.

PRYNNE. It *does* speak!!

CORNFORD. God save me! These are my words!

PRYNNE. I was in a fever, Richard. I conjured up my own voice well enough . . . convincingly so . . . we're only too ready to imagine overstatement in our own heads. But now you hear yours . . . we both hear it . . . the shape of your sounds are thrown back at you too!

CORNFORD. It mimics my words!

PRYNNE. Appropriates, Richard, holds them in storage . . . preserves their shape long after you've disowned them.

Turns spindle.

CORNFORD'S VOICE (*distortion*). Confess it, Ned, the spindle causes the machine to flux.

CORNFORD. It gouges memory from the mind!

PRYNNE. Your mockery too . . . the machine retains even the banter in your delivery!

CORNFORD. Not just the banter . . . it unifies what is said with how it should be spoken! A wealth of opposites . . . contradictory knowledge . . . the scientist as magician!

PRYNNE. It's a challenge to our wit, right enough . . .

CORNFORD. Make it say more. (PRYNNE *turns spindle again*.)

CORNFORD'S VOICE (*more distortion and crackle*). To what end?

CORNFORD. I'd forgotten the order of my words. . . . The machine remembers and I'd forgotten! The event and the memory of the event . . . it's all one now. . . . We can reach out and touch the past! Your device'll unprovide dour history. . . . It's a new beginning!

PRYNNE (*uneasily*). A new beginning . . .

CORNFORD. We school our senses to accept death as an end to our earthly presence. And now you show us how our earthly sounds can be detached from our bodies and stored in *this*! . . . Pity poor history – having to vacate the site on which it has for so long stood!

PRYNNE. The machine's for my pleasure only.

CORNFORD. Your pleasure?

PRYNNE. I can never make it available to the larger congregation.

CORNFORD. Then it's just a toy!

PRYNNE. I'll be purged like so much cess if news of my toy spreads.

CORNFORD. You've too many friends.

PRYNNE. Friends! What good will friends do me? The heavens'll set the sky on me for this!

CORNFORD. These are bolder times than you give credit. You'll receive all the encouragement you need.

PRYNNE. Into the cells with my masterless men!

CORNFORD. No need even to address the ambition of intermediaries. If we take it to Passingham, he could go direct to the Privy Council.

PRYNNE. Is Passingham any less ambitious?

CORNFORD. But the waste . . . so much wasted invention!

PRYNNE (*laughs*). It's a miracle you've survived so long, Richard.

CORNFORD. It seems the machine-maker has made a coward of the Bailiff.

PRYNNE. No – the Bailiff has made a coward of the machine-maker.

Scene 5

Exterior. Courtyard. Day. Horse snorting. Bridle clinking.

PRYNNE. You want a look at my new lad before you go?

CORNFORD. I've all the men I need.

PRYNNE. He comes with a two-year indenture.

CORNFORD. You're too efficient. . . . Our needs are paltry set against this zeal to provide them!

PRYNNE. I have to be efficient . . . it's my craft that funds my art!

CORNFORD (*mockery*). And it's only your craft that keeps a dangerous world in abeyance. And your resource, of course . . . let's not forget your resource.

PRYNNE. The boy in my outbuildings . . . he showed resource. . . . He left his parish to find work. Look at him now!

CORNFORD. What's the real reason, Ned? Why the modesty?

PRYNNE (*eventually*). The sounds you heard were recognisable as fair copies of the words made by you this hour. But imagine the shock to those who did not hear you make them. Words without the visible presence of the minds and bodies that engineered them. Words that cannot be sourced to their masters. Words alone . . . escaped, renegade words! Try to hear them as others would hear them . . . as sounds without a source.

CORNFORD. They shall know them to be my words.

PRYNNE. Then they will say it's a future Cornford . . . a Cornford long dead trying to seep back into our world of the flesh.

CORNFORD. Then explain the science.

PRYNNE. Such a process can never be explained to the mind that sees only magic.

CORNFORD. But if you arrange to demonstrate the machine . . .

PRYNNE. A machine that contrives to outlast flesh? That takes our earthly thoughts and holds them in an unearthly state? They will see only its heretic maker!

CORNFORD. Can earthly immortality be so bad?

PRYNNE. I'll be punished for its powers . . . punished unjustly! I'm not my machine . . . my machine's not me!

CORNFORD. It's a creation of your mind . . . it's part of you.

PRYNNE. Everything I did not wish myself to be . . . it's there . . . in that creation. If my life had been filled with light instead of darkness and fear . . . Well, then there'd have been no cause for me to hide away and work on such an artefact. I would willingly have disdained it in favour of . . .

CORNFORD. What?

PRYNNE. The life of a man.

CORNFORD (*laughs*). And be as other men?

PRYNNE. I *am* as other men!

CORNFORD. Not so much a man as to disdain laxative invention.

PRYNNE. It's a corpse . . . a maggoty bowel lining for dead thoughts . . . a machine for the thoughts of the bowel!

CORNFORD. A machine that'll liberate and transform all who come into contact with it! . . .

PRYNNE. Liberate! Transform!

CORNFORD. A home to the mind. . . . The body's such an insanitary shelter. I beg you, Ned, grant the ghost in us its rightful status. License it as you might one of your masterless men.

PRYNNE. Ghosts now!

CORNFORD. What you've fashioned here . . . it projects even the visions of the stateless mind. . . . It reviews *me* reviewing *it*!

PRYNNE. A generous testimony for such a short, gruesome acquaintance!

CORNFORD. You want to be judged sound in your view of the world. . . . How else do you justify so much fear? And so much pride in that fear?

PRYNNE. Pride?

CORNFORD. Donate the prescription for its assembly, then, if you're so much a woman!

PRYNNE. The world shall have it . . . when I'm dead! Then it shall have the machine and its prescription!

CORNFORD. The dictatorship of magic . . . the magician's assumption that only he knows the mix! . . . Well, shall this satisfy. Your machine's no longer the property of a mind scurrying about in its own bowel . . . it's part of a new wisdom with which the world must and shall equip itself.

PRYNNE. Wisdom's a rich man's luxury . . . certainty's all that matters in times such as these.

CORNFORD (*going*). Then you're about to know luxury . . . like it or not!

Horse cantering away.

PRYNNE (*shouts after him*). I was prepared for this . . . betrayal!
And I know how it is to be resolved. . . . At least the worldly
Bailiff does! (*Under his breath.*) They'll never believe him . . .
the machine has to be seen to be believed. They'll just pity him his
disturbances of the mind. A machine fashioned to retain Cornford's
own forgettable musings as well as give expression to higher, nobler
aspirations? They'll never believe him. (*Shouts after him again.*)
The Bailiff will find it a place of hiding . . . out of your reach!

Scene 6

Interior. PRYNNE's *workroom. Night. Sounds from the forest drift in
through an open window.* PRYNNE *is agitated.*

PRYNNE. Be calm . . . be calm! You're a man of *this* world – not
some whimpering monk.

Turns spindle and addresses machine.

My task is to give shape to the unplanned circumstances of my life
. . . to give pattern to endeavour.

Stops spindle.

Where to start a biography such as this? Start when unplanned
circumstance made you its creature . . . when the child was forced
to prepare and instruct the man.

Turns spindle.

It is a simple matter now for me to renounce before an absent
God my Roman mother and father. Such a time to be Papists!
In the beginning it was just fines for disobeying the Act and not
attending church. Then when the papal bull disposed us to challenge
the Queen's legitimacy . . .

Stops spindle.

This is just a history lesson!

Turns spindle.

A black fear descended upon us. Twice we were to flee for our lives.
Such visions . . . such terrible childhood phantoms. Fireballs chased
me down dark passages . . . rivers of putrefying flesh swept me into
a sea of corpses. Then . . . deafness. No longer did I have to listen
. . . no more women sobbing . . . dogs whimpering. Not a sound
for two years . . . two blissful years . . . never was I to know such
peace again!

Stops spindle.

My mother's Roman philosophers see perfection all around. I could
believe in perfection only while my hearing was impeded. It occasions

me to look out on to their nature. And what I see is perfect enough
. . . the woods . . . the misty hills beyond. But now I know such
perfection to be made up of a million tiny massacres.

Scene 7

Interior. Cells. Day. Echoey acoustic. PRYNNE *showing* PARSON
BLACKTIN *the new intake.*

BLACKTIN. You have to feed them too?

PRYNNE. They're costly to sustain, right enough. And if I don't find
them masters soon . . .

BLACKTIN. They're a poor lot.

PRYNNE. This one's strong . . . the boy. You could do worse than
to find him a place.

BOY. I shouldn't be here, sir, I'm to be . . .

PRYNNE. Shut your mouth! (*To* BLACKTIN.) Always the same
protestations of innocence . . . the sweet nature of the masterless
man! He wants only to embrace prodigality after such abundance
as this!

BLACKTIN. It's to be hoped they have inclination to ponder their
overspreading vices here. Such commonality . . . it can be used to
common advantage. . . . The sumptuous fruits of folly are often
shared in such close confinement.

PRYNNE. So I'm expected to purge the suggestion from their bodies
too.

BLACKTIN (*to the prisoners*). Forbid yourselves pleasuring in each
other, bodged people. Spill no more sin on to the earth and those
who follow will have occasion to thank you.

BOY. Sir . . .

BLACKTIN. Find your own voice . . . unimpugned by the Devil's
frog croak. . . . For in discovering your own voice you do discover
the Lord's.

PRYNNE. Waste of a good sermon, Parson.

BLACKTIN. Disdain the plague of the mind . . . return cock-sore
to the womb of creation that delivered you unto the world.
Recreate yourselves away from the scene of your wickedness . . .
return heart-sick and sore from sin . . . for in sin a whole universe
does miscarry. (*A few dissident groans from the prisoners.*)

PRYNNE (*most amused*). They think your reasoning's duceable to
the good.

BLACKTIN. So now the prisoners have taken to confiding in their jailer.

PRYNNE. By the hour.

BLACKTIN. Then *your* reasoning . . .

PRYNNE. By the hour! Their cries carry to me at my bench . . . they plead with me to consider our shared ancestry.

BLACKTIN. Devils!

PRYNNE. They also instruct me to be as they are . . . to consider their misfortune as I would my own.

BLACKTIN. Do you take their instruction to heart?

PRYNNE (*laughs*). Their every word.

BLACKTIN (*confidentially*). It's difficult with men such as these, Prynne. There's nothing so perilous as the description of sin, for in describing it I give range for imitation. Empty vessels filling with cess.

PRYNNE. Such a generous appraisal!

BLACKTIN. They're unable to read of sin and yet they sin still. They understand my maxims, right enough, but only as inducements to their engorged senses. They wetly enfold them as they would enfold bad maxims.

BOY (*starting to sob*). I don't want to be bad, sir!

The other prisoners hoot derisively.

PRYNNE (*under his breath*). Not to hear again! Not to hear them!

BLACKTIN. You make a poor showing of yourself, boy.

BOY. I'm a boy, sir . . . just a boy!

BLACKTIN. Expunge all jaundiced thoughts from your malleable minds, bodged people, for the disease which so afflicts you could spread and cause even magistrates to fall from reputation.

PRYNNE. A bulky preponderance such as sin floating weightlessly up to the lofty heights of magistrates . . .

BLACKTIN. To a future age also. . . . Sin can be transported to the future age as it can from coney catcher to coney catcher. They are the vessels in which sin is transmitted through time.

PRYNNE. Then they must be cleansed to walk abroad in the new century!

BLACKTIN. The new century must have only the best of what we are. Our new machines are telling ambassadors . . . machines like yours, Prynne.

PRYNNE (*after a stunned silence*). My machine?

BLACKTIN. Cornford said you'd be coy.

PRYNNE. Then he deceives you too.

BLACKTIN. His account was heavily reliant on such imagery! . . .

PRYNNE. Judas!!

BLACKTIN. Such eager rebuttal . . . in advance of knowing what he charges too. (*Going.*) Show me this machine, Prynne, I'll decide if it's worthy of his testimonial.

Door clangs shut.

Scene 8

Interior. Workroom. Day. PRYNNE *turning the spindle on the machine and playing back* CORNFORD's *voice.*

CORNFORD'S VOICE (*distorted*). It seems to have two of everything! . . .

BLACKTIN (*stunned*). He's here . . . in this room with us!

PRYNNE. It's his last appearance.

BLACKTIN. I swear it, Prynne, I thought Cornford mad. You could've bluffed if you'd not been so keen to deny him.

CORNFORD'S VOICE (*distorted*). Confess it, Ned, the spindle causes the machine to flux.

BLACKTIN. It *is* magic!

PRYNNE. The parts are too simple . . . simpler even than the simplest musket.

BLACKTIN. But the balance of these parts . . . how easy it could've been for its proportions to miscarry.

PRYNNE. I don't claim to be its inventor. Doubtless there are many such machines up and down the land.

BLACKTIN. Machines whose proportions are doomed to miscarry.

PRYNNE. No . . . true machines! Machines that carry their maker's purpose!

BLACKTIN. The world has never looked on such a machine. There has never been anything such as you have put before us.

PRYNNE. Men have tried to mimic their own unseen sounds since the beginning of time. The Greeks attempted it three thousand years ago.

BLACKTIN. It isn't mimicry. The machine even points to Cornford's manner. That *is* Cornford!

PRYNNE. It's just a poor thing, Thomas . . .

BLACKTIN. A poor thing, indeed!

PRYNNE. Sometimes even the spindle refuses to function.

BLACKTIN. If only you could perceive the worth of your own device!

PRYNNE (*surprised*). Worth?

BLACKTIN. It'll instruct the new age!

PRYNNE. Then . . .

BLACKTIN. The voice cannot be falsified in the manner of the written confession. My only hope is that you've bestowed it with capacity enough to allow our thoughts safe carriage across time.

PRYNNE. I imagined you'd see it to be the work of a mischievous dissenter.

BLACKTIN. A dissenter? You've trapped the unseen words of Cornford in your machine.

PRYNNE. The words as they were spoken . . . it cannot rearrange their order.

BLACKTIN. Inside this contraption exist the proportions of that other dimension . . . a world unencumbered by our corporeal presence. Don't you see . . . the spirit voice *does* find refuge outside its pitiful husk!

PRYNNE. I'd never make such leviathan claims.

BLACKTIN. That other dimension overspreads into our world and reassures our own doubting mortality.

PRYNNE. It still doubts.

BLACKTIN. Your doubts are refuted by your actions.

PRYNNE (*agitated*). You know I'd not be as I am if I believed any morsel of me could outlast my life here . . . you'd find me free of malice and envy and all other time-bound distempers. And yet you confer upon me such blasphemous divinity!

BLACKTIN. I know you to be good, Prynne, for you follow our Lord and show us worthy intentions in all your deeds.

PRYNNE. It's just a machine . . . it remembers only feeble words.

BLACKTIN. Then make more machines.

PRYNNE. More?

BLACKTIN. As many as you can.

PRYNNE. And how do you propose I fund the time I shall need for its refinement? My only income . . .

BLACKTIN. Your friends shall fund you the time you need.

PRYNNE. If you're proposing charity . . .

BLACKTIN. I'm proposing help to find masters for the beggars in your cells.

PRYNNE. Help?

BLACKTIN. There's another dimension still . . . acquaintances known to me but not to you.

PRYNNE. It would give me more time . . . not to have to find them masters.

BLACKTIN. Then keep your cells well-stocked. You'll soon have reason to be grateful for Cornford's indiscretion.

PRYNNE. Cornford went against me.

BLACKTIN. Maybe the bluster in you always intended for the world to hear the shape of Cornford's voice. . . . Why else would you let me hear?

PRYNNE. I intended . . .

BLACKTIN. You intended the world to hear.

PRYNNE (*eventually*). Let the heavens open up, then . . . let me be scorned and reviled! I was put on this earth to advocate my work and advocate it I shall! Let this be what I was for!

Scene 9

Interior. PRYNNE's *rooms. Night.* PRYNNE *turning the spindle and speaking into the machine.*

PRYNNE. Give thanks to the absent God for all gifts God-given . . . for he is the author of mundane and original creation. Those who dwell in chains would never disdain to drink from my cup. If they had a morsel of what has been bestowed upon me, they'd fall to their knees in gratitude. I would never trade their manly complexity . . . their boredom, their restlessness . . . their need to be so many creatures in a single vessel. My only need is for work of the brain and its calming simplicity. Give thanks, then, for the many hours of repose and contemplation at my bench. And give thanks too for what I have missed in this life, for much of it would've been duceable to the bad.

Scene 10

Exterior. Wood. Night. Dogs barking, etc., as PRYNNE *and his petty constables round up more men.*

PRYNNE. How many's that?

CONSTABLE (*a little way off*). Four!

PRYNNE. Get them into the wagon!

CONSTABLE. All of 'em?

PRYNNE. We've room!

CONSTABLE. They'll just eat our grub and soil our straw. Look at 'em – nobody's going to risk the plague to billet these scarecrows!

PRYNNE. Just keep them moving! For every masterless man there's a master!

CONSTABLE (*to prisoners*). Move if you can, wrinkled brawlers . . . high-born masters are waiting to bid for your muscle!

Chains clank as the CONSTABLE *herds the men on to wagon.*

GIRL (*approaching*). Sir . . .

PRYNNE (*shouts to* CONSTABLE). See that the gate's open in readiness! They're in an ugly temper . . . we'll have to be gone in haste!

GIRL (*closer*). I've some business, sir.

PRYNNE. Not with me.

GIRL. With the Bailiff, sir.

PRYNNE. Careful, child. You put yourself at risk . . . and not just from me! Child stealers abound here . . . they'd slit your throat and then take pleasure in your unquestioning corpse.

GIRL. My husband, sir . . . you have him presently in your cells.

PRYNNE. And you believe he rots there blamelessly.

GIRL. No, sir, not . . .

PRYNNE. Then he's there justly.

GIRL. No, sir, there's been a mistake.

PRYNNE. Stop now! Or else you will force me to go good-faced to my Sheriff with your charges. And then? . . .

GIRL. Sir?

PRYNNE. What then?

GIRL. I don't know, sir.

PRYNNE. He'd look at their detail and find them wanting and would shred your back for your trouble. (*Lets this sink in.*) You're best off without this husband. Let the lice feed off your poor shrunken body and be content.

GIRL. Free him, sir . . . free him and license him.

PRYNNE. I have no power to license. And give thanks to the enemy that I don't look closer at the licences I've inspected already. . . . It's only his ambition that keeps our navy in readiness. And if our navy stood down, Heppenstal and the sweaty exertions of his men'd no longer be encouraged here.

GIRL (*starting to cry*). Free him, sir . . . please.

PRYNNE. How old are you?

GIRL. Fourteen.

PRYNNE. A woman, no less!

GIRL. I'll go with you, sir, if you want me.

PRYNNE. So this is the business you want to transact. And we've scarcely disposed of your wedding!

GIRL. I'm used to the ways of fatherly men, sir. My husband has as many years as you.

PRYNNE. Who married you?

GIRL (*evasive*). I *am* married, sir.

PRYNNE. In the eyes of the Creator?

GIRL. He says we are married.

PRYNNE. The Creator?

GIRL. My husband, sir.

PRYNNE. Such is the state of things that a child . . .

GIRL. You shan't be married to me, sir, if you go with me.

PRYNNE. . . . a child so young . . .

GIRL. It's a fair transaction, sir.

PRYNNE. No, it's not fair . . . it's too late for me to take advantage of you. A sudden acquaintance with that pleasure would disturb my mortality. Its remembrance would torment and rift on me and chastise my peace of mind for having failed to instruct myself earlier. It's labour enough to bear my unnatural life without . . .

CONSTABLE (*off*). Let's be gone from this fetid wood, Bailiff . . . this is an unpredictable rabble!

GIRL. I beg you, sir, give me my husband.

PRYNNE. So he can pleasure himself in those things denied me!

GIRL (*confused*). I'm not denying you, sir.

PRYNNE. So deny me! Pleasure is just the signal for it to be snatched away again! Not just joy . . . life itself!

CONSTABLE (*off*). Bound Bailiff!

PRYNNE. You wouldn't taunt me so if you'd known the parents who made me . . . who so grievously blighted their family . . . who destroyed their own divinity and the lives they had made rather than renounce the Roman church.

GIRL. Sir . . .

PRYNNE. You've good hearing, I see, but you hear only a disembodied voice. For that's what I am – a voice without a body. Remember these words . . . store them for as long as yielding mortality allows. For these are words the Bailiff has never spoken to another living being.

Noise from the mob rises.

CONSTABLE (*returning*). Looks like we'll have to fight our way out of here.

PRYNNE. We'll give 'em their fight, then! I'm ready!

Scene 11

Interior. Workroom. Night. Eerie, distant animal noises from the forest.

PRYNNE. On this day I killed a man . . . the first time in this uneventful life I have killed. It shall be with me forever. If I live to kill a hundred men, I shall see only his eyes. Those eyes hungered for knowledge to the last . . . the need to know what it was like to be as I am . . . the dying man asking his slayer for experience. And in the same instant *instructing* his slayer. Shall this satisfy, murderer, it could have been you at this end of your blade . . . just as you could have been the girl's fatherly husband. Only fear separates this murderer from the beggarly and masterless. What am I destined to lose first? My fear? Or my life?

Scene 12

Interior. Cells. Night. Echoey acoustic.

BOY. Sir!

PRYNNE (*approaching*). I don't answer the summons from the beggars in my cells.

TYLER. Go back to sleep!

BOY. Used to sleeping in the open, sir.

PRYNNE. Be grateful I've found you shelter.

BOY. I look after myself, sir. I find my own shelter.

PRYNNE. I brought you in . . . out of the weather.

BOY. Don't want shelter.

PRYNNE. Sit quiet. You'll be indentured soon . . . gone before any of the dogs you share my straw with.

BOY. Used to sleeping in the air, sir. (*Then angrily.*) I can prove who I claim to be. I can verify my history.

PRYNNE. The long and detailed self-justification of the masterless man . . .

BOY. You're educated, sir. You can write it down.

PRYNNE. Not what you have to say.

BOY. You won't think I need a master when you hear my story.

PRYNNE. Can't hear you, boy.

BOY. I've always looked to myself.

PRYNNE. Still can't hear you.

BOY. Looked to myself since I was eight, sir. Been responsible for myself since before I was just a boy.

PRYNNE. He's simple. The boy's simple.

BOY. I cared for my mother till she died.

PRYNNE. What about *my* history? Why don't you sit quiet and listen to my history?

BOY. Looked after my mother . . . used to mess herself, sir. Had to clear up after her.

PRYNNE. Claims he had a mother. (*Shouts.*) You never had a mother! You're a masterless man!

BOY. Some of them here mess themselves, sir, the old ones. Smell's bad in the morning . . . the old ones make such a stink.

PRYNNE. Sit quiet or else I'll set you cleaning up after them!

BOY. Couldn't be left. She couldn't be left at the end. I hope the girl I marry don't end up like that. The girl I shall choose . . .

PRYNNE. So you've not yet chosen!

BOY. I meant the girl I'm to marry, sir.

PRYNNE. The wife you have *yet* to choose.

BOY. My wife to be, sir.

PRYNNE. A phantom . . . like the mother.

BOY. I *am* betrothed, sir.

PRYNNE. I could find you a wife. A girl your age, she is . . . subsists here within the boundaries under my jurisdiction.

BOY. My wife . . . here!

PRYNNE. She shall never be your wife. She exists only through my recall of her.

BOY. If I could marry her . . .

PRYNNE. Never. She's betrothed to a . . . fatherly man. Used only to the ways of fatherly men.

TYLER. He *can* talk.

PRYNNE. He wants to tell me how he came to be here.

TYLER. Talks and talks and talks.

BOY. A wife . . . of my age . . . in this parish!

TYLER. Settle him down, shall I?

PRYNNE. He won't settle. He's not ready . . . doesn't have the learning.

BOY. A wife . . . here!

TYLER. He needs learning.

PRYNNE. So learn him . . . if you think he needs learning.

TYLER. I'll learn him, right enough. He'll get my learning.

Scene 13

Interior. Workroom. Night. Spindle turning.

PRYNNE'S VOICE (*distorted*). My task is to give shape to the unplanned circumstance of my life . . .

PRYNNE. The sentiments are empty . . . the voice bleats! This is no biography!

PRYNNE'S VOICE (*overlap*). . . . to give pattern to endeavour.

Stops spindle.

PRYNNE. A voice without a body, right enough. My machine does not describe me . . . it describes only my sickness. How will the future age make a picture of what I was before my decline? Will it even have the wit to picture me as I am now?

CORNFORD (*approaching*). I see you've found your own private confessor, Ned. Soon you'll have no further need of friend Blacktin.

PRYNNE. There's to be no further correspondence between you and me.

CORNFORD. An artefact that had its beginnings in its master's vanity too!

PRYNNE (*laughs*). Vanity as well as pride?

CORNFORD. The vanity of a man who refuses to acknowledge the uniqueness of his own creation.

PRYNNE. There's too much creation . . . it's everywhere. Nature invents, forgets, reinvents . . . then admonishes its own confusion by punishing those who try to supplement it.

CORNFORD. Blacktin's been active on your behalf . . . he's found for your device a patron.

PRYNNE. A patron?

CORNFORD. Though, I fear, he won't be interested in the content of your cells as presently constituted. He's after more virtuous stock.

PRYNNE. Unlicensed men are seldom virtuous.

CORNFORD (*not without sarcasm*). They must be young and pure in heart.

PRYNNE. They'd have to be very young, then. (*Then suspiciously.*) And who is my patron?

CORNFORD. Our friend Passingham, of course . . . concerned to create shape where none before existed!

PRYNNE. Create? A mischievous paraphrase.

CORNFORD. I'm talking about the masterless young, Ned, not your machine.

PRYNNE. Then I mistook your . . . (*Catching his breath.*) I shall have to sit.

CORNFORD. Aren't you well?

Chair scrapes back as PRYNNE *sits.*

PRYNNE. My beggars . . . they pass on their stench and sickness to me . . . for all my abstinence. And you and Passingham abound in good health . . . for all your pleasuring.

CORNFORD. Passingham blesses the world with his wealth . . . you with the wit of your invention . . . and you both enrich your friends by your sins.

PRYNNE. Sins?

CORNFORD. Your work can be used as much for heretic purposes
as Passingham's cock. We excuse you this and give thanks for
experiment.

PRYNNE. Report to my patron that I presently have no children in
my custody. No boys who wish to be married . . . no girls already
married to fatherly men . . .

CORNFORD. There was a boy . . .

PRYNNE. I was deceived . . . the boy'll be a man soon.

CORNFORD. There'll be a guinea for him and for those who follow.

PRYNNE. Bidding's high.

CORNFORD. Higher than what might be customary for such . . .

PRYNNE. Young flesh?

CORNFORD. It didn't trouble you before.

PRYNNE. I've men . . . no boys . . . just men!

CORNFORD. I've already given an undertaking to Passingham.

PRYNNE. Passingham is blackest black . . . his heart has closed up
and blackened.

CORNFORD. I can't believe you'd . . .

PRYNNE. *You* are blackest black . . . and I will not be a purveyor
of the flesh of children!

CORNFORD. Be warned, Ned. The Deputy Lieutenant grants licences
and monopolies only to his favourites. And as it's the custom again to
offer the offices of the parish to the highest bidder . . .

PRYNNE. Who'll want my office?

CORNFORD. He's about to appoint a new Subsidy Commissioner . . .

PRYNNE. Then let him appoint a new Bailiff! (*He rises.*) I must
lie down before . . . I have to lie down. Go now. You have my
answer . . . the boy is masterless . . .

CORNFORD. I'll see Passingham gets your answer.

Scene 14

Interior. PRYNNE's *room. Day.* PRYNNE *turns the spindle as he
dictates into his machine.*

PRYNNE. The centre of a cloud . . . a milky cloud . . . it's as if
I'm biting at it and trying to take it down into my unformed body.

And yet I view this cloud from far off . . . from another world. A squeezing sensation . . . life itself is squeezed out of me . . . breathing is suddenly a tedious labour. And there's an overwhelming smell . . . a pungent, cloying, womanly smell. Something takes hold of a handle deep within my gut and propels me through space. Such pain . . . sensation after sensation informs itself only through pain! . . . Don't you see its argument . . . these are the birth pangs of Ned Prynne I re-live here . . . life before the first understanding of awareness. It's here I shall end my account . . . at my birth. A life told backwards is a life *lived* backwards.

Stops spindle.

In truth this is a life that loses in the telling . . . it acquaints me only too vividly with my own miserable chronology. Even the rudimentary innards of my machine can cope with its range. And yet there is only my story to tell . . . there can be no outside concern now. If only Cornford and Blacktin hadn't tantalised me with the prospect of that larger congregation! It rears up at me still . . . the congregation I never had.

Starts spindle.

But nothing overwhelms now. No more do I fear my own poor history. I welcome even its pain . . . the pain is less for the telling. Why are there so many good substances here? Why is it so much harder for me to feel pain?

Scene 15

Interior. PRYNNE's *rooms. Day.* BLACKTIN *confronting an agitated* PRYNNE.

BLACKTIN. We understood you to be with us. You made an undertaking to share the benefits of your fertile mind.

PRYNNE. My fertile mind . . .

BLACKTIN. A bargain was struck. . . . The concern you expressed for the state of your affairs was met by a promise of aid from your friends.

PRYNNE. The machine's mine. And the only story it has to tell is mine.

BLACKTIN. The story of a child . . . a fractious child unable to keep up with the momentum he's set himself. A child too content with the knowledge of his own cleverness!

PRYNNE. Then this child will address his story directly . . . as he would to a biographer!

BLACKTIN. As he would to the Creator himself!

PRYNNE. Tolerate me this one comfort, Thomas . . . to leave to a future age my story . . . a voice from our times!

BLACKTIN. *Your* voice!

PRYNNE. My account'll be all the more honest for being spoken at my machine. A human biographer would . . .

BLACKTIN. Scrupulous honesty is tolerable only when a story is told against the teller. Shame and modesty clearly have no place here . . . there's no intermediary on hand to restrain you. Expect no further support from me, Ned Prynne . . . this is very much against the fashion!

PRYNNE. My machine . . . it pushes me beyond endurance. And yet it's laxative as well as tormentor. You have a corporeal life . . . consider those who have no life of the body!

BLACKTIN. You want pity? You have seldom shown pity for others.

PRYNNE. The machine is the best of me . . . the part of me that's all pity.

BLACKTIN. I'm unable even to care, Ned!

PRYNNE. Thomas . . .

BLACKTIN. Why should I? You care nothing for us! So much is your artefact a product of your own temper that you prohibit its use by others!

PRYNNE. It shares my logic . . . it knows my life has been lived badly.

BLACKTIN. Stop this . . . stop it now!

PRYNNE. You shan't have it! You'll corrode its guts with your black Christian blood!

BLACKTIN (*eventually*). Once the spirit memory passes from the body of its originator it passes into common domain . . . like a masterless man on common land. You're not a jailer of souls, Ned Prynne, the Church has granted you no dispensation to hold souls in a limbo of your own devising.

PRYNNE. I want only a berth for *my* soul.

BLACKTIN. You've no more domain over your own soul than you have over mine. Why, you might be holding it against its will. These are matters for the Church to deliberate on.

PRYNNE. But it won't be able to sustain itself without . . . (*Catches his breath*.)

BLACKTIN. What's wrong?

PRYNNE. Nothing. I . . .

BLACKTIN. What we have to settle is whether your voice . . . your story . . . is suited to the prescription of your machine.

PRYNNE. What?

BLACKTIN. Is Ned Prynne the voice of his own artefact? A future age might perceive you as a voice from the past, right enough, but not *of* the past.

PRYNNE. I *made* the machine!

BLACKTIN. But is it your task to take it forward into the future age?

PRYNNE. If I'm not its true voice, then neither are you or Cornford.

BLACKTIN. The point at dispute is . . . are you pure?

PRYNNE. Pure!?

BLACKTIN. Are you pure?

PRYNNE. I have abstained . . .

BLACKTIN. But has your imprisoned spirit abstained? Are you proposing to despatch into the future age a spirit contaminated by all you have seen and done?

PRYNNE. By all I have . . .

BLACKTIN. You have made men suffer . . . you have caused suffering and you have let that suffering mark you. And now your own machine rifts on you and certifies you as unfit to take it forward to the future age.

PRYNNE. No . . .

BLACKTIN. Pure invention cries out for pure expression.

PRYNNE. And where can an age as this find a voice without blemish or corruption? Where can . . .

PRYNNE *falls to the floor. He starts to make a growling noise.*

BLACKTIN. Are you ill, Ned?

TYLER (*approaching*). What's wrong with Master Prynne?

BLACKTIN. It appears he's having some kind of fit.

TYLER. He'll have to be put to bed, then.

BLACKTIN. Was that all he wanted this machine for? To set down his own bodged life?

TYLER. You'll have to go, Parson.

BLACKTIN. Such a majestic palace for such a poor crabbed soul! (*Going.*) Make sure he doesn't reach out in his delirium and do it harm.

Scene 16

Interior. PRYNNE's *workroom. Day. Echoey acoustic with exaggerated work noises in background – repeated hammer blows, etc. Fade in the spindle turning on machine. Again louder than it usually is. This time* PRYNNE's *recorded voice cues his live voice.*

PRYNNE'S VOICE (*distorted*). Who controls me?

PRYNNE. Who controls . . .

PRYNNE'S VOICE (*distorted*). Do you control me? Who is the machine maker?

PRYNNE. Do you . . .

PRYNNE'S VOICE (*distorted*). Has the parson taken me over? Is he the machine maker now?

PRYNNE. Has he . . .

PRYNNE'S VOICE (*distorted*). Will I be required to take the shape of his words now?

PRYNNE. Will I be . . .

PRYNNE'S VOICE (*distorted*). What's to become of me?

PRYNNE. What's to become . . . You shan't be squandered on Blacktin! I shan't allow it! You'll have a bigger life!

Scene 17

Interior. PRYNNE's *bedroom. Day.* TYLER *waking* PRYNNE.

TYLER. Master Prynne!

PRYNNE. What?

TYLER. The Petty Constable's brought the boy, Master.

PRYNNE. What boy?

CONSTABLE. You instructed me to bring the boy, Bailiff.

TYLER. Down on your knees, boy, the Master's not coming up to you.

PRYNNE. They tell me I have some disorder of the mind.

BOY. What's going to happen to me, sir?

CONSTABLE. Shut your mouth!!

PRYNNE. There's a medical term for it . . . an infection of the mind. The blood's . . . (*Attention wanders.*) It's as if I give expression to the same thoughts over and over again. (*To* TYLER.) Who's this?

TYLER. You asked to see him, Master.

PRYNNE. They tell me I have no recall of words once spoken . . . they come back again and again as if they had duplicated themselves many times over. Blood's polluted . . . the fight's gone . . . there's not much fear left now, either. How easy it is to give up! (*To* TYLER.) Have I said this before?

TYLER. We'd stop you if you had . . . in accordance with your instructions.

PRYNNE. Leave the boy with me . . . we've got business.

CONSTABLE. Bailiff . . .

PRYNNE. Out!

CONSTABLE. We're going, Master.

Door closing as TYLER *and the* PETTY CONSTABLE *leave.*

PRYNNE. The conditions, then. You need to know the conditions.

BOY. Sir . . .

PRYNNE. What I have to say is to your advantage. If you distract me, you might cause me to forget I'm giving you your liberty.

BOY. You're letting me go, sir?

PRYNNE. You see the device on the table?

BOY. Yes, sir.

PRYNNE. It's a new invention . . . my invention . . . a product of my poor infected mind . . . Have I said any of this before?

BOY. No, sir.

PRYNNE. The Church has decreed it a pure invention that pines only for pure expression. All I can offer it at such a point in history . . . is a victim. The purity of a victim.

BOY. Sir . . .

PRYNNE. And what better than one of my victims? A spirit-voice tainted and corrupted by the Bailiff of the forest! (*Laughs feebly.*) That I should have spent so much life fashioning a machine that is interested only in the produce of my base craft! I made it so I could forget my craft. I gave it my heart. And in return it persuaded me

I was better than the work I performed for the Sheriff. And now it pleads for me to reacquaint myself with the work I want so much to be rid of!

BOY. I don't understand, sir.

PRYNNE. It's a machine for a voice without a body . . . it was for this purpose I assembled its parts. Now it miscarries . . . it demands instead the dirt of bodily experience. It demands your filth . . . as well as the filth the other masterless men passed on to you in your confinement. Anger too . . . it thrives on anger . . . it wants the anger you feel for being made a vessel for their filth. The anger you have for me . . . for helping to make possible the passage of such filth.

BOY. Sir . . .

PRYNNE. The machine's yours when I die . . . it must be used to advance the cause of ordinary men. Great men are simple to fathom . . . they want power only to impose the shapes of their imaginations upon a world that discomforts them. But ordinary men . . . they introduce a confusion into history. The story of the world is their story . . . their hardship.

BOY. What do I do with it, sir?

PRYNNE. Astound it . . . it's for you and all those like you . . . men who cannot read or write . . . men who have only their talk. Take it to your grave . . . it'll tell your story to generations yet unborn. (*Cries out.*) Such headaches! . . .

BOY. Should I . . .

PRYNNE. We've done it, boy, we've fooled 'em . . . they were going to confiscate the words stored in my machine. (*Breaks off.*) It's not painful . . . none of it's painful . . . it's just a disorder in the mind, that's all. (*Strains as he sits up.*) Bring it here. I'll instruct you in its use. Or have I instructed you already?

BOY. No, sir.

PRYNNE. If I repeat myself, you must tell me. You mustn't let my mind wander or else I'll forget why I asked to see you.

BOY. You were going to instruct me, sir.

PRYNNE. That's it . . . speak up . . . don't be frightened of my rank. This is where I've gone, you see . . . into the machine. Where I was going. Where I am.

BOY. In the machine, sir?

PRYNNE. Turn the spindle . . . the spindle at the side.

Spindle turning.

Now tell the machine what you want it to know. (*Silence.*) I'm
giving you the machine so it can record your grievances. (*Silence.*)
Address it, then. You have grievances to settle. Address your machine,
damn you. (*Silence.*) I don't hear you, boy! I don't hear anything!

Scene 18

Interior. PRYNNE's *rooms. Day. Spindle turning. During the following*
PRYNNE's *voice is gradually and imperceptibly transformed into a*
filtered, distorted recording from the machine.

PRYNNE. These last moments . . . my last moments . . . will be as
fresh and clear in hundreds of years as they are to me now . . .
preserved in perfect detail. In this machine my poor thoughts form
themselves into an irrefutable pattern. They confidentially give up their
secrets and now challenge the agents of that future age. Render them
false if you will, though it may dispose you to treat them as lies of the
most appealing kind . . . lies that seek only to serve the truth. Satisfy
you to welcome them as peaceful emissaries to your own time . . .
as currency to be made use of in service to your beliefs. They are
absolute . . . doctrinal. And it is my last act to shepherd them from
a world which has known my worldly presence to one that shall
not. Words out of time speaking up for me against the new despots
of your age. Unexplained echoes and shadows . . . as insubstantial
as the spirits of those that might have been. My thoughts vouchsafe
my previous existence and reconstruct me in your century. For exist
I did. Rival ideologies of nature testify to my existence as they battle
for tyranny over my reconstituted state. A score of such phantoms . . .
each with its own will . . . seek a host animal in the spirit of Ned
Prynne. They assemble here now . . . in this room . . . assemble
even as the disease gnaws at my innards . . . as mucus collects in my
lungs. They too will be sealed forever in my machine . . . with the
bailiff and the many things he is supposed not to know. It's a man
trapped outside time itself that speaks to you now . . . as knowledge
itself is trapped outside time. So examine now this apostle from the
past who skims from age to age like an unseeing god. Construct an
aviary for his thoughts and display and prod them as you might his
flesh and tissue. And explore this corridor back to his time. Such a
prize to be had . . . the accretion of scholar and subject . . . such a
prize. . . . (*Pause.*) But I know that not even the felon or the idle
conniver of treason will want to call up this event . . . or any other
part of the life that has gone before. Or the life of my custodian –
the boy. The boy'll look after my machine, right enough . . . hide it
in a place of safekeeping. But to what end? Can *he* make any better
use of it? He will not speak. And for all my vision I did not see
him as he will one day be . . . worn down by anxiety and daily
cares. Is *this* to be the fate of my creation too? Is this what I made
it for? To be put aside and forgotten? Not impounded and ritually

destroyed . . . just forgotten. To have lived in fear all those years . . .
to have thrown away so much in preparation for something that never
happened. Nothing happened . . . they left my machine alone. Now
it'll survive long enough to find it's been thought up all over again.
Or worse . . . some future biographer will summon up my thoughts
from its corroded guts and find in my bodged life the inspiration for
invention of his own devising. (*Pause*.) But there's no profit in
this . . . the story's been told. I am content to abstain now. Content
to be a voice without a body.

A BUTLER DID IT

by David Cregan

David Cregan was born in 1931 and educated at Cambridge University, where he was a member of the Comedy Theatre Group, The Mummers and the Footlights. Before becoming a full-time writer, he worked for several years as an English teacher and mouse poison salesman. He has written one novel and over forty plays, twenty-five of them for the stage and twelve for radio. His radio play, *The Awful Insulation of Rage*, was awarded the Sony Prize for the best drama script of 1987 and in 1990 his Fringe play for children, *Cinderella*, was nominated for the Whitbread Prize. He is a member of the Eastern Arts Drama Panel and a founder member of the Theatre Writers' Union.

A *Butler Did It* was first broadcast on 'Drama Now', BBC Radio 3, on 31 July 1990. The cast was as follows:

PAULA	Melanie Nicholson
(upper-middle-class, 23)	
DANIEL	Simon Treves
(middle-class professional, 24)	
SIR DESMOND LISLE	Hugh Manning
(potent, self-made, Paula's grandfather, 70)	
HONEYMAN	Bernard Hepton
(Sir Desmond's butler, ageless but actually 58)	
HARRY	Roger Hammond
(Honeyman's younger brother)	
SAMANTHA	Anna Massey
(Sir Desmond's daughter, mid-forties, Paula's mother)	
ALFRED	Ian Collier
(Sir Desmond's son, 40)	
ALASTAIR	Neville Jason
(Samantha's husband, Paula's father, gallery owner)	
SEAN	Geoffrey Beevers
(Samantha's lover, TV journalist)	
CLERICAL VOICE	David King
(in Salisbury Cathedral)	
BBC NEWS ANNOUNCER	Simon Milner

Director: John Tydeman
Running time, as broadcast: 70 minutes

The sound of the spring wind in the trees. Two sets of footsteps approach from the distance. Over this the voice of HONEYMAN, *a butler of precise tone, aged fifty-eight, addresses the audience.*

HONEYMAN. That spring, when the young people walked in terrible naïvety through the woods above Salisbury, with the symbolic shoots of nature pushy as ever, they undid more than they knew, more than I, the butler, knew, more than the established world was prepared to admit. Young people, young at least in mind people, can disturb so amazingly much, one is forced to admire it.

The footsteps now stop close to us.

PAULA. Oh! A little yellow daffodil.

DANIEL. I thought you'd never speak.

PAULA. I wonder who dropped it in the mud like this?

DANIEL. Hello! Anyone about, looking for a little yellow daff –

PAULA. It doesn't matter.

DANIEL. Hello!

PAULA. Please don't. They probably want to take it home, to decorate their dinner table. I hate mahogany.

Walking starts again.

DANIEL. Decorate their dinner table?

PAULA. Isn't that what people do?

DANIEL. Not my people.

PAULA. Oh.

Wind noise and walking only. Then:

I hadn't said anything before because I didn't know how to start.

DANIEL. Why?

PAULA. Well, I like to think I know things, I mean we all do know things, don't we, we've been given knowledge, but you seem to know things that are rather far off.

DANIEL. Like people who don't decorate their dinner tables.

PAULA. Yes, I know, I did have friends, you know, at college, and I have visited. It's just –

DANIEL. Yes?

PAULA. It's just . . . the feeling of being overwhelmed, of seeing a face I always dreamed of – I always thought it would belong to someone whose dinner table would be decorated.

DANIEL. Where do *you* have dinner?

PAULA. It's just when you find you've gone this far towards someone, and they're not –

Walking stops.

Please can we kiss?

DANIEL (*close to her*). You're lovely. (*Very close.*) Lovely and lost.

PAULA. Pardon?

DANIEL. I don't know what I meant by that.

PAULA. Yes, you do.

DANIEL. It was presumption.

PAULA. I'm terribly poised.

DANIEL. Let's kiss.

PAULA. All right. No, let's not.

Walking starts again.

DANIEL. Oh, bloody hell.

PAULA. We can get back to Salisbury this way.

Walking is faster than before.

DANIEL. Is this because of a bloody little daffodil?

PAULA. Nothing's so innocent it can't disturb you.

DANIEL. Even if you're terribly poised?

PAULA. We all have insecurity, Daniel. It just gets set off by different things in different people.

DANIEL. Like mention of dinner tables.

PAULA. I wish I hadn't come to Grandpa's for the weekend. I like people to be clichés.

DANIEL. I'm hardly original.

PAULA. You're too original for me.

Sounds of another person splashing along the path.

And someone's coming. He's trying to dodge the puddles of spring. I think the sun is blinding his glasses.

DANIEL. Can you hear what he's saying to himself?

The footsteps are near now. Angry footsteps.

PAULA. Good afternoon.

The man doesn't stop. He is HARRY, *of whom more later, a man in the upper-middle-age bracket.*

HARRY. What? Oh yes, I suppose so.

PAULA. Is something wrong?

HARRY. Never have a brother who's cleverer than you, especially an older one. Goodbye.

He has never stopped walking.

PAULA. What a peculiar thing to say.

DANIEL. Can we kiss now?

PAULA. All right.

They kiss.

HONEYMAN (*voice over*). Why are lips so dangerous? Why is the silken skin of mouths – eating, talking, loving – why is that the place where devastation lurks?

PAULA (*almost a whisper to* DANIEL). I never knew kissing could be so complete.

DANIEL (*also in a whisper*). It's the first time I've never felt the need to make light conversation afterwards, certainly. Let's do it again, because I don't know where to put all this feeling.

The wind continues to blow freshly.

The acoustic of a conservatory, where watering is taking place.
SIR DESMOND LISLE *is doing this. His butler,* HONEYMAN, *is apparently just in the house, and is being called out to his master. When* HONEYMAN *walks, his step is springy and competent.*

SIR DESMOND. Honeyman?

HONEYMAN. Sir Desmond?

SIR DESMOND. I'm in the conservatory, watering.

HONEYMAN. Of course.

He comes out.

SIR DESMOND. There was a man in the kitchen this afternoon, wearing glasses and a suit.

HONEYMAN. My brother, sir. I hope he didn't disturb you. He's a bank manager.

SIR DESMOND. My butler has a brother who's a bank manager?

HONEYMAN. I'm very sorry, sir. I have kept him quiet, though, up to now.

SIR DESMOND. Don't let him out again. Everyman is entitled to climb wherever he can, but I don't want the family disturbing.

HONEYMAN. I'll tell him.

SIR DESMOND. The status quo is what the new rich aim for, Honeyman, so if it disappears when we reach it, our lives have been totally in vain.

HONEYMAN. I sympathise completely, sir.

SIR DESMOND. You can't be rich and powerful unless there's someone to be rich and powerful over.

HONEYMAN. I do appreciate comprehensively the delicate position of the rich and powerful, Sir Desmond.

SIR DESMOND. We need to feel safe.

HONEYMAN. I know. You are fully admired and appreciated by me, and you can put my brother completely out of your head.

SIR DESMOND. Then why was he here?

HONEYMAN. We always spend our holidays together and were talking about the summer. We're going to trace Stevenson's *Travels with a Donkey*, in the Cevennes. It's in southern France.

SIR DESMOND. Not Stockton to Darlington?

HONEYMAN. That was a different family.

SIR DESMOND. You make me nervous, sometimes.

HONEYMAN (*a little anxious*). I don't mean to.

SIR DESMOND. Then get the tea. And the children are coming, so mash it properly.

HONEYMAN. I'll tell Mrs Fellows.

HONEYMAN *walks away and we hear him going down passages and eventually arriving at the kitchen. As he goes, he addresses the listener with this speech.*

HONEYMAN (*voice over*). I was a grammar school boy, like poor brother Harry, fearfully intelligent and deeply in love with the life of the very, very rich, because it purchased so much culture – I mean, to live with Rembrandts and sit on Hepplewhite. However, I also felt scorn and loathing for the way huge wealth was acquired, depressing humanity in general for the benefit of the few. That is the basic immorality of life, the elementary evil. So, to satisfy my longings and to keep my conscience clear, both at the same time, I became a butler, living well and taking no responsibility for it. We all do that, don't we? And as I had long ago rejected loyalty as incompatible with clarity of thought, I also felt no duty to my master, and was prepared always, when the time came, to ditch him. I might've been a very great man, Harry said, but then he was my younger brother, and hated me hysterically, for which I was genuinely sad.

Arriving at the kitchen through a door.

(*Normal voice.*) Family tea, Mrs Fellows. They'll be here at any moment.

The sound of two people's feet on the floor of the conservatory. They belong to SAMANTHA, SIR DESMOND's daughter and PAULA's mother, and to ALFRED, who is younger than SAMANTHA, SIR DESMOND's son.

SAM. Our Father, which art in the conservatory –

SIR DESMOND. Welcome to the simple pleasures, the country –

SAM. We're all so locked into your daydreams, Father, that we almost don't exist. How are you?

SIR DESMOND. Where's your husband?

SAM. At the gallery.

SIR DESMOND. I warned you about art, Samantha. Spoils Sunday, always has done. Hello, Alfred.

ALFRED. Father.

SIR DESMOND. Anything new since Friday?

ALFRED. Just the golf.

SIR DESMOND. Wentworth?

ALFRED. Moor Park.

SIR DESMOND. Near Watford, which isn't up to much. Make it Wentworth next week.

ALFRED. Yes, Father.

SIR DESMOND. And your daughter needs smacking, Samantha. She's been out ever since she came home.

SAM. Home isn't here. It's with us, in London.

SIR DESMOND. She's got her own flat?

SAM. Yes.

SIR DESMOND. Then she ought to have a husband. I don't like the way the young make mock of what we all aspire to. Get her settled, Sam, family-like. Yes?

SAM. We'll see.

SIR DESMOND. We will. Now, tea.

They all move.

Next week you'll come for lunch.

SAM/ALFRED. Er . . .

SIR DESMOND. It'll be no trouble to us, will it, Honeyman?

HONEYMAN (*clattering cups*). It'll be a great pleasure, Sir Desmond.

SAM. What else could you say, Honeyman?

HONEYMAN. It's the truth.

SIR DESMOND. You're not paid to tell the truth, Honeyman, just the credible. And remember you two, if it weren't for me you'd have grown up in the North, in the back streets of Stockport, so you needn't look gloomy at the thought of Sunday lunch.

HONEYMAN (*voice over sound of teacups*). We lived all week in Holland Park, and only came to Salisbury at the weekend. I loved driving the Daimler, low, unshakeable, and I always had the use of it for myself, which made Harry wild.

In the quietly humming Daimler.

HARRY (*an angry bank manager*). You don't know anything about life, Tom Honeyman.

HONEYMAN. I know immense things, Harry. The sheer silk of driving this black dart through London teaches me more about life than all your days struggling up the ladder at the Midland.

HARRY. Struggle teaches you everything that matters.

HONEYMAN. Oh, I know about struggle. I watch television.

HARRY. He's given you that as well. You've never even had to buy a licence.

HONEYMAN. Nor a meal, Harry. You and I are about to feast once again on the Diner's Card he pays for, and you're going to adore it, aren't you?

HARRY. Oh God! I am weak and the food'll be so lovely.

HONEYMAN. Stick with me. Sir Desmond's family are, as always, in my hands, giving me my pleasure.

Differing acoustics.

ALFRED. What would we do without you, Honeyman?

HONEYMAN (*slightly simpering*). Very little, Mr Alfred.

SAM. Part of the family, Honeyman.

HONEYMAN. And its secrets, Miss Sam.

ALFRED. Run me a bath.

SAM. Run me a bath.

HONEYMAN (*voice over*). If it weren't for me – oh, if it weren't for me! That's what I thought, then.

A restaurant. More slurps than indicated, probably.

HONEYMAN (*normal voice*). The truth is, Harry – do you have to slurp your soup?

HARRY. I'm a bachelor.

HONEYMAN. So am I, but I don't offend myself by doing that. The truth is, I'm no different from anyone else, superficially. I serve wealth, like we all do, and I take my pleasures where I can. But, and here's the real truth, very soon I can and will change everything by one, simple –

Very loud slurp. HONEYMAN *has a burst of alarming fury.*

Oh, for heaven's sake!

HARRY (*very angry*). I wish you'd been a great man and left me alone!

HONEYMAN. You'd miss our lovely holidays.

HARRY. Not me!

HONEYMAN. You would!

HARRY. Take someone else!

HONEYMAN. I want you.

HARRY. To treat like dirt?

HONEYMAN. You're a highly intelligent manager of a bank in the West End of London. That's not dirt. It's a rarity on lots of counts.

HARRY. You always make my job sound like a joke.

HONEYMAN. Try to learn about jokes, will you? And try to get hold of some views, so we can tussle brilliantly over our baguettes.

HARRY. I hate Matisse.

HONEYMAN. Is that a joke or a view?

HARRY. You see? Dirt!

HONEYMAN. By views I mean ideals. You must have some somewhere. Convictions, passions –

HARRY. We passed the eleven plus to be purged of those. I don't know how you did it, but you still seem to have convictions and passions and all sorts of things that should've been balanced out of you at school.

HONEYMAN. Oh, school. We were exhorted there to be honest and to be loyal, two mutually incompatible ideals. We weren't purged, Harry, we were simply placed in an impossible position which turned into a trauma. (*Slurp*.) Oh God! The city's full of men who've been shocked into immobility by having to be honest and yet never to reveal the duplicity of their friends. They look glazed, and grin a lot, and talk without inflection. They can't live creative lives at all because they're caught by the balls by English middle-class morality, the seering, almost castrating stiff upper lip, ready to engage its teeth, unless they swear to believe in honesty and loyalty at the same time, which of course, they can't. (*Slurp*.) Well, I've thrown off loyalty. The truth is, Harry, the truth about me, the real truth, is that I am in a position to unravel so much wealth, so much dishonestly acquired money, that I could make the world an infinitely happier place tomorrow. And one day soon, I will.

HARRY. How?

HONEYMAN. Well – you see – I could kill Sir Desmond Lisle, couldn't I?

HARRY. For God's sake –

HONEYMAN. Why not?

HARRY. Human life is sacred.

HONEYMAN. To whom?

HARRY. It doesn't matter whom to. It's a useful phrase to stop us killing people we don't like.

HONEYMAN. Are you showing loyalty to the human race?

HARRY. Yes.

HONEYMAN. How humdrum. How typically colourless!

HARRY. I hate you!

HONEYMAN. Sibling rivalry. And you're not to visit Salisbury again. Sir Desmond says.

(*Voice over.*) I was very nearly part of the family. Even in my little flat, my eyrie at the top of the Holland Park home, with my television window to the world outside, even there, the family visited me, part of their lives.

Acoustic of a room with a TV playing in it. A door opens.

HONEYMAN. Miss Paula!

PAULA. Do sit down.

HONEYMAN. I – er –

PAULA. You've got a new television.

HONEYMAN. Your grandfather provides me, always.

PAULA. Did you choose it?

HONEYMAN. That would've been too much. I'm simply grateful for all the generosity that –

PAULA. Gratitude is dangerously near servitude, don't you think?

HONEYMAN. I am a servant.

PAULA. Part of the family. I came to you because there was no one in and I wanted to tell someone I was happy.

HONEYMAN. I'm honoured that –

PAULA. Oh, for God's sake, how starchy can you be?

HONEYMAN. What made you happy?

PAULA (*acid*). I can't tell the butler, can I? He's just a servant.

HONEYMAN. Love?

PAULA. In the woods above Salisbury. Oh, Honeyman, I'm happy for the first time in my life. That's the rain forest you're watching.

HONEYMAN. Miss Paula, you must've been happy before this.

PAULA. No. What a pity they have to chop it down. Still, we can't have everything.

HONEYMAN. Miss Paula?

PAULA. It's no use, I can't talk to you. We're miles and miles apart.

HONEYMAN (*voice over*). There was, to be frank, an awful lot of triviality. The curly crockery, the embossed silver – rich men so frequently get lost in luxury, and then the shapes of things get blurred, and the sharpness of life is blunted. He had so many art treasures – I swooned daily over his Impressionists – yet it was the chintz that took up all my time, straightening it, dusting it, preparing it as the scenery for his game of happy families.

Sound of footsteps on marble floor.

ALFRED. Honeyman.

Footsteps stop.

HONEYMAN (*on ladder*). Mr Alfred?

ALFRED. I have to speak to you. Come off that ladder.

HONEYMAN. Your father can't abide the possibility of cobwebs in the pelmets, Mr Alfred. Shouldn't you be at the office?

ALFRED. I'm at a business lunch. And I'm not coming to Salisbury next weekend. I'm going to France.

HONEYMAN. La petite maison secondaire in Normandy?

ALFRED. I have to guard my property and see that it's all right.

HONEYMAN. He's set his heart on everyone, you, Miss Sam, Miss Paula –

ALFRED. Tell him it's an investment.

HONEYMAN. I'll do my best.

ALFRED. What would we do without you?

HONEYMAN (*voice over*). I did wonder even then if the rituals were changing me. People are changed that way. They become what they look like. I was almost too good at butling. Drawing baths for instance – (*Chuckles.*) – I loved drawing baths.

Sound of bathwater.

HONEYMAN (*calling*). I'm drawing the bath, Miss Samantha, in your old room.

SAM (*coming upstairs*). No need to mention this to Father, Honeyman.

HONEYMAN. Very well.

SAM (*surprised*). You keep the rooms exactly as they were!

HONEYMAN. He likes to feel his home is solid and secure.

SAM. To keep away the memory of Stockport. (*Laughs.*) Have you ever been to Stockport?

HONEYMAN. I'm happy to say not. Though I know it well from his bath-time lectures.

SAM. Unzip me, will you.

HONEYMAN. Me?

SAM. There's no need to be afraid, Tom. You're practically a member of the family, and, being wealthy, we're not that sort of family, are we?

HONEYMAN. No.

SAM. Besides – oh, besides, besides –

HONEYMAN. Miss Sam?

SAM. Things happen to one. One accidentally looks through a new window and the view's wildly different. Don't you want to know why I'm here at four in the afternoon?

HONEYMAN. It's hardly my place to ask that sort –

SAM. Place? I'm here because my husband – he does have a name, we must try to remember it –

HONEYMAN. Alastair.

SAM. Alastair is at home this afternoon, cataloguing things. And I can't meet him, smelling of another man.

HONEYMAN. I see.

SAM. And I don't think I can make lunch on Sunday, Honeyman.

HONEYMAN. Oh dear.

SAM. You'd better go now, I suppose, though you've seen me often enough in my knickers as a child. And out of them.

HONEYMAN. Good heavens – a dressing gown –

SAM (*laughing*). You prude!

HONEYMAN (*voice over*). She wasn't beautiful, but there are things a butler shouldn't see. And shouldn't be seen to see. Like all the family she was immensely sensual and largely unaware of it. Paula was the same, the most sensual of all of them, drawing you to her without meaning to.

DANIEL's *flat. The sound of a record player playing the final moments of the first movement of the Brahms Violin Concerto.*

PAULA. Daniel, I don't know if I'm into this, yet.

Record player goes off.

People seem to do it all over the place, like Uncle Alfred's golf, and that's confusing. It isn't known I'm here, either.

DANIEL. By whom?

PAULA. I don't know why I said that. What do you do, here in London?

DANIEL. Geology. I work at –

PAULA. Yes, of course, I forgot.

DANIEL. What do you do?

PAULA. Oh. The plan is for me to become an architect's assistant, which I am, and then an architect.

DANIEL. Whose plan?

PAULA. Mine – yes, mine.

DANIEL. Not your grandfather's?

PAULA. They laugh at him where I work. They call him The Dread Developer. Has anyone ever laughed at your relatives?

DANIEL. Isn't that what people do?

PAULA. Not my people. We've had this conversation once. I haven't come for that.

DANIEL. What have you come for?

PAULA. Actually, I feel foolish, and I haven't come for that, either.

DANIEL. I don't think it's my fault.

PAULA. I'd better go away again and do some drawings I'm supposed to work on.

DANIEL. Why?

PAULA. Daniel, I'm a grown-up girl with a job. I'm not supposed to be here.

DANIEL. Supposed by whom?

PAULA. You do pry, don't you?

DANIEL. We met over Saturday sherry in Wiltshire, kissed in the spring woods, and felt very much part of each other. What lies behind all this? Haven't you come to find out?

PAULA. You said I could call whenever I liked.

DANIEL. Is that all?

PAULA. Isn't it enough?

DANIEL. Are you always like this?

PAULA. There you go again, prying.

DANIEL. Oh, for heaven's sake –

PAULA. Well, have you any Mozart?

DANIEL. I'll see.

PAULA. I know I'm disappointing, but that's what I am. I'm a disappointment.

DANIEL. Who to?

PAULA. Well – (*The Mozart Missa Solemnis goes on.*) People float towards me, and then float away again, I watch it happen. I meant more cheerful Mozart than this.

DANIEL. I haven't any. I'm in love with you.

PAULA. You don't know who I am. I'm finished, the end of something. No, don't ask. Do not ask what I am the end of.

DANIEL. Wouldn't you like to know about me?

PAULA. No. Well, I do know about you, from the way you move and things.

DANIEL. How people smell, how they invite you to enquire, how they put you aside. That comes so quickly. But you have to use words, too. And your words are different from the way you smell.

PAULA. I'm a nice girl.

Record off.

DANIEL. I was brought up in Salisbury, so I, too, have suffered niceness. I'm very straightforward, and very interested in what I do, which is research into the platelets of the earth's crust. My father, a solicitor, is very fond of me, as is my mother, and I'm fond of them, though we don't share a single view, I think, we rarely talk about it. My sister's married to a lecturer in art in Newcastle with a family and she's very nice, very contributive, very happy when we meet, because we like each other, and I'm happy about that, it's nice, nicer even than being friends, but I don't know what it is, or even if I ought to try to find out, because I'd have to pick away at things we've only said to each other once, and maybe thought of long ago, and underneath there are questions that are very tender. You've touched those questions, and I am not what I was at midday last Saturday when I parked my car in the drive of the Lancing-Thompsons' large house and walked in for sherry. Something universal has reared up and stared at me.

PAULA. You're prepared to talk about all this?

DANIEL. I have to.

PAULA. Is that what people do?

DANIEL. I do.

PAULA. And you laugh at your relations?

DANIEL. I'd hit them otherwise. I'm going to kiss you now.

PAULA. All right.

DANIEL. It might be a bit unkempt this time.

PAULA. All right.

DANIEL. And then perhaps you'll talk.

PAULA. Can I stay with you in Salisbury this weekend and make love in the woods?

Beginning to kiss.

Bath running.

SIR DESMOND. The green dressing gown, Honeyman. Green eases the spirit after a busy day.

HONEYMAN. Sir.

SIR DESMOND. And now a bath. Oh, I love that bath.

HONEYMAN. Don't we all.

SIR DESMOND. I never thought of you feeling things. Don't go.

HONEYMAN (*turning bath taps off*). Sir.

SIR DESMOND *can be heard getting in.*

SIR DESMOND. Oh, ah, that's marvellous. I'd like to be able to say we kept coal in ours in Stockport, but that would be too colourful. Stockport was stale, the grey stale life of keeping body and soul together, and the great grieving Stockport railway viaduct across the valley.

HONEYMAN. I can never quite see the valley –

SIR DESMOND. The word 'valley' makes it sound like Switzerland that's why, but Stockport was a mud pie of trolley trucks, and cobblestones, and greasy black sludge. It was as if a huge slug had crawled across the banks of the river, and stopped, coughed and died, the whole ugly mess as far as Hazel Grove stinking of smoke and grime. And bloody hell, the Germans missed it in the war, would you believe it. It's all still there, cleaner in some places, drabber in others, but still rotting, dead but endlessly suppurating, and bits of green grass fighting through and withering around Davenport, and motorways skirting round it, derelict buildings in Moss Side. Oh Honeyman, a bath here in Holland Park, with fitted carpets and massive curtains, Old Masters on the heavy wallpaper, I tell you, it's a great fortress against the slug. And the gardens in Salisbury, flowery cushioned ramparts against the oozing North of England. You don't know the terror lurking in the word Stockport. And Crewe and Bury, and those awful, seeping Lowry paintings. And Buxton, the Buxton moors were covered in sooty sheep, like bodies from Belsen. The Peak District had all the soot of Glossop falling on it, you know, black heather till you got to Chatsworth. Chatsworth, now, oh Chatsworth was a sudden waft of Versailles, but I can't think how the Duke lives so near the enemy. Sheffield pushing over the hill, Derby drab to the south, I couldn't do it. I'd be frightened to death.

HONEYMAN. I truly believe you are braver than you think, sir.

SIR DESMOND. Fear makes you do brave things, certainly. I made money because I was afraid. Money keeps me safe. It gives me home. Your brother would know.

HONEYMAN. I don't think he considers money in that way.

SIR DESMOND. For me, money is the power that keeps Stockport at bay. And on Sunday I shall have my family about me for lunch in the country. That, Honeyman, is achievement – a big house in the southern counties, and all my family about me.

HONEYMAN. It's a pity Lady Lillian won't . . .

SIR DESMOND. She used to interrupt. You can go now.

HONEYMAN (*voice over*). I should've killed him then and there, with the word 'family' on his lips. He would've been happy. I would've been happy. As it was, there was that cocky little lover of Samantha's at one of those functions in the art gallery.

Sounds of function in art gallery. Then alarmed SAMANTHA.

SAM. Darling! We can't meet in Alastair's gallery.

The conversation continues in a whisper or low tones.

SEAN. We aren't meeting, we're bumping into one another. Which one is Alastair?

SAM. The one with the pleasant face and the half smile, nodding slowly to the serious man in the Italian jacket, and then nodding fast at the end of each sentence as he laughs nervously.

We hear a nervous laugh.

SEAN. Oh, Sam. He seems nice.

SAM. Yes, he does seem nice. Why've you come?

SEAN. To look. Can't stay long. The mail train goes at four and I have to film my parcel leaving the depot.

SAM. Can't someone else? Then we could –

SEAN. I have to be there myself if I'm to prove it gets interrupted. I just came to get a glimpse of you in your habitat and to ask if everything's fixed for Sunday?

SAM. Alastair will go to Father's in his car, and I'll say I'm picking up Paula from somewhere remote in mine, while she will go up by train as usual.

SEAN. This isn't just an affair, Sam. You won't be going back. We'll kill the ghosts in Salisbury Wood, and then run off together.

SAM. I might be frightened to begin with. A life in jeans, and I haven't worn jeans for years.

SEAN. You worked in television once.

SAM. I was passing time, then.

PAULA. Why are you talking into your catalogues?

SAM. Paula darling!

PAULA. I need to see you. Who's this?

SAM. His name is Sean, he makes investigative television and this is Paula, my only child.

PAULA. Can't you go back to work or something?

SEAN. Yes I can. Goodbye, Sam.

SAM. So nice to bump into you. And what is it?

PAULA. I won't be coming on Sunday.

SAM. What?

PAULA. I might not see you again for ages, actually. I'm not running away, but I am rather sick of you.

SAM. You're twenty-four, Paula. You should've done this at sixteen.

PAULA. Better late than never. Goodbye.

SAM. Paula!

ALASTAIR (*approaching*). Hello, Sam. Hello, Paula. (*Laughs.*)

SAM. Alastair, Paula's leaving us.

ALASTAIR. Goodbye, Paula.

PAULA (*distant*). Goodbye, Daddy.

ALASTAIR. What is it?

SAM. A man I should think. It's time for one.

ALASTAIR. Yes. (*Laughs.*) Is it?

SAM. Oh God, Alastair, you really are the dullest man in art. You make me sicker than brother Alfred, which is saying something.

ALASTAIR. It is. Alfred makes *me* sick. (*Laughs.*)

SAM. Goodbye, Alastair.

ALASTAIR. Paula has a flat of her own, so she's left us already. Have I missed something? Sam?

Church music, hymns, choirs or organ forms the background to the next two speeches.

HONEYMAN (*voice over*). Could I have sensed a need to act sooner? Perhaps quite differently from how I did? I put away so many things I didn't want to know. That Sunday, he still expected them for lunch after church in the Cathedral, because I hadn't managed to tell him otherwise. I didn't believe otherwise.

BBC VOICE. Speculation that the Chancellor may have to raise interest rates even further brought outspoken comment in today's papers. They pointed out that the increase in home ownership is already causing an underlying strain on disposable income, and that any increase in mortgages is likely not only to curb the current spending boom, but to increase wage inflation, thus putting a further brake on domestic industrial growth, already under pressure from the growth of import penetration.

This speech and the church music give way to the echoing voice of a preacher in Salisbury Cathedral.

CLERICAL VOICE. The family, of course, is the centre of all Christian imagery, and the image of the father bears the central weight of that great metaphor. As we all sit together round our family dinner tables today, we should recall that we are part of one of the greatest and weightiest poems of social and religious significance. For the family is the seat of all that is good and right in human life, just as this great building, with its mighty spire, is the centre of all that is good and right in the wider context.

SIR DESMOND. So where the bloody hell are they?

HONEYMAN. Mr Alastair will be here very soon –

SIR DESMOND. Oh, full of sparks!

HONEYMAN. – but Mr Alfred had to attend to his capital investment in France.

SIR DESMOND. French letters, more like.

HONEYMAN. Miss Sam has been called away –

SIR DESMOND. She's got a lover. I've had the correspondence interrupted but there's nothing I can do.

HONEYMAN. And Miss Paula –

SIR DESMOND. An only child and spoilt. I told Samantha, you must have two, like I did, but she's stubborn. Well, I said a family bloody lunch, and I meant a family bloody lunch!

A smash.

HONEYMAN. Your geraniums!

SIR DESMOND. This morning's sermon bore on this, the family, the great poem.

Another smash.

HONEYMAN. The begonias!

SIR DESMOND. And God the Father. Oh, which of my children would hang themselves on a cross at my command?

HONEYMAN. I'm sure they're totally devoted to –

SIR DESMOND. I've made this family safe and all I've got to show for it is a half-wit owner of an art gallery full of cubes and splodges and chairs covered in milk bottle tops – (*Smash.*) – They'd lock him up in Stockport.

HONEYMAN. You loved the cinerarias. I painted them for you.

SIR DESMOND. Why didn't you tell me all this earlier?

HONEYMAN. You had the pleasure of anticipation.

SIR DESMOND. And the pain of disappointment.

HONEYMAN. Well, I'm sorry.

SIR DESMOND. So you should be.

HONEYMAN. I couldn't stop them.

SIR DESMOND. Why not?

HONEYMAN. It's not my place.

SIR DESMOND. Place? Can't you take any responsibility?

HONEYMAN. That's very wounding. I run your home beautifully and you know it.

SIR DESMOND. Yes. And today you'll dine with us to make up for the others.

HONEYMAN. Me?

SIR DESMOND. You're part of the family, paid not to let me down.

HONEYMAN. But I'd be out of place!

SIR DESMOND. You'll be out of place if you don't do what I say. Sacked without a reference. Get the soup.

HONEYMAN (*voice over*). Sacked! It went to my heart like an arrow, confusing me with panic. And I'd never known panic in my life.

The acoustic of the kitchen in Salisbury.

HONEYMAN. I can't help it, Mrs Fellows, I must eat with him, he says, or else be sacked. I know you like my conversation of a Sunday, but there's nothing to be done. I'll take the soup and come back for the joint.

He starts to walk along a corridor.

(*Voice over.*) Why was I so frightened of being sacked? Had I accepted my position as a parasite more completely than I thought? Had I yielded my independence? Was I truly part of the family? Oh, Tom Honeyman, you were an arrogant fool! And up above Salisbury, in the woods, there was more life happening than you could control!

The acoustic of the woods, this time without the wind. Two people are climaxing sexually in a yelp of joy.

PAULA. It *is* your face! Ever since I was at boarding school and had my first crush it was a face like yours.

DANIEL. Am I just a fantasy?

PAULA. Not yet. So far you're still real.

DANIEL. Your stomach is extraordinary.

PAULA. It wouldn't be if it were windy. Stomachs look like tripe when they're cold.

DANIEL. Well . . . sunshine, drying ours.

PAULA. You're kind, aren't you? I've known others and they weren't kind at all.

DANIEL. It's a thing for two people, Paula. It's not just a man and a doughnut.

PAULA. In a way, it does very much concern oneself. One's very own self, which another person is allowed to know and stir. I should be having lunch with the family at Grandpa's. Your parents don't seem to mind what you do.

DANIEL. We have established a way of living between us.

PAULA. Grandpa has a butler for establishing ways of living with us. He calls us Miss Samantha, Miss Paula, Mr Alfred – a sort of parrot.

A sound of giggles.

PAULA. Who's that?

DANIEL. Two other people prancing about without their – good heavens, it's your mother.

PAULA. Picking daffodils for her table?

DANIEL. Not exactly. Pull something on, and don't look.

PAULA. Well, I don't know, should I?

We close on SEAN *and* SAMANTHA.

SAM. Why choose this wood for killing ghosts?

SEAN. Your father's been interfering with the public mail for years, and I have to exorcise my anger over that by making love to you above his house.

SAM. You have made your film about him.

SEAN. Ah, I love you, I love you, I love –

SAM. Just a minute, I've got things to say.

SEAN. And things to do.

SAM. I've often done things with my clothes off, but hardly ever said things. Now then, I've been waiting for you ever since Paula left school. Before, really, since she was at boarding school and I've been bored ever since I packed her off.

SEAN. Are we doing this simply out of boredom?

SAM. Boredom is a formative experience like any other. It makes its mark by sealing you in, denying you existence, forbidding any expression of yourself, withering your feelers into life. And the longer it goes on, the more you shrink, and you squeeze out stuff – little excuses, little jobs, little illnesses, little, little – which thicken the boundaries between you and life. Your thinking limbs shorten and shrivel, so you begin to need the bandage of little doings as protection against the world where once you were. It's a barrier of dozens of little voluntary committees – I don't know what the ones I sat on were for – and if you show any life at all it's as a trapped wasp, a buzz-fly, whirring round charity shows and fancy dress balls – oh, the humming sessions I went to about Shakespeare with well-known actors, the entertaining drone nights I rigged up for Alastair's artists. And no one would've noticed if I'd stopped, mummified by triviality. They won't now. No one will miss the tiny tic-tac of my life, the frantic round of buzzing scratchings, always elegant and pointless. I thought that to want somebody like you, all consuming, oh no, that was immoral, extravagant, whorish. But it turns out that I was waiting for just that. For you to smash my life open.

SEAN. How did I do that, exactly?

SAM. You showed me the thrill of the chase. You took me into the editing room on that tour of the BBC I'd organised for some squeaking ladies like myself, and just shifted my whole perspective, like giving me new glasses. I wanted to be behind the camera where you'd been, hunting the men – my father's men in this case – I wanted to nail those awful people with you, take those prying shots, ask those impermissible questions, feel the unforgivable passion. Then, there you were, sexy as hell, offering it to me. 'You worked in TV before, I'll fix it, if you really want.' And you did. And we made love with such excitement, finding out about each other and not caring for a second that my clothes were underneath and getting crumpled. I was certain then that the whole of me was twice as big, and then twenty times as big as it had been before. What about you?

SEAN. You said, 'This has to be it,' at the end of the editing session, and I couldn't wait to be with you from then on. I also wanted to do this – this love – as near your father's prison house as possible to kill that monstrous connection.

SAM. A sort of St George. How delicious. Someone else is over there, so give me that shirt.

PAULA (*approaching*). Mother?

SAM. Oh my God – Paula.

SEAN. My pants.

SAM. I thought you'd left home.

PAULA. What are you doing?

SAM. The same as you, by the look of it, and I hope you manage it at my age. Hello, er –

DANIEL. Daniel.

SAM. Yes, of course. My name's Samantha, this is Sean, and every time we meet in future we'll know what's underneath, won't we?

PAULA. Where's Daddy?

SAM. Do we need him, too?

SEAN. He's having lunch with your grandfather. The only loyal member of the family.

PAULA. Do you do this often?

SAM. No, do you?

PAULA. No.

SAM. That makes us both innocent as little lambs and learning fast.

PAULA. I'm surprised at you, Mummy. I had to say that.

SAM. Did you, dear? To get everything straight, I must tell you that I'm leaving Alastair.

PAULA. What'll he do?

SAM. It'll be some time before he notices.

SEAN. The weather, please, it's too good to talk about Alastair.

PAULA. He is important.

SEAN. I know. I hate the thought of what I'm doing to him, but I never let go of what I want.

SAM. Sean works in investigative television, Daniel. I used to do that and now I'm going back to it. To work.

PAULA. I didn't think you knew about work.

SAM. Sometimes you're very like your father, too wrapped up in yourself to notice anyone else.

PAULA. I'm here Mother, precisely to unwrap myself, which I am doing, you may have noticed, like mad.

DANIEL. I live in Earl's Court and do Geology.

SEAN. In Earl's Court?

SAM. Where you'll be going, I suppose, Paula? I take it we're all moving into other people's flats and things?

PAULA. Why?

DANIEL. That's awfully definite.

SAM. Sensible and economical for you, surely?

SEAN. Mortgage rates going up –

SAM. Not that we want to talk about mortgage rates, frolicked as we are in the bare skin. Like your grandfather, really, mortgage rates; they dictate so much of what you do and are dull. Will you share our picnic?

DANIEL. Yes, please.

SAM. Clothes will only gather crumbs so don't bother to dress.

PAULA. Are you really leaving home, Mummy?

SAM. That's precisely what I'm leaving.

DANIEL. Which home?

SAM. My father's. His endless rearrangement of other people's lives. Alastair is just a room in my father's house.

PAULA. It will be terrible for Daddy.

SAM. No, it won't. The house is in his name, so he'll potter on quite happily.

SEAN. You're very hard on him, Sam. You didn't have to marry him.

SAM. Having done so, I had to live with him for twenty-five boring years. It would've been our silver wedding in a month, celebrated with dust-collecting rubbish from Harrods and cast-off paintings from Alastair's artists. I've investigated all there is to know about

Alastair and I could make a documentary of insufferable niceness about him, so I know that now he'll be happy as can be without the guilty feeling that he ought to be original. Like so much else, he spins away below me and out of sight.

PAULA. That's brutal.

SAM. Yes.

DANIEL. Duck down everyone. It's the man in glasses again.

SEAN. What man?

DANIEL. On the track, there. He was here last week. Down, go on, down.

Distant footsteps and laughter from HARRY *as he passes by.*

DANIEL. He's laughing.

SEAN. I don't call that laughter.

PAULA. I feel immensely uncomfortable.

SAM. Oh. I feel adolescent. Isn't it wonderful how life turns up all the time.

SEAN. For some people.

HARRY's *angry laughter and some muttering goes on.*

HONEYMAN (*voice over*). It was brother Harry. Harry had called again in spite of my telling him not to. I came on him in the kitchen with his glasses off, wiping the laughter from his eyes as I went down for the joint, and I was cold with fury. I'd learnt how to go cold in the face of strong emotion over the years. Actually, of course, I would've liked to be able to laugh with him.

The kitchen. Laughter.

HONEYMAN. The joint, Mrs Fellows.

HARRY. Dining with the nobs today, are you? You'll be responsible and loyal very soon.

HONEYMAN. I'm dining with Sir Desmond because he said he'd fire me if I didn't. Loyalty doesn't come into it.

HARRY. Oh, loyalty's very close to fear, I'd say. Or love. Do you feel that for Desmond Lisle? (*Laughs.*) Is that why you're planning how to –

HONEYMAN. Mrs Fellows isn't interested in reports of my light-hearted banter with you, Harry. Have you been drinking?

HARRY. I'm laughing at your eating upstairs.

HONEYMAN. Sir Desmond says you're not to visit. Why've you come?

HARRY. To annoy you.

Bell.

You'd better go. You'll get your knuckles rapped by Desmond the Dreadful if you don't.

Laughs.

HONEYMAN (*spitting it out*). Why aren't you married?

HARRY. You frightened all my girls away.
Bell again, imperiously.

Hurry along, Honeyman.

Chuckles.

HONEYMAN (*voice over sound of his footsteps*). It was true. I took a wretched pleasure in humiliating him before women. It was almost a relief that in leaving him alone with Mrs Fellows I couldn't indulge that most unsatisfying pastime. I always wanted to humiliate Alfred, too, in front of his endless girls, but he never had any who would've noticed. As I walked to the dining room, I imagined him in France with another giggling tart, upper-class, lower-class, always tarts.

HONEYMAN's *footsteps. He arrives in the dining room.*

HONEYMAN. The joint, Sir Desmond.

SIR DESMOND. I've been ten minutes on my own with Alastair.

ALASTAIR (*laughs*). I don't think I'm quite on his wavelength.

SIR DESMOND. I've been telling him his house is in his name.

ALASTAIR. I don't quite understand, you see . . .

SIR DESMOND. I've never trusted my own children to be sensible, so his house is in his name. I was right in that.

ALASTAIR. You're always telling us, you're right.

SIR DESMOND. And am I always right, Honeyman?

HONEYMAN. Yes. Oh yes, you are. I sometimes wish you weren't, but you are, Sir Desmond.

SIR DESMOND. Loyal servant, part of the family, better than the rest of them. Pass him this plate, Alastair.

ALASTAIR. What? Oh.

SIR DESMOND. I'm going to screw them, Tom Honeyman. They can't escape all this.

ALASTAIR. Escape?

SIR DESMOND. Samantha's gone, Paula's gone, Alfred's going, you're a fool –

ALASTAIR. I'm sure Sam's just on some committee.

SIR DESMOND. – and you can't marry and hope the cash will fall into your lap with no more effort than a wedding night. It takes a life to do what I've done, and I'm not going to see my money lost to those who won't work to keep it together. Eh, Honeyman?

HONEYMAN. I know exactly how you must feel.

SIR DESMOND. So I'm taking steps to see that doesn't happen. The slug isn't going to get it.

ALASTAIR. What slug?

HONEYMAN. Stockport.

ALASTAIR. I don't understand.

SIR DESMOND. You will when I'm dead, and you're all sitting round this table mourning my passing. I've built a fortress and it's going on. Now eat. Your brother's got some food, I suppose, Tom?

HONEYMAN. I told him to stay away.

SIR DESMOND. I like stubbornness. Part of the family too, your brother.

HONEYMAN. No!

SIR DESMOND. He manages a bank, Alastair.

ALASTAIR. Who does?

SIR DESMOND. Oh, get your beef in you and keep quiet.

ALASTAIR. Is this premature senility, Honeyman?

HONEYMAN. Please! I'm just the butler!

HONEYMAN (*voice over*). What did he mean? A new will that would stop his children escaping from his influence and business enterprises and so prevent me from unravelling his wealth as I'd always said I'd meant to? I had to act or the money would never move away into the world as it should. It hammered me! I must remove that monolithic figure so that everything would crumble! No successor could master the details of it all as he had, no one could make his decisions. That was why at his age he was still chairman, and it was why – oh God – it was why I did indeed love him. Oh, the anguish of that loving – and, as it turned out, the ignorance.

Very quiet, in an office.

SIR DESMOND. Mr Honeyman?

HARRY. Sir Desmond Lisle?

SIR DESMOND. I know your brother. (*Chuckles.*) And of course, you know my kitchen in Salisbury.

HARRY. I have visited . . .

SIR DESMOND. I don't want to know any more, and I don't want you to say you've seen me.

HARRY. Of course, Sir Desmond. Though my brother has a terrible way with him when he wants to know things.

SIR DESMOND. And so have I. Now, bank managers make wills, and I want you to make one none of my own lawyers knows about. Here's the draft. Draw it up by the end of the week.

HARRY. Yes, indeed.

SIR DESMOND. I'll sign it on Friday. Better take care of myself till then, eh?

HARRY *laughs.*

You're a more spineless man than I thought, Honeyman. You'd better correct that. And clean your glasses.

HONEYMAN *can be heard dusting and humming to himself. His voice to the listener comes over this.*

HONEYMAN (*voice over*). Once I'd made my mind up, I was happy, confident, perfectly at ease. There's a certain saintliness in sacrificing a loved one, especially when it is so obviously done for the good of mankind. It even helped me to handle Alastair with a graceful optimism that cheered us both.

ALASTAIR *is pacing about.*

ALASTAIR. She's gone for good, Honeyman. Gone to work in television.

HONEYMAN. That's not for good, Mr Alastair, whatever else it is.

ALASTAIR. Once they're into television, they never move.

HONEYMAN. The escritoire needs polishing, excuse me.

ALASTAIR. So that's that. Over.

HONEYMAN. She'll soon be back, full of fresh perspectives and piercing insights, and you'll start life with a new sense of urgency, and the gallery will sparkle as a centre of excellence you can hardly dream of at the moment.

ALASTAIR. D'you care about art?

HONEYMAN. I paint miniatures. Rural subjects mainly.

ALASTAIR. Oh. Did Sam ever talk to you at all?

HONEYMAN. Just once. She called me Tom and took her clothes off.

ALASTAIR. Good heavens.

HONEYMAN. For a bath. And she gave me powerfully to understand your life is getting a new injection of vitality. Be happy, Mr Alastair. For you, life is on the up and up.

HONEYMAN (*voice over*). For Desmond, though, the down and down, the poor, dear man.

Sound of bath running.

SIR DESMOND. Put my dressing gown ready.

HONEYMAN. The white towelling, I think. There we are.

SIR DESMOND. Why especially the white?

HONEYMAN. It'll set you up for dinner very perkily, the white, and brightness is all before your fellows at a Lord Mayor's function.

SIR DESMOND. I'm not going to the Mansion House in my dressing gown.

HONEYMAN. But you do look nice in it, and if you look nice now, you'll feel nice for the rest of the evening.

SIR DESMOND. Is the bath ready?

HONEYMAN. Oh yes. I think so.

Both go into the bathroom.

SIR DESMOND. You're very chirpy all of a sudden.

HONEYMAN. Thank you.

SIR DESMOND. I never thought of you as having moods. Servants aren't supposed to have them.

HONEYMAN. We have our moments.

SIR DESMOND. Well chirp on. It's nice.

HONEYMAN. White towels, white soap, white face flannel, white bath. And the heat – the exact confirmatory temperature to make you feel comforted yet adult.

SIR DESMOND. You really care about me, don't you?

HONEYMAN. I do. Ready?

SIR DESMOND. Thank you.

He gets into the bath.

Oh, I love the simple pleasures. (*Chuckles.*) The kneeling down, getting the thighs and things used to the warmth and wet. And the sitting – oh – ah – and – bliss – the lying back. (*Chortles of glee.*) Even the poor know this pleasure, Honeyman.

HONEYMAN. Do they really.

SIR DESMOND. Lucky bloody poor. They have no fear of falling.

HONEYMAN. So they say.

SIR DESMOND. What's that?

HONEYMAN. It's a very large, very powerful electric element from the hot water system of an expensive suite in a hotel I once worked in as a lad – Claridges, in fact.

SIR DESMOND. Is it plugged in?

HONEYMAN. Yes.

SIR DESMOND. What are you going to do with it?

HONEYMAN. I'm going to put it in the bath. Like this.

Suitable cries then silence.

HONEYMAN (*voice over*). Not a mark on him. Such a simple pleasure for both of us; he, warm in his bath, I, warm in the sanctity of acting for mankind.

Church music in the background. BBC voice over it.

BBC VOICE. The death has been announced of Sir Desmond Lisle, Chairman of the Stockport and Eccles Building Society and of Allied Southampton Construction. Sir Desmond, a man of considerable influence in the City of London since 1979, was also a great collector of nineteenth-century Impressionist painting and was said to have the finest collection of Odilon Redons outside Paris.

Over this fades the clerical voice in a cathedral.

CLERICAL VOICE. He was, of all the rich the most generous with his wealth, and of all the powerful the least puffed up with worldly pride. His contributions to the arts, including the building of the Dance Centre in Havant and the Museum of Modern Art at Avebury, earned him international fame as a great patron we should all be eternally grateful to.

And over this fades in:

SAM (*in church*). He was a very healthy man. I think he was murdered, Alfred.

ALFRED. Who by?

SAM. Who cares?

ALFRED. Oughtn't we to find out?

SAM. He wasted all our time when living, so I'm spending no more on him now he's dead.

ALASTAIR. When are you coming home, Sam?

SAM. I'm not, Alastair.

ALASTAIR. Honeyman says you are.

SAM. Honeyman is wrong.

The sound of people in a bank.

HONEYMAN. Harry?

HARRY. Aaagh! Go away.

HONEYMAN. I've come about –

HARRY. I know what you've come about.

HONEYMAN. I can't talk through a glass screen so let's go to your office.

HARRY. Leave me alone. I want to forget you.

HONEYMAN. I've only come to say that I've got the tickets for the holiday, but now that –

HARRY. I'm not coming.

HONEYMAN. Why ever not?

HARRY. Because you're a murderer.

HONEYMAN. Don't be hysterical, Harry. There's a queue out here.

HARRY. You can't deny it, can you?

HONEYMAN. I can and do. But it looks as if I might be able to take my holidays earlier, so –

HARRY. You said you were going to do it.

HONEYMAN. Harry, I'm not discussing this through a glass letter box. In fact I'm not discussing it at all.

HARRY. I could have you arrested, now.

HONEYMAN (*close and vicious*). But you're too loyal to your big brother to consider that, aren't you?

A sort of gargling sound.

HARRY. My tie!!

HONEYMAN. Caught, you see, loyalty versus honesty. Muddled by your own impossible ethic, like all the middle classes. Now, if we could go in June instead of August –

HARRY. You cocked it up, you know.

HONEYMAN. Pardon?

HARRY. I told him I wouldn't say, but now – his personal fortune's going to the children provided they both remain directors of his companies for the rest of their lives. But he was going to make a new will divesting them of all their power and money, leaving his fortune to the Tate Gallery – it's an immense sum – and diverting the income from the shares they would have had as directors to the National Theatre and he was putting you in charge of it all at a salary of £60,000.

HONEYMAN. No!

HARRY. But you killed him before he signed. Now everything's locked up exactly as you didn't want it to be.

HONEYMAN. But he's gone! It'll all collapse, surely.

HARRY. Oh, Tom, you don't understand a thing about the world, do you? There are dozens, hundreds, of directors to run the companies.

HONEYMAN. And if he'd signed the new will –

HARRY. Now, go away.

HONEYMAN (*voice over*). I was stunned. He'd meant his fortress to exclude his children, and to include only me, me to preserve his money, and his reputation as a benefactor of the arts. Me. Instead of which – they could of course renounce their directorships to gain their freedom, but somehow I doubted if they would. And in any case, the money hadn't been released into the community, so I had changed nothing, and my younger brother had been taken into Sir Desmond's confidence, which made me mad! But undaunted. Absolutely undaunted.

Sound of a bath running.

HONEYMAN. Your bath, Mr Alfred.

ALFRED. Thank you, Honeyman. It was a very decent funeral for a very difficult old bugger.

HONEYMAN. He'll be missed.

ALFRED. Who by?

HONEYMAN. The shareholders?

ALFRED. They won't notice. He's built the business up so big it's mostly run from the Maldive Islands, or Buenos Aires, or wherever the money sloshes most. My dressing gown?

HONEYMAN. The white.

ALFRED. So though the shareholders or savers or whatever might've thought they were investing in the Stockport and Eccles Building Society, run by our dear old dad, they were in fact contributing to a satellite TV channel using NASA's military technology and taking security photos, supported by several South African Banks, and controlling four supermarket chains and half the world's agrichemical businesses, chopping down the rain forests and doing naughties in the Thames. Let alone the telephone companies and uranium mines, etc., etc. Your plain old family man with a Stockport and Eccles mortgage doesn't think about that, thank God.

HONEYMAN. And now Sir Desmond's dead?

ALFRED. It'll just go on and on, controlling the status quo from no one quite knows where. Am I getting a paunch?

HONEYMAN. Pardon?

ALFRED. Don't want to get so fat I don't meet the girls where it matters. Ha ha ha!

HONEYMAN. Ready?

ALFRED. Thank you, Honeyman.

He is now splashing in the bath.

Ah, such a simple pleasure.

HONEYMAN. Even the poor know it, they say.

ALFRED. Bugger the poor. What's that, Honeyman?

HONEYMAN. It's a very large heating element from Claridges, Mr Alfred. Would you just move your legs? Thank you.

Death sounds again.

HONEYMAN. This could go on and on.

Church music becoming choral Palestrina and BBC voice.

BBC VOICE. The death has been announced of Mr Alfred Lisle, whose father, Sir Desmond Lisle, died of cardiac arrest several days ago. Shares in the Stockport and Eccles Building Society, and Allied Southampton Construction remained unchanged.

CLERICAL VOICE. He was a man who carried the greatest of responsibilities, and one who will be sadly missed among a wide circle.

HONEYMAN. Balls! Nothing in art lies like those who practise the business of living.

The sound of the Palestrina – sung in the Cathedral – goes on. After a moment the sound of SEAN *whispering to* SAMANTHA.

SEAN. What is it, Sam?

SAM. There's Honeyman, Father's butler. You've never seen him have you?

SEAN. He isn't implicated in the interference with the mail. The BBC have cancelled the film, by the way – *de mortuis nihil nisi bonum.*

SAM. He's in ecstasy. That is ecstasy.

HONEYMAN (*over the choral music*). The ecstasy of the jealous is enormous. If I'd had one more drop of talent in my veins, I would've overcome the lethargy I knew at heart I suffered from. I might've been standing there and singing with full throat, rendering the music of the great creators with unstoppable majesty, sending waves of beauty into that ancient, perfect house. My pleasure in such sounds, always so vast because of that fantasy, was deeply tainted with hideous despair – if only, oh, if only, I'd been someone else. (*Weeps.*)

Rain outside the Cathedral.

HONEYMAN. Miss Sam?

SAM. Tom. Aren't you getting wet?

HONEYMAN. It was a beautiful service, and I'm always transported by Palestrina.

SAM. Did you kill Father and Alfred?

HONEYMAN. I am the butler, and (*Laughing.*) you know what they say about butlers.

SAM. So did you? (*Silence.*) I'm going away, you know. I'm not taking up the directorship. Alastair can do that if he wants. What'll you do for a job now?

HONEYMAN. I had assumed, somehow, that you would – I don't know.

SAM. Nobody has butlers these days. They're very old-fashioned affairs.

HONEYMAN. We still serve the rich.

SAM. Do you? Anyway, goodbye. My lover's waiting for me in the car park.

HONEYMAN. You're not going back renewed and refreshed to Mr Alastair?

SAM. It would kill him. And don't you do that, Tom. Off you run.

HONEYMAN (*voice over*). Old-fashioned. Old-fashioned executioner of a modern monster that wouldn't, couldn't die, grown too big to be a simple fortress against Stockport and become instead a threat to all mankind. Oh dear, how small I was.

At an exhibition.

PAULA. Honeyman! What are you doing, sitting amid all this screaming, blinding colour?

HONEYMAN. Should I not?

PAULA. I didn't realise you liked art.

HONEYMAN. I have a small interest.

DANIEL. Picasso is very big, of course. And all these genitalia – green ones, red, yellow –

Nothing.

Doesn't it turn you on, even at the basic level of . . . you know?

Nothing.

You just think it's an old man drawing dirty pictures.

Nothing.

Well, I'm a geologist and I think it's wonderful.

PAULA. I don't suppose we'll meet again, Honeyman.

Nothing.

You look absolutely awful, sitting there like a cross between a vulture and a refugee. I can't bear it.

DANIEL. Paula!

PAULA. Well, it's true. He's like a retired headmistress who used to be frightening. Servants are always frightening, though, giving their lives to others like virgin sacrifices. It's consenting rape.

HONEYMAN. I am a man of passion! I love justice! I'm giving my life for humanity!

PAULA. Good heavens, Honeyman, do you have feelings?

HONEYMAN. Enormous ones. Only I painted – smaller stuff.

HONEYMAN (*voice over*). The end was obvious. Alastair was there to see it.

In the hall of the Holland Park house.

HONEYMAN. Mr Alastair.

ALASTAIR. Is there any news of Sam?

HONEYMAN. She's left for good.

ALASTAIR. Oh. (*Laughs.*)

HONEYMAN. Didn't you meet her lover at Alfred's funeral? He's a virile man in tight corduroys whose eye is sharp and whose expression is the lively blank of one who assimilates everything. Your daughter, Paula, is in love and is rejecting those she grew up with, especially me.

ALASTAIR. Is there a drink?

HONEYMAN. No.

ALASTAIR. What?

HONEYMAN. May I introduce you to my younger brother, Harold?

ALASTAIR. Oh, the bank manager! (*Laughs.*)

HARRY. I'm not a joke!

HONEYMAN. The cynical gentleman over there is an inspector from Scotland Yard who has come to arrest me for the murder of Sir Desmond and Mr Alfred.

ALASTAIR. Really?

HONEYMAN. So the house is yours, and you'll have to get your own drinks.

HARRY. Sir Desmond's last words to me were that I should try to get some spine. I've done that. It was me who called in the police.

HONEYMAN (*laughs*). You call that spine? You loyal little creep, you couldn't get a spine into your back with major surgery, let alone with moral exhortation. You have the life and spirit of a dead condom.

HARRY (*shouting*). Take him away!

HONEYMAN (*voice over*). But who was I to talk, who was old-fashioned? The empire born from Sir Desmond's simple fear of Stockport grows and grows, and floats about the globe gobbling the ozone layer, killing Indians, putting up inflation, swallowing people's savings, evicting people who can't pay their mortgages, that sort of thing. It sheds compound interest on those who bow to it, and withers the hopes of many who know nothing about it. Some other way than mine is needed to be rid of it. I misread things, you see. The children, they seemed to know more than I did after all. The women, whom I thought of as prisoners, they weren't prisoners at all. They were like some beneficial dry rot, working away inside their family to destroy it and transform it. They didn't think what they were doing. They just rotted their part of it away. I still don't quite understand about being out-of-date. It's such a patronising criticism one can hardly bring oneself to believe it. Quite often I don't. But I don't know – I don't know . . . The monster cannot be allowed to become the master, can it?

DEATH AND THE TANGO

A Comedy Thriller on Themes of Metaphysical Fantasy

by John Fletcher

John Fletcher has written extensively for television, stage and radio. His television plays include *Stargazy on Zummerdown* and *Mrs F* and plays for radio include *Wandering in Eden*, *The Trumpet Sound* and *Suddenly*. He has also written several plays for the Bristol Old Vic and is currently adapting Fritz Lang's version of *House by the River* for Zed Films Ltd. He lives in Somerset. *Death and the Tango* was the BBC's 1991 entry for the Prix Italia.

Death and the Tango was first broadcast on 'Drama Now', BBC Radio 3, on 18 September 1990. The cast was as follows:

JEFF	Steve Hodson
BYRON	Christian Rodska
LORETTA/LYDIA	Mary Wimbush
CELIA/GRACE	Maureen O'Brien
CHARLIE/MC/SYMPOSIUM MEMBER 1/ ONLOOKER 3/INSTRUCTOR 1	Roger Hume
INSTRUCTOR 2/MAN 2 (RENNIE)/ SYMPOSIUM MEMBER 3/ONLOOKER 2	Christopher Scott
WOMAN 2/SYMPOSIUM MEMBER 2/ ONLOOKER 1	Judy Bridgland

Director: Nigel Bryant
Running time, as broadcast: 75 minutes

A strong, rhythmic tango. Down, but continues insistently beneath.
Acoustic of empty, rainy canal bank. JEFF, *30, a reflective Brummie.*

JEFF (*voice over*). 'It is said the City of God hath no need of the
Sun, neither of the Moon to shine in it; for the Glory of the Lord
doth light it.'

Oh Birmingham, Birmingham – what darkness is this upon you?
Where is the lightness in Perry Bar, West Bromwich, Bloxwich and
Dudley, the bustle and industry and good cheer that once blazed
forth?

Here by the waters of the Fazeley and Walsall Junction Canal,
amid old tyres and dead prams and dismembered plastic dolls, my
fishing rod in my hand, I sit down and weep when I remember
Birmingham.

Music up then down. Still insistent under sound of hurried footsteps
down wet cobbled backstreets. BYRON, *25-year-old Brummie,*
impulsive, passionate, walking rapidly along.

BYRON (*voice over*). Where is it? Where is it? Reservoir Street?
Skinners Lane? Brickkiln Row, Paradise Court? I know it's here
somewhere. Navigation Way, Oxygen Street, Small Brook and
Floodgate Gardens.
    I can scent it, sniff it down some bleak old back street. Oozing
out through the cracked windows of some run down old church
hall or gym. Its cheap, illicit stench, its Latin aroma slithering
down these dark back streets. It's here. I know it. Somewhere. The
tango.

Music up. The tango. Credits. Music down, out.

Canal side acoustic. Drips as JEFF *sits fishing.*

JEFF (*voice over*). 'And this Mass, or Undigested Matter, or Chaos,
created in the beginning, is without Form, which it shall after Acquire,

when the Spirit of the Lord hath digested it from the waters. And our earth is void, that is, not producing any creatures, nor adorned with any plants, Fruits, or Flowers. But after THE SPIRIT OF GOD SHALL MOVE UPON THE WATERS, and work this Undigested Matter into that form which it SHALL retain, then the Earth shall bud forth the Herb, and the seed and the Fruitful Tree, the bright-eyed bird in the sky and the fish in the waters, and God shall see it is good, made perfect. Yeah. For perfection is that to which nothing is wanting.'

Oh Birmingham. Oh Birmingham. The rain has seeped right down me back and down me bum. Not so much as a minnow has bobbed me float. (*Rises, reeling in line. Preparing to go.*) Time I was going. Time I was finding a bit of warmth and light.

Jump cut to . . .
Banging chord as bad, discordant, trio of musicians embark upon a virulent tango. Microphone pans back. It is a large, dusty, rundown hall. We hear the almost-in-time steps of BYRON *and* LORETTA, *a 75-year-old Brummie. The actors should have cans on so they can synchronise with the music.*

BYRON (*voice over*). I made it! I made it!

LORETTA. Push out your left leg, young man. Further. Thrust mine aside. Harder, there. And . . . push . . . that's it!

BYRON (*voice over*). Somewhere, I knew, somewhere in Birmingham there must be someone, people who still dance the tango – I found them.

LORETTA. Faster, young man, faster. I'm not some porcelain antique.

BYRON. Sorry.

LORETTA. You can jolt me, throw me.

BYRON. No I can't.

LORETTA. Go on. Right over your knee and gaze down into my eyes. Strut and prance, strut and prance – just as when I was a young woman.

BYRON. I'll try.

LORETTA. Not hard enough.

BYRON. But you're quite . . . old.

LORETTA. Seventy-five years.

BYRON. And your bones are probably quite . . . brittle.

LORETTA (*intimately*). Press yourself against me. Right against me. (*They come together.*) Imagine this body only twenty-five years old. Sinuous as flowing water, panting softly in your ear, drawing you across this floor subtle as a serpent, our steps spidering, stamping. Can you imagine? What Birmingham was once like?

BYRON (*voice over*). I tried. I tried very hard. But every time I stared down into her rheumy, red-veined eye, studied her upward-turned mouth caked in lipstick . . .

LORETTA. Draw me in, harder, nearer. Then throw me out . . . (*slightly pathetic.*) please.

BYRON (*voice over*). Each time, cheek by jowl, we strutted the width of the floor, ungainly as cockerels . . .

LORETTA. My bones aren't brittle. The sap rises in them fierce as ever. Toss me away like straw – draw me in like fire.

BYRON (*voice over*). It wasn't her. I could have danced with her until Eternity washed up and God hung out the tea towel to dry. It was the place. That griminess that works its way into everything in Birmingham. Infested with dinginess, an ancient Masonic hall of cobwebs and cracks, smelling of loo disinfectant. A paraffin heater in the corner. It dampens your soul, dooms your melody.

LORETTA. Don't be silent, young man. I can remember the times of Birmingham when everyone danced the tango and the sunlight shone all day, every day. We had sunlight in our veins.

BYRON. Yeah.

BYRON (*voice over*). Floorboards rough and unpolished. Paint dull and peeling. And the OAPs sat round the edges on their cheap chairs and tables, begging with their hound-like eyes for just one dance, just one flame to rekindle their ancient bodies. I dance one dance with each of them – even a couple with the blokes. Then I leave. This is not where I shall dance MY tango.

Cut to . . . a dusty library. JEFF *surrounded by ancient and dusty tomes.*

JEFF (*reading*). 'It hath been said of Prometheus that he, an excellent man and teacher of wisdom, might form men out of clay, and, with the fire of that wisdom, breathe life and quickness into them. It hath also been said that he invented fire not as he discovered flames and their consumption of materials and fabrics, but in as far as his keen, hungering curiosity reached the Stars and other Celestial Bodies and set them ablaze in the imagination of other men. He bringeth fire to all men's minds.'

Beat.

Cor. Can you imagine that? Up above the clouds they're meant to be. Stars, planets, moon – the sun itself. Burning away. I knew a man that knew a man who once said he saw the sun shining in the sky over Birmingham. It's up there still – apparently. (*Sighs, turns page. Reads.*) 'And that the legend of Prometheus being bound to the top of the hill and his Entrails devoured by an Eagle, is meant to represent that inner ache and Desire he had to investigate the Natures, Motions, and Influences of the Heavenly Bodies.'

Yeah! (*Louder.*) Yeah!! (*Louder.*) Yeah!!!!

SEVERAL. Ssssssh!

JEFF. Oh – pardon me. (*Voice over*). I'm in the library. Brum public library. One dim light bulb, endless shelves groaning beneath cobwebbed tomes. Old codgers gathered about, drily reading their dusty tracts. I come here for my sustenance, my intellectual gravy my daily sunrise. Then, suddenly, I see it. Pinned to the public services notice board. Situations vacant in the lighthouse business. Two volunteers required to person a lighthouse.
     Yes!

Jump cut to . . . BYRON *and* JEFF's *digs. Small rather bare room acoustic. In the middle of an argument.*

BYRON. No!

JEFF. Yes! Bringing light to darkness, form to chaos. We've got to do it.

BYRON. Never!

JEFF. Broadcasting into the void. (*Beat.*) Byron . . .

BYRON. Jeff?

JEFF. We're mates . . .

BYRON. None truer.

JEFF. Where you go, I go. Where I go . . . soulmates.

BYRON. Jeff, mate, someday – I mean this – someday I'm going to dance the tango. Proper. Find me a young girl as keen, as needing to dance the dance as I am. And we shall dance it upon a proper parquetted ballroom dance floor, with revolving lights and purple drapes and . . . truth!

JEFF. Think of that lighthouse – out there . . .

BYRON (*voice over*). And as I dance I shall have a red rose – a proper blood red rose clamped between me teeth – with proper thorns on its stem so the blood from my lips runs down over the redness of the rose and smears across her marble-white cleavage and drips on to the floor as we stamp and steam across it and . . .

JEFF. Byron?

BYRON. Jeff?

JEFF. I just want you to think of it, for a second. Picture it – out there. Darkness – and light!

BYRON (*uninterested*). Right.

JEFF. What does your soul crave for more than anything?

BYRON. The tango!

JEFF. Passion!
      Can you imagine the darkness out there. Not night like we've got here – a smudgy orange half-light like some dreary disease – no – utter endless darkness. Blackness to match the blackness of your soul.

Beat.

And then, coming out of it – these seas, these mountains moving. Great passionate havocs of water turbining and tumbling each upon the other, towering above our tiny erection of rock and light, crashing down and around, then thundering on and on in their immense heroic obsession – off into infinity, oblivion.

Beat.

I see a light in your dark eye, Byron. Birmingham is finished. You're finished in Birmingham. You'll never find a tango partner here.

BYRON. I'll find one on a lighthouse in the middle of an ocean?

JEFF. I'll dance with you. I'll even put on a wig and make-up.

BYRON. What?

JEFF. Byron – when you tire of those endless seas out there – pacing round and round the balcony – you can come inside, into the fierce white light – and I'll offer you a glass of wine, you can put on your tango records – I'll dance round the floor in your arms.

BYRON. With your bald patch and glasses?

JEFF. You can teach me. I'll study a tango instruction manual. What is there in Birmingham, Byron? All these years and what have you come up with – one bingo hall full of old age pensioners. No one else wants to know. Think of it. Even when you're inside – snug and warm – outside you'll be able to hear the sea snarling and moaning – a wild beast stalking you. Fate.

Your oily black locks are shining. I see a glow in the gold ring through your ear. You, Byron, are a romantic – a romantic curable only by death.

Acoustic out.

JEFF (*voice over*). And so, Byron and me joined the lighthouse service.

Cut.

Fade in. Interior Portakabin-type classroom. Intense neon light. Instructor at front of class. Brummie, 60, hard.

INSTRUCTOR. This lamp is a stationary fixed multi burner. It has incandescent oxygen mantles here, here, and here. Around the mantles you will see its lenses – flashed and occulated – here, here and here. They are driven, propelled about this ring here by compressed air supplied by this pump here.
   You're following me?

JEFF. Yes, sir.

BYRON (*more slowly*). Yeah.

INSTRUCTOR. This is a most exquisite piece of engineering you're looking at. Stuck in the height of a lighthouse tower, it can throw a single beam of light fifty miles into the darkness. It relies not only upon your constant intelligence and vigilance to keep its machinery and moving parts in perfect working order . . . you listening, Smith?

BYRON (*touch of non co-operation*). Of course, sir.

INSTRUCTOR. . . . But also endless, loving elbow grease. You must have no greater passion in your soul . . .

JEFF. Yes, sir.

INSTRUCTOR. . . . than to care constantly, in extremis, to the cleanliness and perfection of these lenses and refractors.

   (*Touch of anger.*) You listening, Smith?

BYRON (*slightly aggressively*). Of course, sir.

INSTRUCTOR. As you will find as you live out your lives upon a lighthouse – it is in the nature of the purest light to attract the purest dirt. Light is a very fragile commodity in this universe – like intelligence, like reason. But you are her champions, her technicians.

Fade out.

Fade in. Interior of cabin of helicopter. INSTRUCTOR 2, still a touch of Brummie, but young, smooth, technical.

INSTRUCTOR 2. As you two gentlemen are aware, modern lighthouse management techniques include a requirement to operate a helicopter. A small scout craft.

JEFF. Yes, sir.

BYRON. Yeah.

INSTRUCTOR 2. Be able to fly it through the most inclement weather – both so that you can gain access to your place of work – and, if conditions so demand, to use it in furtherance of an actual rescue mission scenario.

BYRON. Pulling dead bodies out of the sea, you mean.

INSTRUCTOR 2. Er, yes. Well, Smith and Miles, the moment of truth. Good luck, gentlemen, your first flight. You're cleared for takeoff. (*Exit shutting cabin door.*)

JEFF. Right. Ready.

BYRON. Are you ready, Jeff?

JEFF. Of course I am. Ignition.

BYRON. Ignition. (*Rotor blade starts to revolve.*)

JEFF. Full aerilion extension, blade elevation.

BYRON. Full aerilion extension, blade elevation.

JEFF. More boost.

BYRON. More boost. (*Higher engine sounds.*)

JEFF. Rotor elevation?

BYRON. 54.

JEFF. Here we go. (*Beat.*) Takeoff.

BYRON. Takeoff.

JEFF. One metre. Two metre. Four metre. Four metre. Byron, why aren't we rising?

BYRON. Good question, Jeff.

JEFF. Give me more boost.

BYRON. More boost.

JEFF. Rotor elevation?

BYRON. It's falling. Down to 32.

JEFF. Oh my God.

BYRON. We appear to be falling.

JEFF. I can't do anything.

BYRON. You're panicking.

JEFF. I'm not panicking.

BYRON. It's only a flight simulator.

Cut. Single alone atmosphere.

JEFF (*voice over*). In the end Byron and me got our lighthouse persons certificates, our helicopter pilots licences. We were ready. Byron packed his tango records into his kitbag, I stuffed mine with volumes borrowed long term from the public library – Walter Raleigh's *History of the World*, Ficino's translation of the *Corpus Hermeticum* – proper reading – then we all bundled aboard the helicopter.

Sound of helicopter starting. Acoustic changes without interrupting speech.

Up into the night air, so that Birmingham's orange street lights lay below us like meadows of buttercups. Then dipping, away to the north, up into the darkness. Above us, at two thousand feet, a blanket of streaming never-ending cloud. Beneath us the black land unreeling, and then, suddenly, out over precipitous cliffs, waves crashing far beneath, out onto the desolate ocean, white combers and rollers far below. We were over her, suspended above her monstrous, untamed form.

We hear the sea beneath, strains of the tango start to be intertwined electronically with sounds of ocean.

Lonely. Sandwiched in a black tunnel between cloud and sea we travelled on. Fifty miles, a hundred, two hundred miles of darkness. Suddenly, far ahead, a tiny needle, a point of light lancing through the darkness, bouncing sometime off ocean, sometime off cloud. Let there be light. Hallelujah. Our lighthouse. Our home.

Fade out.

Fade in. Crew's quarters, inside lighthouse. Sea distant outside. JEFF *seated at dressing table reading. No campness nor butchness nor innuendo in voice – dead straight. Same with* BYRON.

JEFF (*reading*). 'It hath pleased the Almighty to insinuate into my harte an insatiable zeale and desire to knowe his truth, proceeding and ascending by degrees, from thinges visible to consider of thinges invisible . . .' Wish these eyelashes would stick on. I really don't think pink lipstick goes with my dress.

Sighs. Sound of page turning as starts reading again.

'. . . from thinges bodily to consider of thinges spiritualle; from thinges transitory and momentary, to meditate of thinges permanente; by thinges mortal to have some perceiverance of immortalitie. And, to conclude most briefly: by the most merveilous frame of the WHOLE

WORLD philosophically viewed, most faithfully to love, honor, and glorifie alwaies, the FRAMER and CREATOR thereof.'
(*Sighs.*) My hair. My hair. God do I look a mess.

Door opens. Enter BYRON.

JEFF. Byron?

BYRON. I've been out there.

JEFF. You've checked the mirrors, the rotational apparatus?

BYRON. You spent your entire watch checking them. I've been outside.

JEFF. Any ships on the radar?

BYRON (*slightly impatiently*). If there were the automatic alarms would alert us, wouldn't they? I've been out there, on the balcony, staring out into the nothingness, letting the blackness and wind and spray feed on my face, letting the seas wind (*As in 'wind up'.*) and ratchet my blood.

JEFF. Knew you'd like it.

BYRON (*just noticing*). You're wearing a dress.

JEFF. Best my seamstressing could run up. And I've stuck on some eyelashes, lipstick – got a wig going. What do you think?

BYRON. Passable.

JEFF. I even bought a book – *How to Dance the Tango in Ten Easy Lessons – Diagrams of All Essential Foot Movements Included.* Our first night on our lighthouse should be memorable. You play your tango tapes, I open some tins of wine, we dance the night away.

BYRON. That sounds – (*Moved.*) very nice. It's very kind of you.

Sounds of sea and wind up, then down and sound of tango and BYRON and JEFF's footsteps dancing.

JEFF (*voice over*). We danced that night – light and darkness together – cheek by cheek – drinking many tins of wine – all the time Byron with this maniacal glare in his eye – breathing heavily, strutting majestically – and me with my mascara running, my tights slipping – but with contentment in my heart.
I'd never seen him this way before – he seemed to drink demonic in all the elemental forces loosed in the world – tide, wind, rain – till all focused minute within him, blazed out from him black, hard as a diamond.

BYRON. I'm happy. I'm happy.

Music down. But sea up slightly. Slightly different acoustic.

JEFF (*voice over*). Of course, it couldn't always be like that. Week passed into week, month into month. We settled into a routine. No ships came on our radar screen. I cleaned the glass and mirrors, hoovered the living quarters, kept the log – Byron paced the helipad, restless. I tried to tempt him with the food – Tinned faggots I mixed with marrowfat peas from a tin and new tinned potatoes, then I tried baked beans from a tin and frankfurter sausages – fresh from their tin. All tried in new, endless permutations to tempt him, perk him, lift him.

But he fell into a decline, grew listless, withdrawn.

One day, finally, he failed to come on watch. I found him in his room, slouched across his bed, a litter of emptied wine tins about his feet.

Interior of BYRON's *small room. Occasional rustles of tins.* BYRON *on bed. Sea in distance.*

BYRON (*tired and emotional*). Death, you see. Death. It's got to be done with a young girl. A wonderful young girl full in the fire of life, brimming with youth. And she must be in black. And I must be naked – utterly naked except for the red rose stuck in my mouth. And at the end of the dance, I must die. Utterly. My blood – hot, sticky, drains down into the earth beneath. A graveyard. It must be a graveyard over which I dance. A pit filled with bones and skulls and blood. A royal pit, in which sleep the king and queen surrounded by their courtiers. That earth must be special. Know why?

JEFF. No?

BYRON (*rattle of tins*). Open another tin of wine. The tin opener's over there somewhere.

JEFF. No thanks.

BYRON. 'S proper, fizzy stuff.

JEFF. No, thanks.

During this speech the strains of the Tango Sinister are heard for the first time – ethereally.

BYRON. I'm not getting at you, brother. I know you try. With your dresses and roses and whathaveyous. Champion, better than Brum any day. But it's not proper. The tango, see, 's got to be danced on proper earth, sacred earth of sacrifice, because the tango is about death – about the life that can be created only out of death – that can arise from an earth of slaughter, of bones.
    They used to do this in the old days, see. If the kingdom wasn't going quite right – crops weren't growing proper, livestock was sickly

– the queen would decide they'd all got to die. First of all she'd kill the king – cut his throat or whatever – then bung him in a butt or casket of honey or wine or summat to preserve him – then they'd get down to organising this great Festival of Death. Proper job. Weave the most fantastic head-dresses and colourful clothes, bright beads and precious stones and silver and gold bracelets, gorgeous feathers, and all the courtiers and slaves would have all these baths in precious liquids and they'd cook these most delicate pies and cakes to feed them on their journey through the underworld and the wagons on which they'd travel would be decked out beautifully and the white horses groomed and groomed to perfection.

Then everyone'd shake hands with their relatives, their friends, they'd kiss and hug, climb into the wagons, ride down into the earth, to the bottom of this pit that had been dug, into this stone tomb, and the king's body would be laid out in the centre, the queen would say this prayer, all would sing songs, chant chants, embrace each other – mothers, fathers, little children, aged grandfathers – (*Sobs.*) all going down into the earth – then, as the horses were slaughtered, a wine would pass round from mouth to mouth – slowly, solemnly – a rich dark red wine laced with hashish or opium to make you dream the dreams of the dead, with cinnamon and nutmeg to sweeten the bitter hemlock that makes you sleep the sleep of the dead. And all together, limb to limb, cuddled head to warm breast and against snug lap, would lie down to dream and dream such dreams of death as above them the workmen bricked in the walls and filled and covered all with earth upon earth, layer upon layer.

That ground was pregnant with their life, their dreams, ripe and bursting with it. Can you imagine its kindness, its gentleness, its power. (*Sobs. Cries. Pulls himself together.*) And so come the dancers. The drawers up of life. Man and woman together. Pulling up life from that great reservoir, passing it out through all the land. Shaping, embodying, giving life to their dreams. (*Pulls himself together.*)

When I dance my great tango, my dance of sacrifice, I shall be immaculate, freshly bathed, in black evening dress. Patent leather shoes. Braided trousers, black velvet jacket and tie, each pleat and fold in my cummerbund, my waistcoat, each frill and tuck in my white satin shirt – all shall be perfect. My rose shall be torn fresh from the bush. (*Pause.*)

JEFF (*gently*). Byron? (*Pause.*) Byron?

BYRON (*absent-mindedly*). Yeah?

JEFF. We are not on some grand imperial dance floor – we are not above some ancient burial ground – we're on a lighthouse. A lighthouse that needs . . .

BYRON. No!

JEFF. A lighthouse that must maintain the principles . . .

BYRON. Don't tell me that – you hear?

JEFF. . . . maintain the principles of order in a universe of chaos.

Distant bell ringing.

BYRON (*voice over*). What's that?

JEFF (*not hearing*). That amidst much darkness . . .

BYRON (*voice over*). Shut up! That ringing . . .

JEFF. The radar alarm!

BYRON. Yeah.

JEFF (*going*). Come on.

Whoosh and sweep of radar screen centre mike. JEFF *and* BYRON *looking at it.*

It must be huge. Look at it on the radar . . .

BYRON. Fifty miles off. In the pitch dark.

JEFF. If it keeps up that course it'll be on the rocks.

BYRON. Raise it on the radio.

Buttons, etc. pushed.

JEFF (*into mike*). Hello. Hello. Unidentified ship on our radar screens bearing 172 degrees south. Lighthouse Charlie Foxtrot Tango here. Do you read me?

BYRON. It's huge.

JEFF (*slight beat*). Repeat, we have a most urgent message. Do you read me?

BYRON (*pause*). Not a sausage. Maybe we'd better raise it visually, from the helicopter, with flares and so on.

JEFF. How long's it got before it runs on to those rocks?

BYRON. Not long.

JEFF (*going*). Come on.

Cut. Fade up. Night. Sound of wind. Rain, seas, helicopter taking off.

Change to interior of cockpit.

BYRON. God – it's a filthy night.

JEFF. Give me more boost.

BYRON. More boost. Like being a ping pong ball in the table tennis championships.

JEFF. How's our course?

BYRON. West north west. We should have visual contact within seven, 07 minutes.

JEFF. Right.

BYRON. Ever known blackness like this? Just infinite.

JEFF. Keep your mind on your instruments. (*Pause. Voice over.*) Then we saw her . . . (*Sound of waves, sea up slightly.*) ploughing her majestic course through the towering waves, sleek and swift as a greyhound, climbing each new wave proud, conquering the crest, sliding down in the next trough – never for a moment deviating nor hesitating. A great Edwardian liner, four funnels smoking, ablaze from stem to stern with electric light.

BYRON. My God!

JEFF. That ship must be a hundred years old.

BYRON. She's beautiful. A dream

JEFF. But what's she doing here? Drop a flare. Try and raise her. (*Beat. Reminding.*) Byron . . .

BYRON. Yeah?

JEFF. The flare.

JEFF (*voice over*). We tried seven flares in all. No response. In the end we had no choice. We had to board her, perilously land upon her heaving deck, set off across it to raise the alarm. (*Appropriate sounds of climbing, etc.*) Clambered up ladders, along companionways to the bridge, standing gaunt and dark above the deck.

JEFF. Here's the door.

BYRON. Right.

Opens door. Interior acoustic of bridge. Fusty. Silent. Groan of wheel. Door shuts.

JEFF (*voice over*). Deserted, cold, silent as the grave. All the instruments – compasses, speed indicators, chart tables – standing silent and stiff as sentries. A layer of dust over polished mahogany. (*Groan of wheel up.*) Only the great wheel moved and chafed, held to its course by a gigantic iron chain.

BYRON. Blimey.

JEFF. Not a soul.

BYRON. Spooky . . .

JEFF. Yeah.

BYRON. . . . but fun. (*Going.*) Come on.

JEFF. Where are you going?

BYRON. Search the compartments, cabins. There's a whole huge ship here.

JEFF. But if there isn't anyone on the bridge . . .

BYRON. Enjoy it, Jeff. This doesn't happen every day of the year. Lie back and enjoy it.

Fade down. Fade up.

Long corridor. JEFF *and* BYRON's *footsteps echo down it. Sea in background.*

JEFF (*voice over*). Along decks and cabin-lined corridors ablaze with light we walked, searching for one single human soul – me a bit hesitantly.

BYRON. Jeff – you mustn't draw back. In all this darkness there are unformed pieces of flesh and bone and gristle floating about – as yet chaotic – the future unformed – but you must join in. What we're involved in here is an act of creation – understand?

JEFF. Well . . .

BYRON (*stops*). Wait.

JEFF. What?

BYRON. Listen. Hear what I hear?

From a distance we hear the strains of the Tango Sinister.

BYRON. My God – here?

JEFF. It's from down the corridor – the first class section.

BYRON. It'll be the ballroom. (*Going.*) Come on.

JEFF (*stopping*). Byron – this ship has only got four hours – till it hits the rocks.

BYRON (*going*). I know. I know. Come on.

JEFF. God – if only life wasn't so complex. (JEFF *follows. They hurry towards sounds of tango. Voice over.*) We hurried down posh corridors – teak gleaming, brass polished, blood red carpets – turned a corner and . . .

CELIA. Good evening.

BYRON (*stopping*). My God.

JEFF (*not getting it*). What? (*Seeing.*) Oh.

CELIA. I said 'Good evening'.

BYRON. Er.

CELIA. Articulate, too. Are you ready for the dance?

BYRON. Pardon?

JEFF. Where's the captain? You see we've got to . . .

CELIA (*ignoring. To* BYRON). Everything's arranged. You'd better come in, I'll introduce you to our opponents . . .

BYRON. Opponents?

CELIA. There's nothing to panic about. I've worked everything out. Follow me.

BYRON (*following*). Right.

CELIA. My name is Celia.

BYRON. Oh – right – 'Celia'.

JEFF (*quiet hiss*). Byron.

BYRON (*stops*). Yes.

JEFF. We're on this boat to save it, right?

BYRON. Of course, Jeff. God – look at her – she is magnificent – imperial as Rome.

JEFF. And twice as nasty. Leave this to me. Excuse me – er –

CELIA. Celia.

JEFF. It is absolutely imperative we immediately meet the captain of this vessel.

CELIA (*to* BYRON). I hope your friend isn't normally like this. If he were to keep it up all evening he would get exceedingly boring. (*Going.*) Come along.

BYRON. Right.

JEFF (*groans*). Byron.

CELIA. And remember, 'Byron', whatever happens, you are mine. *My* partner, my property.

BYRON. Yes, Celia.

CELIA. Here we are.

Opens enormous doors. A great ballroom. Tango orchestra, folks whirling round, other folks sat at tables, chattering, drinking champagne.

BYRON. My God! My good God!

JEFF (*voice over*). It was extraordinary. A great light-filled ballroom – chandeliers ablaze, gold sheened walls, all set about this dazzling dance floor alive with exotic creatures mincing and stomping in triumphant tango. In the very centre, utterly deserted, never crossed by any human being, an enormous polished gold circle of metal – mysterious and pristine.

CELIA (*dismissively*). Look at them.

BYRON. Them?

CELIA. Those creatures there. Pathetic. Invalids. They don't stand a chance against you and me.

JEFF. Look, I've got to explain . . . (*Silence has fallen. Voice over*). But silence had already fallen. Everyone in the ballroom had stopped, stepped forward to gawp.

Low interested gabble as they step forward to inspect.

MAN 2. I say, take a look.

WOMAN 2. Extraordinary.

CHARLIE. Good gracious.

JEFF (*voice over*). I didn't lose a second. Leapt on to a nearby table to address the crowd. (*Leaps on to table.*) Ladies and gentlemen. Passengers on this liner. You are in the utmost danger. Do not panic but you are in the utmost danger. The ship on which you are travelling is at this very moment bearing down upon the most terrible rocks.

A murmur of voices has grown as dancers pass by JEFF, *moving towards* BYRON *and* CELIA *at door.*

LYDIA. It's extraordinary – he's got a ring through his ear.

JEFF *hesitates briefly at this, but carries bravely on.*

JEFF. It is imperative, imperative, that I meet your captain and speak to him immediately concerning the imminent peril his vessel is in, the imperative fact that it changes course immediately. You have less than four hours before . . .

Voices meanwhile have grown as they comment on BYRON *and* CELIA.

CHARLIE. I say – he's a bit young.

LYDIA. Sweet meat on the bone, eh?

MAN 2. Trust Celia.

WOMAN 2. Frightful dress sense, though.

CHARLIE. Says something about (*Reading.*) 'lighthouse person' on his jacket.

WOMAN 2. Lighthouse?

MAN 2. Specialises in insubstantial erections. (*Brittle laughter.*)

LYDIA. Just look at those curls clustering round his nape, though.

CHARLIE (*as a joke*). Steady, girl.

WOMAN 2. Those hanging eyelids.

LYDIA. That pouting lip.

ALL. Golly!

JEFF (*in the distance. Hint of desperation*). Ladies and gentlemen. Ladies and gentlemen . . .

CHARLIE. That's a piece of prime beef you've got, Celia.

WOMAN 2. Well hung, I bet. (*Titters.*)

LYDIA. Where did you discover him?

WOMAN 2. Let's feel him.

CHARLIE. Got pretty strong arms.

MAN 2. All his own teeth.

LYDIA (*giggle*). Feel his legs.

CELIA. Step back. Step back all of you. This is mine. Magnificent. Together we shall beat all, triumphant Tango Champions.

CHARLIE. No.

LYDIA. Never.

WOMAN 2. We'll win.

MAN 2. We'll win.

CELIA. Byron – lead me to the floor. We shall show these creatures our stuff.

BYRON. But . . .

CELIA. We'll change your clothes later – now we must dance.

JEFF. Byron – we've got to . . .

CELIA (*voice over*). Byron – do you wish to dance the tango – or do you not wish to dance the tango?

BYRON (*beat. With excitement*). I do – wish to dance the tango.

Strident, bold, dramatic chords, leading to strident, bold dramatic version of the tango. BYRON *and* CELIA *are dancing alone on floor.*

It's like I'm in a dream. You're in a dream. We're dancing in a dream. I can't tell where you end and I start.

CELIA. What other way is there to dance?

BYRON. Er – none.

CELIA. We are gods. Tasting immortality.

BYRON. Couldn't have put it better myself.

JEFF (*voice over. Different part of ballroom*). I watched them for a moment. All the other dancers gathered about the floor, watching hawk-eyed as they glided over the parquet – Byron mind-dead, entranced, frankly – gob-smacked. I turned. About my business. (*Pushes through doors. They shut behind him as he walks off, footsteps ringing down an iron corridor.*) Somewhere on this ship there must be someone that could help.

CELIA's *posh cabin.*

CELIA. Keep still. It's almost there. (*Strangled sounds from* BYRON.) It's very tight.

BYRON (*half strangled*). You can say that again.

CELIA (*effort*). There. A bow tie. The final detail in place. Black shoes, black trousers, white shirt and tails, a blood-dripping rose. Everything immaculate.

BYRON. Thank you.

CELIA. Think nothing of it.

BYRON. You're very particular, about dressing me. These clothes – did they belong to someone else?

CELIA (*beat*). Yes. My old partner. Reginald.

BYRON. What happened to Reginald?

CELIA. Unfortunate. Most unfortunate. We were out – dancing on the floor – and quite suddenly Reginald collapsed – in my arms. Dead.

BYRON. I'm sorry.

CELIA. Yes.

BYRON (*beat*). Another thing. On the dance floor. There's this great central circle of golden metal – no one dances on it . . .

CELIA. Byron . . .

BYRON. Celia?

CELIA. . . . shut up. Thought and tango dancing do not go together.

Rusty, iron bowels of the ship. A vast boiler room. Occasional iron clangs and groans. Drips of water. Sea heard vaguely in background. JEFF *walks up to microphone.*

JEFF. Frankly, I'm down. Down, down down. I've gone down through first class, second class, third class, through the officers' deck, the crew's deck, right down to this vast deserted rusty boiler room.

And everywhere – not a person.

Chatter of guests about tables – general sounds of ballroom, dancing, tango orchestra in background.

CELIA *and* BYRON's *table.*

BYRON (*beat*). Celia.

CELIA. Byron?

BYRON. You're magnificent. I mean, brilliant. Great. Frankly – amazing.

CELIA. Thank you, Byron.

BYRON. Such colours, richnesses – like a bird of paradise. Cerises, vermilions, ochres and azures, jacinths and jades . . .

CELIA (*voice over*). Byron – we have guests.

CHARLE *and* LYDIA *have approached.*

CHARLIE. Mind if we join you?

LYDIA. Come and ogle the new boy?

CELIA (*not delighted*). Charlie – Lydia.

LYDIA. Call me Lids.

CHARLIE. Thought we ought to come over . . .

LYDIA. Say hello.

CHARLIE. Well – shall we sit down. (*Beat. Sits.*) There. We've sat down.

LYDIA (*to* BYRON). Naughty old Celia – keeping you all to herself.

BYRON. Well . . .

CHARLIE. Brought a bottle of bubbly over. How about cracking it. (*Pop of cork.*) There. Let's have your glass.

BYRON. Thank you – but I've had rather a lot already.

CELIA. Here's a glass, Charlie – you have some anyway.

CHARLIE. Acid on the stomach, old girl. Can't.

LYDIA. So – you're the opposition.

BYRON. Opposition?

LYDIA. In the tango.

BYRON. I suppose so – yes.

CHARLIE. I see Celia's got you dressed to kill . . .

CELIA (*warningly*). Charlie – your tongue.

CHARLIE. Spect Celia brought you in to replace Reggie.

LYDIA. Poor old Reggie.

CHARLIE. Sure you don't want some champers, young fellah.

BYRON. Oh – all right.

CHARLIE (*starts to pour*). Here we go. (*Pours.*)

CELIA (*standing*). Don't drink that. (*Knocks it away.*)

BYRON. What?

CHARLIE. You bitch!

CELIA. Look at it. (*We hear acid hissing.*) How it eats away the table cloth – burning and hissing.

BYRON. Poison.

CELIA. Acid, more like.

CHARLIE. Time me and Lydia were going.

LYDIA (*going*). See you on the dance floor.

BOTH. Byee!

BYRON. They tried to kill me.

CELIA. It's time we were taking our places for the first round of the contest.

BYRON. He tried to kill me.

CELIA. All part of the rough and tumble of tangoing. An old trick. He was merely trying to unsettle you before you went on the floor.

BYRON. Unsettle? Murder!

CELIA (*going*). Comes to the same thing.

JEFF *on dead steel.*

JEFF. I think I've reached the final depths. The grating beneath the coal bunkers. Six inches of solid steel beneath me and then the seething black waters of the ocean. No one. Not one other human soul I can warn about the impending tragedy . . .

They say love is blind. God is Love. Therefore God is blind. A great monstrous, eyeless, noseless, mouthless, earless creature, utterly unaware of the outside world, an enormous dark impervious skin wrapped all around him, so rolled in a ball he knows nothing of the outside, only his own internal world of light and reason and joy. I am on the dark outside. (*Leaves*.) I journey on.

Dramatic chords of tango.

The dance starts. Sounds of ballroom, dancers, etc. Up. CELIA *and* BYRON *are dancing.*

BYRON. With countless other bodies – we whirl and strut endlessly about the dance floor. (*Voice over*.) I swoon. I sag and balloon like sex on a water bed that's gone on too long but you've forgotten how to end it.

CELIA. All right, darling?

BYRON. That's one way of describing it. Personally, I'd use words like delirious, ecstatic.

CELIA. Watch out for that couple over there.

BYRON. Who – the couple with the lady in orange?

CELIA. Sidney and Daphne Swinton. See the way he keeps dipping his shoulder. Dance and dip. Dance and dip.

BYRON. Yes – they're coming our way.

CELIA. Be very careful – do exactly as I say.

BYRON. What's happening?

CELIA. Don't lose the rhythm of the dance. When I push – you fall. Here they come. (*Pushes*.) Ooh.

BYRON (*being pushed off away*). Aah.

CELIA. There – they're past.

BYRON. My God – I saw it – a six-inch steel blade, slicing through the air – skewered the place I'd have been if you hadn't . . .

CELIA. We're a team. Now follow me.

BYRON. Where are we going?

CELIA. Following Sidney and Daphne Swinton. You don't think I'm going to let them get away with that, do you?

BYRON. But . . .

CELIA. You do a double spin to the left, I'll do a feint right, and then . . .

BYRON. But . . .

CELIA. Go! (*A whirling heard, then a cry of pain from Sidney.*) Take that, Sidney Swinton. (*More groans from Sidney.*) Always vulnerable to a specially sharpened stiletto in the calf.

BYRON. But that's two men tried to kill me now.

CELIA. Don't lose your rhythm – the judges are watching.

BYRON. But . . .

CELIA. Such actions are common. This is a tango competition. Already we're in the quarter finals.

BYRON. You're right. (*Beat.*) Life at the extreme. (*Beat.*) I love it.

Darkness. Dankness. Iron echo.

JEFF (*voice over*). I tried everywhere. The bakeries and laundries and telephone exchanges, the purser's office. Not no one. Not nowhere. My own iron echo in the darkness.

Starts to move. Footsteps.

Just over an hour to go. I return to the ballroom . . .

Sounds of ballroom – tango etc. approaching.

. . . but just outside, I see a sorry figure, lurking, indecisive.

RENNIE. Maimed, I was. Maimed for life. By Geoffrey.

JEFF. Geoffrey?

RENNIE. Yes. Maimed for life. By Geoffrey.

JEFF. I see.

RENNIE. Maimed for life.

JEFF (*pause*). This is a difficult question.

RENNIE. Maimed . . .

JEFF. For life. But what I'd like to ask you is – what do you think of as life?

RENNIE. What?

JEFF. I mean – there's this ballroom here – right . . .

RENNIE (*doubtfully*). Yes . . .

JEFF. There's the staterooms where you all sleep – and the dining room where you all dine – you're following me.

RENNIE. Possibly . . .

JEFF. Well – what do you think exists beyond these things?

RENNIE. I don't follow you.

JEFF. If I was to tell you that at the end of this corridor – turn left –
second right – there is open air, a great sea crashing on the deck, that
you and everyone of you tango madmen were on a massive luxury
liner that at this very second is bearing down at thirty knots on a reef
of rocks which will tear your hull out – if I was to tell you this . . .
(*Pause. Sighs.*) . . . then you really wouldn't be interested – not
in the slightest – would you.

RENNIE. Know how I was maimed?

JEFF. No. Tell me.

RENNIE. I was in the final. The final! Me and my girl Glenda. We
were on the very edge of dancing in that golden circle – the supreme
honour for all dancers – when Geoffrey, damned Geoffrey – had this
sort of poison dart affair hidden in his waistcoat – bloody great thing
– these sort of doors rolled open in his waistcoat – this cannon sort
of stuck out – he turned to face me – fired a broadside – and I lay
upon the floor – maimed for life.

JEFF (*beat*). How long has this sort of world – dancing the tango
– in here – been going on?

RENNIE. What do you mean 'how long'?

JEFF. Well – since you were young? Since your grandparents were
young? Since the beginning of time?

RENNIE. Time? What is time?

Cut to interior of ballroom. CELIA *and* BYRON *are at their table.*
CELIA *is trying to stick something on to the heels of* BYRON's
shoes.

BYRON. Eggshells?

CELIA. We're in the final, Byron. You and I have won through.

BYRON. I know. But why do I need half an eggshell glued to the
heel of each of my shoes?

CELIA. It is the ultimate . . . (*Correcting herself.*) Sorry, the
penultimate test of the skill and precision of a male tango dancer.
If you can dance a whole tango – never once coming off your toes
back on to your heels – as a proper tango dancer should do . . .

BYRON. Yeah.

CELIA. Then the eggshells remain unbroken – you have danced a
perfect tango – your opposition is in disarray. Geoffrey over there
would never dance on eggshells.

BYRON. That fat man with the extraordinary waistcoat?

CELIA. That's him. Him and Loella. Our opponents.

BYRON (*beat*). Celia.

CELIA. Byron?

BYRON. What's that great golden circle in the middle of the floor – the place where no one ever dances? . . .

CELIA. Byron . . .

BYRON. Celia?

CELIA. Shut up!

Cut to back of ballroom. JEFF *seated at table. Anticipating.*

JEFF (*voice over*). I slipped in through the door, sat at a back table, sipped a flat lemonade. Fifty minutes to go. I would try one last time to rouse them. Then I would extricate Byron, we'd take off, it would be every person for him or herself.

A fanfare. Quite distant amplified MASTER OF CEREMONIES.

MASTER OF CEREMONIES. My lords, persons and gentlemen, assembled here, we come now to that moment, that special moment, we all live for. Another Grand Final of another Grand Tango Competition. Who shall be our winners? Who shall be allowed to dance all alone upon the great golden circle? Persons and gentlemen, we have . . . (*Roll of drums.*) on our left, Geoffrey Waistcoat Higgins and his formidable partner Loella . . . (*Fanfare. Cheers and boos.*) and on my right, wearing eggshells upon his heels, the daring and reckless young tangoist Byron and his exotic lady person, Celia. (*Fanfare. Cheers and boos.*) Now, Maestro. Music. (*Sharp, incisive tango.*)

JEFF (*voice over*). Celia was dressed all in crystals, angles, refractions – she shimmered and crackled across the floor. Not so much fatale as catastrophique. She and Byron danced sharp, incisive. Tubby Geoffrey and thin Loella circled them warily.

Cut to BYRON *and* CELIA *dancing.*

BYRON. I love you.

CELIA. I love you too – but keep an eye on Geoffrey.

BYRON. If I were to do nothing else – if I were to die now . . .

CELIA (*pushing him*). Watch out. (*A bang.*)

BYRON. What was that?

CELIA. Geoffrey firing a poison dart . . .

BYRON. I don't care. I love you.

CELIA. Watch out for those eggshells.

Cut to – ballroom noises in background.

JEFF (*voice over.*) Byron and Celia twisted and dodged while Geoffrey lumbered after, firing broadsides from his waistcoat. (*Distant boom.*) An onlooker fell here. (*Distant boom.*) An innocent saxophonist there, but ever the vigilant Celia picked and stepped a safe course for her and Byron.

Byron!

I mean – look at them. Creatures of the night. Eye paint. Artifice.

Not like that in heaven. Know what the precise theological word is to describe angels having it off – commingling. See them two ethereal persons over there – getting their onions – they're commingling. Angels are not like us, see. They're all spirit. They can totally intermingle, commingle, everything. But when we make love, when we mingle our two bodies, try to fuse them in one, we're not that successful. Except for a general mingling of the genital areas, we by and large stay resolutely apart.

Cross mix immediately . . .

Sounds of BYRON *and* CELIA *making love in* CELIA's *cabin or at any rate* BYRON *making love while* CELIA *smokes a cigarette totally detached. In the studio you could try for a surrealistic effect by having* BYRON *doing press-ups on a bed while* CELIA *sits in a chair beside bed.*

BYRON. Oh God. Oh God.

CELIA. Do hurry up.

BYRON. You're beautiful. So beautiful.

CELIA. The really important part of the evening is still ahead of us.

BYRON. This is it. I think this is it. I really am . . .

CELIA. I've got a really special wardrobe laid out. And your 'appliances'.

BYRON. Here I go. I'm going . . . going . . . (*Comes.*) gone.

CELIA. Do be a dear and move your leg. (*Groan from* BYRON.) There. Now I'll slip into my clothes. You must do the same.

BYRON (*not taking it in*). What?

CELIA. You'll wear all the clothes you wore for the contest – except for these.

BYRON. These? What are these?

CELIA. Specially adapted shoes.

BYRON. And these things – on the heels.

CELIA. Remember how you danced the last dance with eggshells on your heels? Well, those things are a tiny bit different.

BYRON. They're . . .

CELIA. Electrodes. Copper electrodes.

BYRON. But . . .

CELIA. You and I are going to dance across the golden metal circle solo – a privilege granted only to winners of the tango contest.

BYRON. But what are the electrodes?

CELIA. The circle is electrified – several million volts. If your heels touch . . . (*Pause*.)

BYRON. What about you? Your feet?

CELIA. I will wear rubber soles. I am the woman.

BYRON. So that's what happened to poor old Reginald.

CELIA. He made a mistake.

BYRON. Snap crackle and pop. A puff of smoke in your arms.

CELIA. There is no reason why you should not dance perfectly. Is there?

BYRON. No.

CELIA. You are a tango dancer. You know what it's all about.

BYRON (*swallow*). Death.

CELIA. If you don't dance perfectly. Want it any other way?

BYRON (*swallows*). No.

CELIA. Then let's get dancing. Our audience awaits.

The ballroom. Animated talk. Desultory tango.

JEFF (*voice over*). Twenty-five minutes. Twenty-five minutes till the whole caboodle goes down.

MASTER OF CEREMONIES. My lords, ladies and others . . .

JEFF. What?

MASTER OF CEREMONIES. . . . It now gives me great pleasure to introduce to you once again our winning couple – Byron and Celia – who are to dance for us our Grand Ceremonial Tango to discover whether Byron really is to be our new captain.

JEFF (*voice over, stands in surprise*). Captain?

MASTER OF CEREMONIES. Ladies and gentlemen – Byron and Celia.

   Fanfare.

JEFF (*voice over*). Captain?

CELIA. Do you want to dance the tango or not?

BYRON. Of course I do.

CELIA. Then get a move on.

BYRON. I would. But I can't get my legs to move.

CHARLIE (*onlooker*). He's chickening out.

LYDIA. Lost his bottle.

JEFF (*close to* BYRON). Byron – we've got little more than twenty
   minutes . . .

BYRON. What?

JEFF. Before the boat hits the rocks.

BYRON. What?

JEFF. Look – I'll give them one last speech – try and convince them
   of their danger – then we've got to leave.

BYRON. Leave? I'm not leaving – I'm going to dance the tango.

CELIA. Then let's go.

LYDIA. Yes!

CHARLIE. About time.

BYRON. Only trouble – my legs won't move.

JEFF. You won't leave till you've danced?

BYRON. This is the ultimate tango.

JEFF. But you can't dance it.

MAN 2. Coward.

JEFF. So what if I dance it?

BYRON. You?

JEFF. I dance it. I become captain.

LYDIA. Captain.

JEFF. Then perhaps the fine folks here will listen, for once, to a bit
   of common sense.

CHARLIE. Rather.

WOMAN 2. I'd say.

BYRON. The only trouble is – you can't dance the tango.

JEFF. I have my *How to Dance the Tango in Ten Easy Lessons – Diagrams of All Essential Foot Movements Included* here (*Brandishing.*) in my hip pocket.

BYRON. Jeff – you don't understand. You wear these shoes I'm wearing. You go out on the floor. Unless you stay on total tiptoes throughout the dance – a million volts will pass through your body. This requires perfect tango dancing.

JEFF. Which you can't do. (BYRON *swallows*.) Give them to me.

BYRON. Jeff . . .

JEFF. Give them to me. (*Voice over*.) I fitted my metal executioners to my feet, stepped gingerly towards the floor – getting my instruction manual out as I went. Suddenly – I found myself dancing.

Tango Sinister up and under as he speaks.

JEFF. To the left three four then to the right, three four. Position A, three four, position B three four – turn, turn, and turn again.

CELIA. Do you have to read that instruction manual?

JEFF. I am one eighth of an inch above destruction – one two three four – turn your partner – one two three four . . .

CELIA. You should let go.

JEFF. Thank you – but I value my person.

CELIA. It's more fun.

JEFF. Spoken from a position of rubber-heeled security . . . Turn your partner, position A once more, and turn your partner.

CELIA. Let go.

JEFF (*voice over*). It's a matter of concentration. The floor crackles and shimmers beneath me.

CELIA. It's a great liquid pool. Wanting to baptise you.

JEFF (*voice over*). Concentrate! Concentrate!

CELIA. Slowly let yourself down.

JEFF. No – never.

CELIA. Then throw away your *Instruction Manual*.

JEFF (*beat*). All right. (*Throws it away.*) There – I've thrown it away.

CELIA. Dance a bit faster.

JEFF. You think you can get me – don't you. Frying tonight.

CELIA. Dance faster.

Music speeding up.

JEFF. All right – and you. Come on.

CELIA. Not too fast.

JEFF. Why not? Scared? Come on – I'll turn you.

CELIA. Not so fast. If I fall . . .

JEFF. You're not scared of falling. Faster . . . and faster . . . and faster.

CELIA. That's it. I give up. Stop! Stop!

JEFF. I'm captain.

CELIA. You're captain.

JEFF jumps on chair, addresses crowd.

JEFF. Right. Listen the lot of you! This is your captain speaking. You have five minutes now. Literally five minutes – in which to abandon ship.

CHARLIE. Abandon ship?

MAN 2. What is the fellow talking about?

JEFF. If you do nothing else, I, your captain, beg you that you will at least follow me out on to your boat's deck, so you can at least see . . .

LYDIA. See?

MAN 2. Boat?

WOMAN 2. Deck?

JEFF. Please.

CHARLIE. Fellow's been drinking.

MAN 2. Lids – how about another tango?

LYDIA. Smashing.

MAN 2. Time we got another contest going, eh?

WOMAN 2. Super.

CHARLIE. Come on, folks, – back to the floor – take your partners.

Crowd move off. Moment's silence.

JEFF (*voice over*). I'd done – I'd done my bit. I lifted up Byron.

BYRON. You bastard.

JEFF (*voice over*). He fought a bit.

BYRON. You've ruined my life, you bastard.

JEFF (*voice over*). I carried him hurriedly back down the corridor, out on to the deck . . . (*Sound of sea and wind.*) . . . where the helicopter stood.

JEFF. We've only got a few seconds left.

Door of helicopter opens.

BYRON. You know when I hated you most? The second you threw away that *Instruction Manual* (*Hum of rotor starts.*) . . . up until that moment I'd been able to kid myself – you're dancing because you're just following the book – but after that, as you started sliding over that floor – over that death – I hated you.

JEFF. Full aerilion extension, blade elevation. Byron?

BYRON. Get stuffed.

JEFF. More boost. (*Rotor noise up.*) Here we go. (*Beat.*) Takeoff.

JEFF (*voice over*). We lifted into the black night – alive. Rose – till the liner climbed and lunged beneath us – then – she struck the rocks – a sunken reef – full. Her momentum carrying her on – but her hull being peeled off beneath her like a lid on a sardine can.

I flew the copter lower – right down by her side as the waters clawed and ate at her – her decks and lights slipping below – into the darkness – and – I had one last glimpse – through a state room window – for one last time heard the strains of a distant tango . . . as oblivious, upon their floor, the dancers once more set off about their endless tango, while the ship disappeared down into the darkness, between the jaws of an eternal womb.

Sound of helicopter.

BYRON. I am shattered. Totally shattered.

JEFF. Take it easy. We survived.

BYRON. I mean, there I was, with the chance to dance above the great lips of Death, knowing that any second I might be sucked down – the ultimate – but, at the vital second my true heart faltered – I – I could not. Life – (*Laughs.*) *life* became a thing I saw as – desirable like a two-up-two-down-separate-toilet-bathroom-full-kitchen-facilities maisonette in Solihull.

JEFF. Poor Byron.

BYRON. Don't patronise me.

JEFF (*voice over*). But I could not help but feel a certain frisson, a joy infuse my hands and body. I gripped the joystick. I mean, I had seized my destiny – in both hands – with the help of *How to Dance the Tango in Ten Easy Lessons* – I had steered us up to some sort of salvation.

Now all my life I had been surrounded by clouds, drizzle and darkness – I had only dreamed about light, beauty, transcendence, but now my hands glowed on the controls – I can do things – I increased the boost – the revs – the craft danced beneath my direction – bobbed lighthearted. Why not go up?

BYRON. Jeff – what are you doing?

JEFF (*voice over*). I mean – our mundaneness, our earthboundness – is only a matter of choice. We can alter that fate. Below, darkness, dirt, wet – up above . . .

Sound of helicopter increasing.

BYRON. Jeff – we're climbing?

JEFF. Climbing – climbing – I mean – if there are clouds – then above the clouds – eventually . . .

BYRON. Let's get home. To the lighthouse.

JEFF. Suddenly – the lighthouse is home. Safe. No.

BYRON. But this craft is only a tiny . . .

JEFF. It's a matter of will-power. Somewhere, if we go on upwards long enough, above all these clouds – there must be . . .

Helicopter up, revs high, craft getting quite a shaking.

BYRON (*to himself*). Mum – I'm sorry, Mum – I'm sorry I never used to tidy me room. I'm sorry the vaseline and hairs from my comb used to block the plug hole in the bath. My attitude never was . . . one hundred per cent. But I loved you, Mum. I loved you.

BYRON goes under. Helicopter sound continuing. JEFF's voice over comes up.

JEFF (*voice over*). Climbing through these clouds is like battering up through porridge – but we rise and rise –

BYRON. We're running out of fuel. Look at the dial.

JEFF. Doesn't matter. It's a matter of logic. Pure reason.

BYRON. Stuff the reason.

JEFF. Somewhere up here . . . somewhere . . .

The sound of the helicopter and the violence it is receiving changes in tone – melts into an electronic sound. Broadening out as they speak into a sort of level of exaltation.

JEFF *and* BYRON *look at this world for a while in awestruck silence.*

JEFF. Oh my God.

BYRON. Sweet Jesus.

JEFF. Heaven be praised.

BYRON. I'm gob-smacked – frankly.

JEFF (*voice over*). Light. There was light. (*Laughs.*) The sun is laughter, for by him laugh all mortal minds, and the boundless universe beyond.

Oh Lord,
    When I look at thy heavens, the work of thy fingers the moon and the stars which thou hast established; what is man that thou art mindful of him?

JEFF. Do you realise where we are?

BYRON. Yeah.

JEFF. Stars, moon, planets – laid out before us.

BYRON. My gast, Jeff, is well and truly flabbered.

Sound of electronic switch in pitch of helicopter as it changes course. Then under, opening bars of lugubrious Messaien's 'Et expecto resurrectionem mortuorum'.

BYRON. Where are we going? You're changing course.

JEFF. Where do you think?

BYRON. No.

JEFF. Yes.

BYRON. Jeff, I'm not . . .

JEFF (*voice over*). Heaven, Byron – you and I are going straight to Heaven. It's what I've dreamed of all these years. Pure, ethereal, unending Light.

BYRON. Yes, but . . .

JEFF. Illumination. Understanding.

BYRON. Jeff . . .

JEFF. Truth. At last I will uncover, live through, become Truth. Total Spiritual Oneness. Half an hour ago, Byron, what were we but gross, anoraked creatures of the night, but now we shall become ethereal, elfin entities . . .

BYRON. That's as may be, but . . .

JEFF. I'm landing. Can't you smell the love.

Sound of electronic helicopter coming down.

BYRON (*voice over*). A great white infinite plain, and in its midst the towers and spires and golden domes of the Eternal City, endless marble stairs and steps rising, causeways and forums, and gliding through and across them heavenly personages, staring ahead, mumbling sacred mantra.

Helicopter lands. Down and out. Electronic swishes and hums heard of passing ethereal personages.

JEFF (*getting ready to go*). Isn't this exciting.

BYRON (*unconvinced*). Yes.

JEFF. Come on.

BYRON. Where are you going?

JEFF. Where do you think? We are on the Parnassus, the Olympus of Truth. All these sages and philosophers, virtuosi of argument – and I have the answers. By God, after a lifetime in Brum, Byron, I have the answers.

JEFF. Look, there's a signpost (*Pointing.*) 'To the Symposium'. (*Pointing again.*)

BYRON. And there. 'To Another Symposium'.

JEFF. More and more. Thousands of them. (*Going.*) This is it.

BYRON. Jeff!

JEFF. What?

BYRON. Wait for me.

JEFF. What?

BYRON. Me. I'm coming.

JEFF. Coming? Are you sure you should, Byron? Symposii, metaphysics – not really your cup of ambrosia.

BYRON. I could try.

JEFF. But look at all these etherea passing us – pale, translucent, cranial. You are a bit – fleshly. You have been known to sweat. And that earring!

BYRON (*strongly*). I'm coming.

JEFF. Very well. But no yawning. This is Heaven. Positively no yawning.

Symposium acoustic. People sat around. BYRON does an extraordinary yawn. Catches himself half way.

BYRON. Sorry.

JEFF. My name is Jeff. Jeff. Gentlemen, ladies, ethereal persons, welcome to this, my symposium. I am from Birmingham. I – from Birmingham, from darkness, through sheer power of the intellect, metaphysical reasoning – have created light. By the creasing of my brow I have passed up the Great Chain of Being – from mere fleshly things . . .

BYRON *yawns*.

Byron!

BYRON. Sorry.

JEFF. . . . I have passed all the way up to . . . here. Heaven.

MEMBER 1 (*bored*). That's great.

MEMBER 2 (*bored*). Fascinating!

MEMBER 3 (*bored*). So what exactly do you want to talk to us about?

JEFF. Light!

MEMBER 2. Light?

MEMBER 3. Not light!

MEMBER 2. We've had light up to here.

MEMBER 1. What about a bit of darkness.

MEMBER 3. Excitement.

MEMBER 2. Rough trade.

JEFF. No! We shall not talk of darkness – excitement. We shall talk about light. The Great Chain of Being. The progress of the Almighty – as revealed to me.

The same later. Increasing coughs, scraping of chairs, yawns, during speech.

JEFF. For diverse living things represent diverse spirits and powers. For God as a whole is in All Things; and as the Divinity descends in a certain manner and communicates itself to Nature, so the light which shines in natural things mounts up to the Life which presides over them. Thus crocodiles, cocks, onions and turnips were never worshipped for themselves, but the gods and the divinity in crocodiles, cocks and other things, which divinity was . . .

Other members of the symposium starting to talk among themselves.

JEFF. . . . is, and will be found in diverse subjects in so far as they . . . (*Breaks out.*) Look – I want to communicate with you – do you understand – get through to you – so we can . . .

MEMBER 1. What?

MEMBER 2. Can what?

JEFF. So we can catch light – mutually combust – become greater, more creative . . .

MEMBER 1. Creative!

JEFF. . . . mysterious . . .

MEMBER 2. Mysterious!

JEFF. . . . wonderful . . .

MEMBER 3. Fellah's a bit cracked.

MEMBER 1. One over the six.

JEFF (*emphatically*). We are all a part of the Great Chain of Being – Creation – progressing upwards . . .

BYRON *yawns*.

JEFF (*shouting*). Byron.

BYRON. Oops, sorry.

JEFF. Get out of here!

BYRON. But . . .

JEFF. This instant! Out! For ever!

BYRON. But . . .

JEFF. Off!

BYRON. But it's strange out there, Heaven. Unfriendly. You and me . . .

JEFF. Do I have to throw you out?

MEMBER 2. Ooh – that would be interesting.

MEMBER 3. Completely unspiritual.

MEMBER 1. Crudely physical.

BYRON. But Jeff . . .

JEFF. Out!

A street corner in Heaven. Electronic whooshes as spiritual beings pass and repass. A slight wind.

BYRON (*voice over*). I went. Out into Heaven. What to do in Heaven? I stood on a street corner. Surrounded by blanks and nothingnesses. Could have been Birmingham on a Saturday night. Essences and vapours waft past – whey-faced, disengaged. An unsympathetic wind blows. Stand my hair on end, raise my collar, scuff my heels. Whistle up a whistle.

Whistles a bit.
Nothing connects. Everything spills, plummets off into eternity. I sort of teeter on the brink. Must get a grip of myself – or I won't be here . . .

GRACE. Hello.

BYRON (*startled*). What?

GRACE. I said hello.

BYRON. Oh – there you are. You aren't very – composed.

GRACE. I'm a heavenly being. I've been listening to you. 'Sensing' you.

BYRON. Oh.

GRACE. Smelling you.

BYRON. Eh! What do you mean? I'm as well washed as the . . .

GRACE. Know what I imagined as I smelt you? I imagined flesh, skin, blood, sweat, boils, pimples, hairs and dandruff.

BYRON. Charming.

GRACE. Lips, armpits, private parts . . .

BYRON. You're a very forward young lady.

GRACE (*correcting*). Angel.

BYRON. Unfocused but forward.

GRACE. What's it like?

BYRON. What?

GRACE. Eating. Eating flesh. Swallowing it down. Dissolving it in your stomach juices, then cleansing it out so you're just left with the waste – passing it out, excreting it. Tell me what it's like to have genitals . . .

BYRON. Um . . .

GRACE. I want to know. I am innocent. Pure – disgustingly pure.

BYRON. You have a problem or two.

GRACE. Tell me what you look like.

BYRON. Black leather – can't you tell?

GRACE. I'm an angel. Can you see me?

BYRON. Sort of.

GRACE. My mohican hair cut, the ring through my nose . . .

BYRON. An angelic punk . . .

GRACE. A fallen angel. I've dropped out.

BYRON. I know the feeling.

GRACE. Look into my eyes.

BYRON. Your eyes?

GRACE. Deep.

BYRON. There's nothing there.

GRACE. Light. Only light. Perpetual light. Blank bloody endless light. I want to see.

BYRON. What?

GRACE. I want to feel. I want to smell. All the colours. All the rainbows and richnesses of earth.

BYRON. Er . . .

GRACE. They tell me about it sometimes. Whisper it to me. Till they drive me mad.

BYRON. What?

GRACE. Stories about . . . earth. It does exist, doesn't it?

BYRON. Yeah.

GRACE. But I might just be imagining you. You might be inside my head. I can't see you. Heaven is full of speculation. When you die, you go to earth. God lives in places like – where do you come from?

BYRON. Birmingham.

GRACE. Birmingham. God lives in Birmingham. You're sure earth really exists?

BYRON. Er – yes. To the best of my knowledge. Earth exists. Birmingham exists. Mum definitely exists.

GRACE. But how do I know you're not just me – telling myself stories?

The symposium.

JEFF *quietly, intensely, meaningfully, audience actually listening.*

JEFF. I tell you. God eternally loves this universe. He rides it like a bull a cow, ruts like a stag, pricks like a wren his jenny. It is from this perpetual swyving and lusting that the Universe, in her immensity, brings forth abundance.

So it is with man and woman. Their loving, their caring together. It has a deeper meaning than we realise. From God, the master and round of all generative powers, has been passed down to all his creatures, this sacrament of joy and happiness and perpetual fertility.

I wouldn't tell you of the compulsion which binds each one of us to each other, were it not that each of us, if he focuses his thoughts in upon him or herself, might learn it from his own inmost being. Remember that supreme time when, through loving without end, you arrive at last at that moment when both commingle with the other – one giving forth his life, the other eagerly taking hold of it and laying it up within her. At that very moment, through the total fusing of two natures, is it not the truth that as the female gains masculine vigour, the male relaxes in feminine langour? So this sacramental act, sweet as it is, is nevertheless a thing done in guilty secret, for, if it were done publicly, the ignorant might jeer and the godhead, manifest in both sexes at that second, might be brought to naught.

The plain.

GRACE. Tell me about feelings.

BYRON. Feelings?

GRACE. Yes.

BYRON. That's a very big subject.

GRACE. Try.

BYRON. You feel with your body. With your bowels and heart and guts and . . .

GRACE. Genitals.

BYRON. Yes. Feeling flows in and out perpetually like a great black river at night, leeching away the banks and roots and gravel, carrying all away, hungry only for the sea. Never satisfied. The stuff of life.

GRACE. I wish I could feel.

BYRON. You will. You will.

GRACE. I won't.

BYRON. I . . . I . . . Is there a place? Away from here?

GRACE. We could go to the Great Plain. Beyond the City.

BYRON. That white place? With the great white sky?

GRACE. Yes. Why?

BYRON. Let's go. I'll explain on the way. I really like you.

GRACE. I really like you. Even though I can't see you.

BYRON. We might do something about that.

GRACE. Kiss me.

BYRON. Kiss you? A spiritual essence?

GRACE. Try.

BYRON. All right. (*Gooey sounds.*)

GRACE. What was it like?

BYRON. I missed your lips. I think I invaded a portion of your nose.

GRACE. This could be the start of . . .

BYRON. Something new. Quite definitely something new.

White plain acoustic.

BYRON *and* GRACE *walking on it.*

BYRON (*voice over*). We passed out of Heaven on to this great white plain – a vast dome of white above us. Soon the city was left far behind, fell beneath the horizon. There was just the two of us.

We turned – sort of faced each other.

GRACE. What are we going to do?

BYRON. In Birmingham, see – where I come from – we have this sort of tradition – where if things are bad and low – when we want to bring a little life and warmth and emotion into our lives – we do this dance, this ancient fertility dance.

GRACE. Dance?

BYRON. Come into my arms.

GRACE. I'll do my best.

BYRON. Now – follow me – as I move.

GRACE. As best I can?

BYRON. As best you can.

We hear his steps as he starts to dance. Her more hesitant breaths and movements – but not footsteps as she tries to follow him. Rhythm in his step.

GRACE. What is this thing? This step?

BYRON. An ancient step – the tango.

GRACE. It's difficult.

BYRON. All good things are difficult. Come on.

We hear the music starting from nowhere, but gradually getting stronger, more virile.

GRACE. The tango.

BYRON. Life.

GRACE. Extraordinary. Can feel it. In my arteries, in my veins. In the tiniest capillary and nerve end. The running of blood.

BYRON. It's a great raiser of the blood.

GRACE. All these things in my body – my body! Starting to form.

Immediate cut to JEFF/Symposium. JEFF *with power, authority. Silent audience.*

JEFF. Eternity is the Power of God. The Work of Eternity is the World which has no beginning but is perpetually becoming by the Power of Eternity. Therefore nothing that is in the world shall ever perish or be destroyed, for Eternity is imperishable.

The dance. They are dancing to a powerful tango. Music.

GRACE. I can feel my stomach, sitting on my bowels, resting in my pelvis. Muscles snapping and stretching in my leg as I kick and glide – left and right, to and fro, round and round.

BYRON. You have a body.

GRACE. Hallelujah!

Symposium. A powerful chord from tango. Silence.

JEFF (*carried away*). And all this great body of the world is a soul, full of intellect and God, who fills it within and without and vivifies the All.

Another great chord from the tango. Silence.

JEFF. It is so you must conceive of God; all that is He contains within himself like thoughts (*A chord.*) The world (*A chord.*) Himself (*A chord.*) The All. (*A chord.*)

Full music resumes from chorus.

GRACE. This is glorious.

BYRON. This is the tango.

GRACE. If only . . .

BYRON. If only?

GRACE. Throw me out further.

BYRON. Further?

She cries out as she spins away.

GRACE. And back again. (*Returns.*) Hold me tighter.

BYRON. Tighter.

GRACE. I can feel you.

BYRON. I can feel you.

GRACE. If only . . .

BYRON. If only? . . .

GRACE. If only I could see you.

They dance.

You've gone quiet. What are you thinking?

BYRON. I'm thinking. If there is a way. You might see. Dance on. Dance on.

Cut to JEFF *at Symposium. As* JEFF *speaks we can start to hear tango in distance. Audience hear it, mutter among themselves. Some rise to leave, but so emphatic is* JEFF's *delivery that they and we listen to what he says.*

JEFF. Therefore, unless you make yourself equal to God, you cannot understand God: for the like is not intelligible save to the like. Make yourself grow to a greatness beyond measure, by a bound free yourself from the body; raise yourself above all time, become Eternity; *then* you will understand God. Say no longer that God is invisible. Do not speak thus. For what is more manifest than God. He has created All only that you might see Him through it. That is the miraculous power of God, to show himself through all things. The intellect makes itself visible in the act of thinking, God in the act of Creation.

Silence from the shattered JEFF. *Shattered by his climax. Expecting applause, but instead it slowly dawns on him that his audience is leaving.*

(*Voice over.*) My audience. Getting up. Leaving. They can't. I have just proved God's Glory. This is my moment of triumph. I should be receiving plaudits, telegrams, delegations of celestial . . .

Hears music.

That music. In Heaven? The tango in Heaven? Byron! Where is Byron?

Final seat upends, listener leaves.

(*Voice over.*) That's it. That does it. My final listener leaves me. Goes out to join that limpwristed piss artiste and fandango dancer from West Bromwich.

Corridor sounds, people.

The thoroughfares are filled with people, once holy folk with pious glazes on their faces, now animated, greedy, hungry for sensation – pouring out of the city, on to the great white plain.

Plain acoustic. Sound of tango coming up.

Look at him – just look at that gilded serpent upon the white plastic. Oiling about the place. Shameless as a raised toilet seat in a nunnery.

Music up. BYRON *and* GRACE *dancing.*

BYRON. It strikes me there are two basic things in this life – Order and Chaos. We're never satisfied. When we have Order, we crave Chaos. When we have Chaos, we love Order.

GRACE. Yes . . .

BYRON. They used to be able to deal with it. In the Stone Age when you were buried you went through a moment of great chaos – you had to adjust to a totally new world.

GRACE. I see . . .

BYRON. So they stuck everything in your grave upside down – jars upside down, human heads, wooden bowls, deers' antlers – sometimes a whole millstone with the pestle underneath – all deliberately upside down – and then they'd smash everything – upside down *and* smashed to pieces – to make it even more chaotic – all to prepare you for the shock, of that moment. They know this from this archaeological dig they've been doing near Peterborough . . .

GRACE. Peterborough. Oh.

BYRON. There's another dig they've done near Peterborough. Bronze Age. In the peat they've discovered this colossal wooden causeway joining together the old mainland to an old island. Millions of pieces of timber half a mile in length. If it had been built in stone in Egypt or Peru they'd be saying 'Oh wow, what an extraordinary ancient monument' – but because it's near Peterborough . . .

GRACE. Yes.

BYRON. Anyhow, where the causeway leaves the mainland they've discovered the remains of sacrificed men and boys, impaled dogs and along its length they've found the most exquisite swords and bows and spears, thrown into the water, the other world, upside down, opposite, inside out to ours.

GRACE. I see.

BYRON. Finally, an artificial island with some houses on it – where the dead might rest and accustom themselves – before the causeway ends on the real island, the Island of the Dead, the Island of the Reborn.

GRACE. This is all very interesting.

BYRON. Do you understand what I'm saying?

GRACE (*beat*). No.

BYRON. All right. One last site. Not near Peterborough this time . . . Near Ipswich.

GRACE. Ipswich?

BYRON. Now, there was this great king. Redwald. He dies, they bury him at this place called Sutton Hoo in all his finery – crowns, sceptres, oils of unction – on board this whacking great boat which they then bury under this mound. That in itself is not important.

GRACE. Oh.

BYRON. You know what is really important? What they've dug up around. All these bodies, people, who died in frenzy. Hold this object.

GRACE. What? What is it?

BYRON. Just hold it.

JEFF (*voice over*). Byron handed the girl this long thin silver object. A knife.

BYRON. This mass graveyard. All sorts were found there. Buried singly, in twos and threes and whole lots of 'em. Some strangled, some decapitated, their heads between their legs, others shot through, others with animals – sheep, dogs, stags – women and children embracing each other. All, each one, died in frenzy.
  You've got that thing I gave you?

GRACE. Yes. What is it?

BYRON. Hold it out straight.

JEFF (*voice over*). The girl held the knife out straight.

Music stops abruptly.

BYRON. You realise what Death is, don't you?

GRACE. Why do you keep talking about Death? Why has the music stopped?

JEFF (*voice over*). I saw what he was going to do.

BYRON. Death . . .

JEFF (*voice over*). I should have moved. That second I should have moved, knocked the knife from . . . but I stuck still. For one second an ancient worm of hatred, jealousy . . .

BYRON. Death is being f . . . (*Receives impact of dagger.*) . . . d by God.

Groans from BYRON, *cries from crowd.*

JEFF (*running forward*). Byron, Byron – what have you done?

GRACE. I can see. I can see.

JEFF. Oh my God – he's stabbed himself.

ONLOOKER 1. Run on to his own dagger.

BYRON. Jeff. Fancy meeting . . .

GRACE. What? What is this I see? (*Screams.*)

BYRON (*slipping down*). I had to do it.

GRACE. You didn't have to do any such thing.

BYRON. To let you see.

GRACE. My sight for your blood? Never!

BYRON. Death – sacrifice – rebirth – it's the point of the tango.

GRACE. Rubbish.

JEFF. Byron – for one second – I could have saved you.

BYRON. No one could have saved me.

JEFF. Forgive me.

BYRON. Of course I forgive you.

JEFF (*voice over*). There wasn't anything that could be done. On that great white plain, beneath its great white dome, the crowds gathered about the young hero, his blood red upon the white. Grace lay beside him, cupping his face desperate in her hands.

GRACE. I've never seen your face before. Never.

BYRON. You can see. You can see.

GRACE. Oh God – how marvellous is your face – which youths cannot think of but as youthful, men but as manly, old men but as an old man's. Oh marvellous face, whose beauty all those who see it are insufficient to admire. The face of God. The face of faces that is veiled in all faces but seen in each face.

JEFF. Byron – don't leave me . . .

BYRON. I . . . I . . .

JEFF. We're mates.

(*Voice over.*) Then, at that very moment, that very moment when God leaves a face and the clay comes in . . .

A distant crashing and rumbling. Sounds of consternation from the crowd.

ONLOOKER 1. What's happening?

ONLOOKER 2. What's going on?

GRACE (*pointing*). Look – up there!

More sounds of crashing and rumbling above.

JEFF (*voice over*). High up, in the very vault of the great white dome
came a massive crashing and breaking. Something huge, white, round
was smashing down through – a vessel like a stately barrage balloon,
swinging slowly down towards us.

Bass. Paul Robeson? Starts singing 'Sweet Chariot'.

ONLOOKER 1. What is it?

ONLOOKER 2. What can it be?

ONLOOKER 1. It's beautiful.

JEFF. It's the hull, the hull of a great white ship.

ONLOOKER 1. My God.

JEFF (*voice over*). In a way like the ocean liner we had voyaged
on earlier, but now pristine clean and white, lowering itself towards
us.

Byron's funeral barge. Come to collect him for his journey.

Singing as GRACE shouts.

GRACE. No! No! You shall not have him.

JEFF. But, Grace . . .

GRACE. Look at him. He's not dead. Not dead yet. Fight, Byron,
fight. Never surrender. (*Looking up.*) Good Lord wherever you
are. Far away from the false absolutes of darkness and light, good
and evil, chaos and order, wherever you have chosen to make your
private home, hear me now I pray you. Hear me. Show your tender
mercy to this good, brave man. Break the rules, for one second step
down, show your face, show mercy.

JEFF (*voice over*). All the world paused. Waited on bated breath.
Then somewhere, a decision was taken.

Distant bangs and crashes from liner.

ONLOOKER 2. What's going on?

ONLOOKER 3. What's happening?

JEFF (*voice over*). Bangs and crashes upon the deck of the ship. A
hurried clattering as gangways and staircases started to be lowered
over the side, down to where we stood. Great broad white staircases.
Lights flashed on and off. People gathered on the decks.

ONLOOKER 1. What are they doing?

ONLOOKER 2. Wish I knew what was happening.

JEFF (*voice over*). A cough (*A cough.*) rent the air. A baton tapped (*A baton tapping.*) the rostrum. Then, it started. Down, from the ship's side, lights flashing, music playing, a great torrent of humanity started to cascade down the stairs.

Over the noise the music – suitable thirties Hollywood musical with mass tap dancing.

Men dressed in white top hats, white tails and gloves and trousers, women in white evening dresses.

Music up, then down.

Descending in glory and ecstasy, thousands of toothy singers, thundering out their rhythms of tap, bouncing their canes, shaking their hands, grinning the grins of the saved, laughing the laughter of the Almighty.

Byron arose.

'Ooh's from those around him.

Grace embraced him. I embraced him. Everyone embraced everyone, before the human tidal wave hit us, swept us away in a fury of dance and ecstasy.

A climax of music and dancing and shouting. Then a drunken solo trumpet.

When that party finished I shall never know. When the last champagne bottle sailed through the air, the last streamer flew, I cannot remember.

Trumpet out.

But eventually the three of us, honoured passengers, climbed back upon the mighty liner, followed by half the inhabitants of heaven, determined to make a new life on earth.
    We weighed anchor.

Ship's mournful hooter.

Set our course across the mighty waters of the firmament, glided down towards earth.

Start of deep, luminous, rising English music – Vaughan Williams, Tallis, Butterworth's 'Shropshire Lad', 'Banks of Green Willow', 'English Idylls'.

One evening, after supper, we walked out upon the deck.

JEFF. You reckon it's worth it?

GRACE. What?

JEFF. Saving the universe.

BYRON. Every time.

GRACE. I mean – just look out there – isn't it a fantastic sight.

JEFF. Awesome.

BYRON. Moon's so close we can almost touch it.

GRACE. Do you think we'll have another . . . adventure? The three of us.

JEFF. Possibly.

GRACE. It would be fun – you know, saving the universe again. Dancing the tango in exotic locations. Scraping through by the skin of our teeth. How about it, Byron?

BYRON. Yeah. Why not? How about you, Jeff?

JEFF. Me? All I'm thinking of at this moment is getting home to Brum.

(*Voice over*.) We descended slowly toward earth. Were enveloped once more in the turmoil of clouds, nosing our way down till suddenly we broke through the clouds above a dark, drear Birmingham.

Out of their houses and hovels they started to come, the people, the sad, sodden sons of darkness, and our sons of light started to disembark, pass down the gangway. They approached each other. Then it happened. A flash of light. A crack of dark and doom across the universe. And then they were together, light and dark – peering, touching – light striking darkness, dark being made visible – colours coming forth. Suddenly a yellow sun was sailing in a blue sky. Brickwork, masonry, ground which for millenia had absorbed rain suddenly started to dry, change, glow with colours. In the streets, instead of puddles – dust – instead of mud, green, blades of grass, mouths of flowers, hums of insects, heady bird song.

The people stepped out into the street. Stretched, yawned, bathed their limbs in the sun. In the backyards and courtyards businesses started to flourish again. Nailmakers, cutlers, dyers and casters, blacksmiths and whitesmiths. Along the streets bakeries, dry cleaners, ironmongers, greengrocers, started to re-open. Green leaves spreading over red buildings.

A hum of humanity. Starting to turn to a roar. Relationships deepening – becoming emotional – children forthcoming. Running out in the busy, careless streets.

The liner stayed for a while, moored to the university clock tower – but then, one day, no longer needed, it drifted away. We were free once more. Emerged from our tunnel of too much darkness, too much light.

These days I live above a launderette. Have a small workshop. Byron and Grace live down the street. With lots of kids. Every Saturday night we go down the Locarno Ballroom. While the kids drink coke and discuss Kylie Minogue, we talk, reminisce about the old times, and Byron still takes Grace for a spin round the floor, old rhythms waking their old limbs. On Sundays I go fishing. The banks of the Fazeley and Walsall Junction Canal. Only this time what comes to my hooks are not old prams and bicycle wheels but fat perch, carp, and rudd. Perhaps I'm getting old.

Tango music up.

SONG OF THE FOREST

by Tina Pepler

For my mother

Tina Pepler was born in the Middle East and spent most of her childhood either living abroad, or in boarding schools. In 1983 she became a postgraduate student at Bristol University Drama Department, where she was awarded a doctorate for her thesis on early radio drama. Her work for radio includes *Waiting*, Radio 4, 1986; *Snow Bubble*, Radio 4, 1988 and *Easy Traumas*, Radio 3, 1991. Her first play for television, *Say Hello to the Real Doctor Snide*, was broadcast on Channel Four in March 1991. She is currently working on an adaptation of two novels by Edith Wharton for a television mini-series. *Song of the Forest* was the BBC's official entry for the Morishige Award International Radio Drama Contest in 1991, the first time that this Japanese contest had been held. The play was also nominated for the Sony award.

Song of the Forest was first broadcast on 'Monday Play', BBC Radio 4, on 16 July 1990. The cast was as follows:

HELENA	Maureen O'Brien
JACU	Mamta Kaash
LAURETTE	Shelley Thompson
HARRY	Bill Wallis
BERNIE	Peter Whitman
MOTHER	June Barrie
SISTER MARINA	Ann Morrish
LIZZIE	Susan Sheridan
JONATHAN	Stephen Garlick
SAM/SURGEON	Vincent Brimble

HELENA 1/HARRY 1/BERNIE 1 represent an inner voice, unheard by the other characters. JACU only ever has an inner voice (except where she is chattering and screeching).

Director: Shaun MacLoughlin
Composer: Elizabeth Parker, Radiophonic Workshop
Running time, as broadcast: 75 minutes

Scene 1

JACU. In the beginning, there was only light. There was no darkness. No one could sleep. They say that in the forest where I come from, man is changing the face of the earth. They say he wants to make it like the beginning again. No forest. No darkness. No green darkness of the forest. No more quiet of the soul.

Music: JACU's *theme. Forest sounds.*

In the trees, listen, listen, the sounds of the night, the whispers of the forest, the whispers of the soul. Jacu. Forest bird. Bird-daughter of the juruna who climbed the ladder in the forest, climbed up into the sky, where the daughters of Alapa washed him in magic water and made him young again. Bird-daughter on earth, girl-daughter in the sky. Home sounds. Home far away.

End music.

If I don't move, man won't notice me. If I don't move, he'll notice something else instead. Like the beginning. No forest. No darkness. No green darkness of the forest. Jacu.

HELENA 1. When I stopped moving, night and day made no difference any more.

JACU. Always daytime. No one can sleep.

Music: HELENA's *theme.*

HELENA 1. Always daytime. Helena, they say, don't give up. Always the harsh daylight, reality, this is how it is, this is how it will be for ever more. Night and day make no difference now. Life and death make no difference. No life without the night. No one touches me now.

Fade music out.

Scene 2

Laboratory acoustic. Monkey noises: the Research Centre and Breeding Colony for Capuchin Aides to Quadriplegics.

JONATHAN. She's so little, isn't she? Her face is like a little child's face. D'you think they miss their mothers?

BERNIE. They're monkeys, Jonathan. Stop projecting.

JONATHAN. They're chosen because they're like us, though, aren't they?

BERNIE. She's making her public début today.

JONATHAN. Joining you at the lectern?

JACU. They say that in the forest where I come from man is changing nature. No more green darkness of the forest. (*Pause.*) Where is my mother?

Scene 3

School acoustic. First day of term.

MOTHER. Don't you want to say goodbye to me, Helena?

SISTER MARINA. Let her go and make friends, Mrs Francis. It's better she doesn't realise you're leaving.

MOTHER. I hope I'm doing the right thing.

SISTER MARINA. It's better for everyone that way.

MOTHER. No, I mean she needs . . . She's an odd little girl. I don't know what to do with her. I thought perhaps friends her own age. I thought . . . I don't know really.

SISTER MARINA. Don't worry, Mrs Francis. We'll take care of her for you.

MOTHER. Yes. Well. I'd better go, then.

HELENA 1 (*as a child*). Mummy?

Scene 4

Jungle: a South American Indian village. Shouts. We hear women and children crying, men shouting.
    Interweave under HELENA *sounds of school playground.*

JACU. They took me from my mother when I was a child. A man from the Indian Protection Service came and took us all away. To school, he said. They made us work.

HELENA 1. Mother. I remember your perfume. I remember you sitting on my bed reading me a story before I went to sleep. I remember finding my clothes ready in the morning.

JACU. There was a mill for crushing the cane, and to save the horses they used four children to turn the wheel. One day the Indian Protection Service agent called in a carpenter to make an oven for the farmhouse. When the carpenter had finished, the agent asked him what he wanted for doing the job. He said he wanted an Indian girl. The agent took him to the mission school and told him to choose one. No one saw or heard of her again.

Start to drift background away. Deadish acoustic.

HELENA 1. When they send you away to school you cry at night and something dies inside you. Perhaps you never really go home again after that. Love means pain. Home is somewhere far away. Darkness means a time at last to cry.

JACU. Later I heard my mother was very ill and I wanted to see her before she died. I ran away to see her. When I got back they thrashed me with a raw hide whip. Perhaps the missionary couldn't hear me crying.

Scene 5

Lecture room acoustic. BERNIE *telling the students about the Simian Aides Scheme.*

BERNIE. This little one is something of a pet at the centre. She's called Jacu. That's a word used by the Bororos tribe of Brazil, where she comes from, and it means, forest bird. She is, as you can see, quite socialised. She doesn't mind being held by me, in fact she likes it. She has been living with me at home for nearly three years. I've just brought her back to the Centre, ready to train her. I gave her her name. She knew it was her name right from the start. Didn't you, Jacu?

Cut to:

Scene 6

JACU. Jacu. My father called me Jacu, because he said I was like a little forest bird. The juruna who was made young again by the magic water in the sky, he made his daughter into a little bird when he came to visit his village on earth. She was a girl only in the sky. In the village, she hopped around her father's feet, as I hopped around my father's feet. Where is my mother now?

SISTER MARINA (*very slight echo*). We're a bit concerned about Helena, Mrs Francis. She seems to be pining.

HELENA 1. Sister Marina doesn't know how to touch people. None of the nuns do. Nobody touches you here.

Scene 7

Lecture room.

BERNIE. All the monkeys in the Simian Aides Scheme have to spend a three-year period with a foster family. What happens is, the baby monkey transfers to the foster family the attachment it would normally feel for the mother. It believes itself to be part of a tribe, with a hierarchy, such as there would be in the wild. It is very important that at the start of its life, the monkey is in constant physical contact with a member of the foster family.

Hold back background acoustic.

JACU. I don't remember my mother very well. I only remember I loved her very much.

Lecture room.

BERNIE. Someone must hold her and touch her ten hours a day minimum. Someone must carry her in their arms as they go about their daily life. The aim is to humanise the monkey.

Hold back background acoustic.

HELENA 1. When I grow up, I'm not going to touch anyone. I'm not going to let anyone touch me. I'm going to be a beautiful princess, and no one will be allowed to touch me.

Lecture room.

BERNIE. It's what the Indian mothers do, in South America. For the first few months of the baby's life, she always has it with her as she goes about her work. Indians believe that makes the baby grow up contented.

Hold back background acoustic.

JACU. My mother kept me always with her when I was very tiny. I knew this because I saw other mothers in the village carrying their babies with them, all the time, like a monkey carries her young. Munducuru Indians say capuchin monkeys are children really, human children. They have been changed into monkeys. They die as children but they are born again as monkeys.

HELENA 1. Nobody touches me now. Nobody touches me now. Nobody ever touches me now.

Scene 8

Over HELENA's *previous speech, fade in scene 8.*

South American Indian music, and shop acoustic. A shop in England selling South American crafts.

HARRY. The mask is beautiful.

HELENA. It comes from Venezuela.

HARRY. I know. Is the true face as lovely as the mask?

HELENA 1. When I grow up, I'm going to be a beautiful princess.

HARRY. Can I touch the mask? Can I hold it in my hands?

HELENA 1. I won't let anyone touch me.

HARRY. I know how delicate it is. I know it comes from far away.

HELENA. You have to pay if you break anything.

HARRY. You must always pay if you break things.

HELENA. How do you know about the mask?

HARRY. The Indians of South America. So strange, so far away. This music. These flutes, jakui they are called. Do you know about these?

HELENA. I only work in the shop.

HARRY. No woman must ever hear them play.

HELENA. Why mustn't she?

HARRY. The tribesmen of the Alto-Xingu in Brazil play four-foot-long jakui, the name for the flute and for the spirit that lives at the bottom of rivers and lagoons. A woman should not even see the jakui. It is a symbol of the malevolent supernatural and of human male sexuality.

HELENA. What happens if she does see it?

HARRY. When the flutes are played and the men dance to the music, the women are kept in sealed houses. If they should see the jakui they would be raped by the tribesmen. The tribesmen become spirits when they are playing the instruments.

Flute music cuts across shop music to become a variation of HELENA's *theme. Suddenly:*

HELENA. Don't.

HARRY. Why not?

HELENA 1. I won't let anyone –

HARRY. Afraid? Afraid because of what I told you? Don't worry. I don't think it counts here, in England, in a shop. All the potency is gone. I'll take the mask. Then I can break it if I like, and pay for it, if I like.

End music.

Scene 9

Dead acoustic.

JACU. Don't worry about what men may do to you, my mother said.
That doesn't matter. The brothers sun and moon were the children
of girls made out of dead logs, sisters sent to marry the jaguar,
and of the five sisters who set out on the bridal journey, two died
because they were raped by creatures too big for their slender girls'
bodies. And yet those who lived, though they mourned the deaths,
did not mourn the violations. They journeyed on and submitted
to the jaguar, and so the sun and the moon were born. Men will
take your body. Your soul they cannot take. Where would we be
without the brothers sun and moon? There would be no difference
between the day and the night. She told me these stories so I would
be free.

SISTER MARINA. Helena doesn't seem to see the beauty of an ordered
life, Mrs Francis. She doesn't seem to settle down.

JACU. My mother said, Jacu, if all you ever do is make corn-cakes,
then do it gladly. Grind the corn better than anyone else, and sing
when you go to fetch the water.

HELENA 1. Sister Marina told me this life didn't count. Only the life
of the soul. Here, in this life, we are bound in chains, the body is
our prison.

JACU. Sing when you go to fetch the water. Live gladly in the forest.
If I die, bury me the way we buried your father.

HELENA 1. When my father died, we went to church for the first
time in three years.

JACU. We buried my father the Bororos way. We put him in
the ground in the centre of the village, till his body rotted, and
the vultures wheeled in the sky. They could smell a forbidden
feast.

HELENA 1. If there's no such thing as the life of the soul, if this is
all there is – where is my father now?

JACU. Then we dug him up again, we cleaned his bones and painted
them red and blue, we adorned them with feathers, and we took
my father deep into the forest, into the heart and soul of the
forest, and left him there so his soul could go on its way, alive
again.

HELENA 1. Since the accident my body is dead. Why am I left here
in a dead body? Why don't they kill me instead of leaving me here
to rot?

Scene 10

Shop acoustic, with music.

HARRY. The mask is from somewhere far away. Like an eternal face, an ageless face, that has seen everything, that has also seen nothing. Smooth and unmoved. Drop the mask. Tell me your name. I'll pay if the mask breaks.

The music shatters.

Scene 11

Airport acoustic.

MOTHER. Goodbye, Helena.

HELENA. Goodbye, Mother. It won't be long. You'll come at Christmas.

MOTHER. Harry will look after you, won't he dear? He'll be a good husband, won't he?

HELENA. You'll be all right. I'll call as soon as I get there.

HELENA 1. I left her at the airport. She left me at the school. Let her make friends.

Dead acoustic.

JACU. When my mother died, the missionaries wouldn't let us bury her our own way, the way we buried my father. Next time they thrashed me I decided not to get better. Where was her soul, if it had not gone into the forest, after the soul of my father, and his father? Those who loved me best knew not to intervene. Those who didn't know me didn't care, they pretended not to see that I was dying, taking my own soul somewhere else. The missionary looked the other way.

Sound of aircraft taking off.

HELENA 1. Goodbye Mother. Goodbye England.

Scene 12

Lecture hall acoustic.

BERNIE. Capuchin monkeys were chosen for the Simian Aides Project because of their intelligence, small size, fastidiousness, and manual dexterity. A mature capuchin weighs about five pounds and stands eighteen inches tall. Once socialised under the scheme, it will form a loyal attachment to its human owner and will have a life expectancy of about thirty years.

LIZZIE. Sir? I have a question, sir.

BERNIE. Yes, Lizzie?

LIZZIE. Doesn't the monkey mind?

Laughter of students.

BERNIE. Quiet now. It's a good question. We have taken her from her natural environment. The human race is entrusted with the care of this planet. We meddle with nature and nature's course. I am holding in my arms a capuchin monkey, cebus species, who was taken from her mother at six weeks old, placed with a foster family of humans and encouraged to believe that the human family was her natural family. By what right?

SAM. For science, sir, for the quadriplegics.

BERNIE. Not long ago, many of the quadriplegics who are still alive today would not have survived. Medical progress has changed that. People live in motionless bodies, with their cognitive and, if they're lucky, their communication skills normal, and if they're unlucky, with their life expectancy normal too. We take one little monkey. We give it to a paralysed person to make that person's life more bearable.

Lose lecture hall and introduce music.
  Echo of JACU's theme.

HELENA 1. Not long ago I would have died instead. That would be kinder. Things were kinder then.

JACU. They say that in the forest where I come from, man is changing the face of the earth. No more green darkness of the forest, the trees up above letting in daylight all the time now, no more peace of the night and the little bird calls sadly as if she knew time had no answers any more, as if time had gone somewhere else.

Scene 13

Outdoors. Florida, a poolside, someone dives in.

LAURETTE. So beautiful, so cool. Doesn't she want to be friends, Harry? Doesn't she do anything but swim and lie in the sun?

HARRY. She needs time. It's all very strange for her. This isn't her place.

LAURETTE. This isn't her planet, if you ask me. England! The moon, more like.

HARRY. I know. She's from somewhere far away.

LAURETTE. So how did you seduce her? Did you just throw a sack over her head and drag her on to the plane? How did you do it, Harry?

HARRY. I told her stories. Stories of South American Indians and flutes and masks.

LAURETTE. Why doesn't she come and lie over here with us?

HARRY. Because you're here.

LAURETTE. Oh, pardon me for being here, I'm sure, don't let me get in the way of anything, will you?

HARRY. No, Laurette, don't go.

LAURETTE. Christ, did you ever hear such a put down and then get asked to stay?

HARRY. Give her time.

LAURETTE. Life is short, Harry.

HARRY. I loved her from the first moment I saw her. I wanted to get behind the mask.

LAURETTE. First time I've heard it called a mask.

HARRY. That face. It hides everything.

LAURETTE. You're old enough to be her father.

HARRY. That's why she married me.

LAURETTE. That's the only reason?

Scene 14

Flashback: a bedroom. Over sounds of lovemaking, the flute, HARRY's *voice, and* HELENA *saying his name; lovemaking and* HELENA *saying 'Harry' continue under* JACU.

HARRY (*echo*). A woman should not even see the jakui. It is a symbol of the malevolent supernatural and of human male sexuality.

HELENA. Harry . . . Harry . . .

JACU. A long time ago, it was the Iamuricuma women who knew the joy and the mystery of the jakui. In those days if a man saw the jakui or the ceremonial dance to its music, the women would grab him and rape him. It was the moon who wanted to take the secret from the women and give it to the men. The moon did not like to see the women dancing, singing, playing the jakui and the curuta, and laughing, while the men were shut up indoors. So he asked the sun to help him steal the jakui from the women. But though the moon gave them the power, men still remember that it was the women who had it first. Perhaps they are still a little bit afraid. That is why they want women.

HELENA 1. When I grow up, I'm going to be a beautiful princess. Beautiful, so no one can touch me.

Scene 15

Poolside again.

HARRY. She married me for things that being older gives me. For my stories. For knowing more than she knows. For my stories of South America and the Indian tribes who sing to another tune. For knowing what she wants.

LAURETTE. Such as?

HARRY. When to speak, and when to keep silent. When to hold her, and when to let her alone. She married me because I know that I have to pay if I break anything.

LAURETTE. Well, aren't you just the perfect couple then. (*Going.*) I need a drink. I can't take the heat.

HELENA (*calling*). Laurette! You're not going already?

LAURETTE. My God, she spoke to me! No, honey, just going to get a drink. With ice.

HELENA. Good idea. I'll follow you.

HARRY. Helena?

HELENA. Yes?

HARRY. What are you thinking?

HELENA. Nothing.

HARRY. I want to please you. I want to make you happy. Are you happy, Helena?

HELENA 1. Was I happy? Presents from South America. The jewels of the women of the Munducuru tribe, the paintings from the Bororos, figures, and masks. Happy?

HELENA. Of course I'm happy. (*Going.*) I'll go in after Laurette.

Scene 16

The lab.

JONATHAN. How did it go?

BERNIE. Oh, she did just fine. She's a star. I'll tell you what though. There was another one like you in the audience.

JONATHAN. What d'you mean?

BERNIE. One of the students asked me whether she minded.

JONATHAN. Good. What did you say?

BERNIE. Oh, you know. The sin of scientific progress and all that stuff.

JONATHAN. How can you be so cynical, Bernie? I don't see how you can have lived with her for three years then treat her as a scientific specimen. I just don't see it at all.

Scene 17

BERNIE 1. She'll get used to being here, to living this new life, and then we'll change things for her again. Playing God, but without his wisdom of all the ages. She has bright darting eyes, bright and darting like a little bright bird. How can she know anything? What does she know of life? And yet, her eyes carry that wisdom, her eyes are as old as time, she is like a little ageless timeless thing, suffering, accepting. She sits, quietly, watching, she will sit on my lap or look out of the window, quietly watching. And I wonder what she's thinking.

Scene 18

Poolside.

HARRY 1. I was lying by the pool with my eyes closed. I was dozing. I knew she wasn't there: I could feel her get up and go to the edge of the pool. I heard her dive in.

Sound of someone diving. Then stillness. The poolside acoustic, with no sound of swimming.

Then I began to feel something was wrong. There was no sound. There hadn't been that small noise of her surfacing. I opened my eyes. She was floating in the water, face down, like a water lily. Only the water lapping. No other sound.

HELENA 1 (*over sound of heartbeat*). Harry!

HARRY. Helena, I cried, but no word came out of my mouth.

Scene 19

Lecture room.

BERNIE. When the three-year period of socialisation is complete, and the monkey is fully adult, it undergoes a full mouth extraction. This is done so that they will not harm anyone. (*Pause.*) So that they will not harm anyone.

Scene 20

Music interweaving with the voices.

JACU. A long time ago, in another country, my mother told me the story of how the monkey invented creative fire. There was a time when the monkey was like man. He had no hair on his body, he sailed in a canoe, ate maize, and slept in a hammock. One day the monkey was sailing back from the maize plantation with the water rat. The water rat gnawed at the maize in the bottom of the canoe until he had made a hole in the canoe, and the monkey had to swim to the shore.

HARRY 1. She was just floating, still, silent. I could see the back of her neck.

JACU. The monkey was a good swimmer, and as he made for the bank he caught a piranha fish, which he dragged to the bank.

HARRY 1. I dived in. I turned her over. Her eyes were closed. Her face was a mask.

JACU. On the riverbank, he met the jaguar, who greatly admired the catch, and invited himself to dinner.

HARRY 1. I got her to the edge of the pool. She felt so heavy. Her skin was smooth and warm.

JACU. The monkey pointed to the sun setting red in the sky and told the jaguar to go and fetch fire to cook the piranha fish. The jaguar ran off to try to catch the sun.

HARRY 1. I thought she was dead. I got her out of the water and lay her down beside the pool. The water ran in little rivulets on her body. She made a dark damp place on the paving stone. I kissed her. I tasted the water on her skin. The sun had gone from the sky.

JACU. But the jaguar could not catch the sun, and he came back after he had run a long way. But look, said the monkey, there it is, all those flames in the sky! Go, go and catch the fire! And the jaguar went off to try again.

HARRY 1. When I kissed her mouth, I found she was still breathing. It was like a miracle. Oh, God, it seemed then like a miracle.

JACU. While the jaguar was gone the second time, the monkey rubbed two sticks together, made a fire, cooked the fish, and ate it all up. He left only the bones.

HARRY 1. While I waited for the ambulance to come, I sat and held her hand. I dared not take her in my arms. I wanted to cradle her head in my lap, but I did not dare. I couldn't hold her.

HELENA 1. No one touches me now.

HARRY 1. So I put my hand on her forehead, golden and warm from the sun, damp from the water. I stroked back her golden hair. But I couldn't hold her.

Hold music back.

HELENA 1. No one.

Keep music going.

JACU. But the invention of creative fire, which later mankind was to copy from the monkey, did not come without pain. The jaguar wanted revenge, when he got back from trying to catch the sun, and found that he had been tricked. He tried to shake the monkey out of the tall tree, to break his neck.

HARRY 1. They said her neck was broken. The fourth vertebra in the neck. I didn't know how to tell her. What does it mean, I asked them.

JACU. My mother told me these things, far away, a lifetime ago, so that I would be free. Out of the fire, the phoenix rises.

Start to fade music.

HELENA 1. They spoke to me and I heard them, but as if it was all happening far away. Then I had a horrible dream while I was still half asleep. I dreamed that I tried to move my legs in the bed. I knew I was in a bed. I tried to move because I was stiff, but my leg wouldn't move. I tried to lift my hand but something was holding it down. As the dream became more and more frightening, I tried to sit up. But the dream wouldn't let go of me. And then I tried to scream. But when I opened my mouth, no sound came out. I filled my lungs, I got all my muscles ready for the scream, I screamed; but there was no sound, and I knew the dream was not a dream.

HARRY. Helena.

HELENA 1. I had woken up. I could not move. I could not speak. I could not remember what had happened before I went to sleep. Only water. I could remember water.

HARRY 1. I kissed the damp skin of your neck. If I had known it would be like this, I would have pretended to be asleep.

HELENA 1. I looked up. I couldn't move.

HARRY 1. I looked down. Her lovely face like a mask.

HELENA 1. I couldn't make any sound. I moved my lips, but no sound came out.

BERNIE. Jacu. We have to put you to sleep now.

JACU. I spoke to the man. He did not understand me.

HARRY. They're going to put you to sleep, Helena. Helena darling.

HELENA 1. I should be dead. That would be kinder. Not long ago I wouldn't have survived. Things were kinder then. They knew then, there's more to life than breath in your body, more to life than a heart beating, more to life than a flicker in the mind.

HARRY. Don't give up, Helena. They're going to do what they can.

HELENA 1. I know what they are going to do. Flicker, flicker.

BERNIE. God knows I don't want to hurt you.

JACU. I think of what my mother told me. Don't worry about what men do to you. They can take your body, but they can never take your soul.

HARRY. They won't hurt you.

HELENA 1. They are going to put cement in my neck, so it won't accidentally move, because if it did, I would die. When I wake up there'll be a thing like a halo round my head. I will lie in prison, in the prison of my body, in the prison of my own silence, people will look down at me as if I'm another species and inside me –

Creep in music.

HARRY. I'll learn to lip read.

BERNIE. All their teeth. For science. The needle –

JACU. Never lose faith in the life –

HELENA 1. Inside me, there'll be –

HARRY. I'll bring the flute, I'll play the flute to you, Helena!

BERNIE. For medical science, I must – I have to do it, Jacu – believe me –

JACU. Never lose faith in the life of the forest – never lose faith –

BERNIE. Her eyes are bright and darting even when she must be afraid and in agony. Still she is like a little bright bird of the forest. Jacu. God. Bright bird of the forest. Sing, little bird.

JACU. Sing, Jacu, when you go to fetch the water! We painted his bones, red and blue –

HELENA 1. If this is all there is, if there's no such thing as the life of the soul – why must I stay here? Why won't they let me die?

BERNIE. When you wake up it'll all be over. It'll be all right, little Jacu, it'll be all right, little girl.

JACU. Inside me, the forest still lives.

HARRY. When you wake up –

HELENA 1. Inside me are words I cannot speak, inside me, if there's no such thing as the life of the soul, inside me a silent –

JACU. Inside me the life of the forest.

HELENA 1. Inside me, a silent scream –

JACU. Life of the forest

HELENA 1. No life of the soul

JACU. Life of the forest

HELENA 1. No life of the soul

JACU. Life of the forest

HELENA 1. No life of the soul

JACU. Never lose faith

HELENA 1. Inside me

JACU. In the life

HELENA 1. Inside me

JACU. Never lose faith

HELENA 1. No life of the soul

JACU. Never lose

HELENA 1. Inside me

JACU. Never

HELENA 1. A silent

JACU. Lose

HELENA 1. Scream

JACU. Faith – never lose faith

HELENA 1. A silent – (*A scream, far away.*)

JACU. Out of the fire the phoenix rises. Out of pain the creative
fire. Never lose faith in the life of the forest.

Cut music, silence.

HELENA 1. When I was a child, I couldn't cry, in case someone heard
me. Now when I scream, no one hears me, no sound comes.

Pause. Time passes.

Scene 21

Quiet hospital room.

HELENA 1. I wake up. For a few moments, my mind is clear. Then
reality creeps in like poison.

LAURETTE. Hello, Helena.

HELENA 1. Laurette.

LAURETTE. You still can't talk, then.

Pause.

Harry told me not to come. He said you don't want visits. I guess I don't know when I'm not wanted. I brought you some fruit.

HELENA 1. I can't touch it. I can look at it though. It's beautiful. I never noticed before, how lovely the colours are. They are perfect. Nature's colours.

JACU (*echo*). Never forget the life of the forest.

LAURETTE. May I sit down? Harry doesn't want to see me either. I feel a pretty useless kind of friend. No one wants to see me. Look, Helena – You wouldn't let me in before, so I'm not expecting you to let me in now. But if there's anything practical – anything I can do – bring you things. Write letters.

HELENA 1. I lie still as stone. Only my heart is still beating. I can hear –

Heart beat.

LAURETTE. You mustn't give up hope, Helena, medical science is a wonderful thing, a few years ago you wouldn't even have got this far – oh God, there I go, I boobed, didn't I?

HELENA 1. I am so still, I can hear my heart beating.

LAURETTE. I'd better go. It's no good telling the truth. But I want to anyway. If I were you, I'd rather be dead, and if there's anything at all I can do to make it more bearable that you're still alive, try to find some way of telling me.

HELENA 1. Laurette . . .

Scene 22

Lecture.

BERNIE. Jacu has now undergone full mouth extraction. Training can begin. Lizzie will be in charge of Jacu's learning programme. Students in their final year are well suited to this type of work. They will train Jacu for two to three hours a day, five or six days a week. Training will take about six months.

Scene 23

The hospital. Also doubles as JACU's *training room.*

SURGEON (*slight echo*). We'll keep her here for about six months, Mr Traub. She needs time to adjust and meantime there's a lot we can do in the way of physiotherapy. She's still benefiting from the traction and weights. We'll have her in a chair in no time.

HARRY 1. I didn't even see her moving the last time she moved. I didn't see her walk to the edge of the pool. Walking to the pool, not thinking about walking. Now she'll never move again, I'll never see her move again. She doesn't want me here. In her eyes, what is it behind her eyes that she won't give me, that she never really gave me?

LAURETTE (*slight echo*). What treatment are they giving her? Will she ever be able to talk again?

HELENA 1. I make no sound. But inside, I am silently screaming. Inside me, no life of the soul, though I make no sound, the silent scream –

LAURETTE (*slight echo*). When will they take that halo thing off her head? She looks like a punk angel. Why isn't he here?

HELENA 1. Harry.

SURGEON (*slight echo*). We can't know for sure why she's still not talking. It's perfectly normal in a case like this for speech to be temporarily lost. Shock. But physically, there's no reason – It's been long enough.

LAURETTE (*slight echo*). On the assumption that you can still hear, sweetheart, I'm going to talk as crassly as ever. Irritation is good medicine.

SURGEON (*slight echo*). We've got to try and teach her how to live her new life. We should be building her towards going home, and living her new life.

HELENA 1. Life and death, day and night, make no difference now.

BERNIE. Jacu must learn to perform a variety of quite complex tasks.

LIZZIE. Food, Jacu!

JACU. I spoke to the woman. She did not understand.

LIZZIE. Cage, Jacu!

JACU. Long ago, and in another country, my mother told me the secrets of the forest, so that I would be free. It doesn't matter what they do with your body.

A buzzer sounds. JACU *chatters.*

BERNIE. She has to wear a mechanism for the administration of a small electric pulse.

LIZZIE. There are off-limit objects and areas in any home. For the safety of the monkey and the quadriplegic. If the monkey goes near forbidden areas she gets a warning. If she ignores the warning, she gets a small electric shock.

BERNIE. For science. Progress. Progress, Jacu.

JACU. Where's the forest?

LIZZIE. Also, if she fails to obey a verbal command, she gets a small electric shock, and is sent to her cage.

The buzzer again.

LIZZIE. Music, Jacu!

Cassette starts playing something harsh and too loud.

LIZZIE. Volume, Jacu!

SURGEON. She must learn to use the mouth-stick.

HELENA 1. Where's Harry?

JACU. Where's the forest?

LIZZIE. Fetch the mouth-stick, Jacu!

SURGEON. Why don't you use the mouth-stick, Mrs Traub?

The buzzer.

JACU. Where's my mother?

SURGEON. She must learn the use of the mouth stick. It is the quadriplegic's primary tool. It can be used for turning pages, dialling a telephone number, changing TV channels, even typing.

HELENA 1. Why isn't Harry here to help me?

LAURETTE. You must help yourself, you know, Helena. There are limits.

Buzzer.

LIZZIE. Off limit, Jacu.

JACU. Where's my mother?

SURGEON. She's doing fine, with the traction and the physiotherapy and the weights, but she still won't talk. Don't you want to go home?

BERNIE. She must be lonely.

LAURETTE. Why won't you talk to me?

BERNIE. Why can't I talk to you? I wish you could talk. Then you'd understand. Jacu? I want you to understand.

HELENA 1. Where's Harry?

HARRY. I'm here. Say something to me, Helena, tell me what you're thinking.

HELENA 1. Harry. Touch me.

LIZZIE. Cage, Jacu!

JACU. The jaguar could not catch the sun. My mother told me these things so I would be free. Free . . .

HARRY. Tell me, Helena. Let me help you. I want to help you. I want to understand.

SURGEON. Let me help you. I want you to use the chair.

LAURETTE. Let me help you. I know you never wanted to let me in –

JACU. The juruna climbed the ladder in the sky and the magic water made him young again. He started a new life in the sky.

SURGEON. It's time. It's a new life. You must want to be home again.

LAURETTE. Your ears are still working, OK? I've got news for you. I'm sure it's meant to be a surprise, but I've always thought surprises are a bit unkind. Harry's getting your mother over.

HELENA 1. No!

LIZZIE. Change music, Jacu!

Cassette music changes to something jangling or strident because HELENA's *mother is coming.*

LAURETTE. Now don't look like that. He told her very carefully, he's a very sensitive man. Anyway, she'll be here in two days.

Frantic music.

HELENA 1. No!

LAURETTE. You mustn't worry, Helena, mothers are more resilient than you think. She'll cope.

HELENA 1. No!

Buzzer.

LIZZIE. Cage, Jacu!

JACU. When they took us away from home they made us work. They didn't lock us up, but when I ran away to see my mother because she was ill, they thrashed me when I got back.

Buzzer.

LIZZIE. Cage, Jacu!

JACU. They thrashed me with a raw hide whip. The missionary looked the other way.

Buzzer.

BERNIE. I look the other way.

JACU. Don't worry what men may do to your body.

LIZZIE. Sandwich, Jacu!

JACU. Live gladly in the forest, my mother said. Where's the forest?

BERNIE. Why are you crying, little Jacu?

JACU. Where's the village?

LIZZIE. How can you tell if she's crying? It's just a noise.

JACU. Where are all the other children?

BERNIE. I'll put her back with the others.

JACU *now, with an effort, dominates the noise; it starts to recede as she says 'once'.*

JACU. Once, in the forest, my mother told me the origin of the stars. There was a little boy gathering corncobs with the women, and the women pounded the corn ready to make corncakes for the men when they came home from hunting in the forest. The little boy stole some of the maize and took it home to his grandmother. He asked her to make a corncake for him and his friends. When she had made the cake and the children had eaten it, they cut out her tongue so she could not tell what they had done. And then, fearing their parents' anger, the children climbed up a creeper into the sky.

Sound of aeroplane.

LAURETTE. She's probably on the plane even right now.

JACU. The mothers came back to the village looking for the children, and questioned the tongueless old woman, but to no purpose, for without her tongue, she could not speak. Then one of the mothers saw the creeper with the children climbing up to the sky, and all the women began to climb up after the children.

HELENA 1. She left me at school. I left her in England. When I grow up, I'm going to – I'm not going to let anyone touch me.

JACU. But the last child, the one who had stolen the corn, cut the creeper, and the women fell on the ground and were changed into howling beasts.

Sound of forest and wild beasts, merging into sound of aircraft.

LAURETTE. Harry's going to bring her straight here from the airport.

HELENA 1. She'll see me. She'll look down at me, like all the others, as if I'm from another planet.

JACU. As a punishment for their heartlessness, the children were transformed into stars, and now for all eternity they must look down at the plight of their mothers. It is the children's eyes that can be seen shining in the sky. The stars are the eyes of heartless children.

LAURETTE. She has a right, Helena. Every mother has a right to help her child.

JACU. I don't remember my mother very well. I only remember that I loved her very much.

HELENA 1 (*as a child*). Mummy!

Very brief pause, then as if answering HELENA:

MOTHER. Helena.

JACU. My mother said the beasts still loved the stars. Your mother will always love you, Jacu, mother love is enduring as the forest, no matter what you do, no matter where you go.

MOTHER. I'm so sorry. So sorry for you and Harry.

JACU. But you can cut the creeper, if you want to. You can cut yourself off and be like the stars in the sky.

MOTHER. They say you're doing very well. Is it painful, my darling? Why don't you try to talk to me? Shall I just talk to you instead? . . . I've never known what you wanted. Your eyes haven't changed. When you were a child, those eyes . . .

JACU (*echo*). The stars are the eyes of heartless children.

MOTHER. I want to help you. Let me help. I've never known —— Your eyes still speak, don't they, Helena? Don't they, my darling? It hurts. They speak to me and it hurts.

HELENA 1. Let her make friends.

MOTHER. I want to make it better. I want to stop it hurting. Tell me what I can do. Tell me with your eyes, Helena. . . . I do go on. (*Then, in a different key.*) Still, you've got some lovely friends here already, haven't you? You've always been good at making friends. Laurette, now she's a lovely girl. It must be a great load off your mind to know there's someone like that looking after Harry for you. Oh, don't look like that, dear, it's not a bit like that. Laurette's your friend, dear, and Harry's much too upset, I know men, I know when a man is. And Harry isn't. Ah! Here they are, Harry and Laurette, arriving together.

Fade.

Scene 24

Home. Indoor acoustic.

HARRY. I'm sorry you didn't want your mother here. I'm sorry I did the wrong thing. More sorry that I didn't understand that when I brought her here. I think you must need understanding more than anything else right now.

HELENA 1. Harry. Harry. Nobody touches me now.

HARRY. Anyhow. She's gone, and you're home. Thank God, you're home at last. Laurette helped me get it all ready for you. She's been wonderful.

HELENA 1. Harry and Laurette.

HARRY. Now, I've brought you a present, it's here for you, and I'm scared, scared to death you won't like it. I used to bring you presents without thinking that. Now I'm thinking, please God, let her understand that I'm doing the best I can. Let her know that if this is the wrong thing to give her, at least I wanted it to be right. OK, Bernie. You can bring her in now.

BERNIE (*approaching*). Jacu. This is Helena. This is your new home, and your new mistress. Helena, this is Jacu.

JACU. Where's the forest?

HELENA 1. He's going to leave me.

JACU. Where's my mother?

A pause.

BERNIE. Hello, Helena, my name is Bernie Seldon. I'm a senior researcher at the Helping Hands study centre. I've been on the Capuchin Aides project since the start.

HELENA 1. This is done so he can leave me.

BERNIE. Normally a student trainer would be introducing her to your home. Jacu happens to be a favourite of mine. I fostered her for three years, the normal three-year socialisation period. I've formed quite an attachment to her. She's a very unusual little animal. But she and I must part. She has to live a different life now.

HARRY. We'll look after her, won't we, Helena?

BERNIE. Your case is rather a difficult one. In the Simian Aides scheme, the capuchins are trained to obey verbal commands. I gather you haven't spoken since your accident, Helena. We'll have to see if you and Jacu can develop an alternative means of communication. Of course your husband could speak the commands, but for one thing, that's defeating the object a bit, because the monkey is supposed to give the carer a break from attendance and the disabled person a degree of independence.

HELENA 1. He wants to leave me.

BERNIE. For another thing, the success of the scheme has in the past come from a close one-to-one relationship between the monkey and the disabled person.

JACU. Where are the other children?

BERNIE. Now perhaps you wouldn't mind if I put Jacu on your lap for a moment? Just a little introduction ceremony.

HELENA 1. He wants to leave me!

Commotion. HELENA *is pushing* JACU *away. Monkey screeching and chattering sounds; also* HELENA *imitates the monkey noise.*

HARRY. Helena! Helena, even if you don't want the monkey, there's no need to be rough with her.

BERNIE. There, Jacu, it's all right.

JACU. Where's my mother, who used to hold me all the time, hold me in her arms?

BERNIE. I've got you, it's all right.

HARRY. I'm sorry, Bernie.

BERNIE. As I said, Jacu is a favourite of mine. I'd much rather take her away than leave her where she's not welcome.

HARRY. Let us try it for a few days, Bernie. I'll take care of her. Helena needs time. It's probably my fault for not warning her. I wanted to give her a surprise.

BERNIE. The scheme is over-subscribed, you know, we won't have any difficulty finding someone else who wants her. She's a particularly intelligent animal.

HARRY. I've said I'm sorry.

BERNIE. It's not you I'm worried about. It's not you Jacu is here to help.

HARRY. It sounds like you should be keeping her yourself.

BERNIE. I wish I could. But it doesn't work like that. I have to part with her. She must start a new life now, whatever I may think about that. She has a new life ahead of her.

JACU. A new life, singing on its way. Goodbye, Father.

HARRY. I have seen them in the wild. I've travelled a lot in South America. I met Helena on a selling trip to England. It seems strange, a monkey in a house like this, clinging to you as if you were a monkey too. A monkey mother.

BERNIE. Or as if she was a child. I've never seen them in the wild. Most of ours so far have been rescued from some other life a man has made for them. Organ grinder monkeys, they're called. Some are donated by people who've got tired of their pets. I've no idea what they're like in the forest.

HARRY. What about Jacu? Where did she come from?

BERNIE. A priest brought her to us. An evangelist. He brought her from South America when she was a tiny baby. He said he'd rescued her because her mother had been killed.

JACU. When my mother died, the missionaries wouldn't let us bury her the Bororos way. I don't know where she went. Her soul is locked up somewhere, it could not go free, living its new life. Next time they thrashed me I decided not to get better. Where's the forest?

BERNIE. We've set up a breeding colony now. Breeding little capuchin monkeys who will never see the forests of South America. They'll never know who they really are. Disney World instead. The colony is at Disney World. Isn't that strange?

HARRY. Life is very strange.

BERNIE. Well. Goodbye, Jacu. I'll see you tomorrow.

HARRY (*going*). Shall I see you out?

JACU. I spoke to the man. He did not understand. Goodbye, Father. (*Pause.*) My mother kept me with her all the time, she held me in her arms all the time. Why doesn't the lady touch me?

HELENA 1. I can't even touch her. She sits looking at me. Unblinking, unflinching, like someone's conscience. I almost want her to talk to me. If she'd talk to me, I'd talk back. If you can understand. Jacu –

HARRY (*approaching*). So. He's gone. Helena? We've got to try and make Jacu feel at home. She must be feeling very lonely and afraid. I've got a videotape here, and a sheet giving us details of what Jacu has learned to do.

Scene 25

A loud bird screech: a forest sound for LAURETTE.

LAURETTE. Well, sweetheart, he's excelled himself this time, hasn't he? A monkey, my, my! Is it a he or a she? Does it have a name? Oh, never mind, I know you can't talk.

HELENA 1. Inside me – Harry and Laurette.

HARRY (*approaching*). Hello, Laurette, you've met Jacu, I see.

LAURETTE. I couldn't wait. You're certainly original, Harry, I'll give you that. Is it a pet or a mini-person? Isn't he cute?

HARRY. She.

LAURETTE. She's gorgeous. Don't you love her, Helena, don't you just love her? Look at those eyes. She has such a sad little face. Like she's lost something. What have you lost, little one?

JACU. Where's my mother? Where's the forest?

HARRY. Her name's Jacu.

LAURETTE. Jacu? What kind of a name d'you call that? And what can she do? What can you do for Helena, Jacu?

JACU. There were guariba monkeys in the forest. Howler monkeys. They made a lot of noise.

HARRY. She's still not talking. It means I have to keep Jacu in training for the time being. Her trainer will be back again today.

Fade.

Scene 26

Later the same day.

BERNIE. Jacu will respond to a series of verbal commands. If she does something bad, she gets sent to her cage. Cage, Jacu!

LIZZIE (*echo*). Cage, Jacu!

JACU. Out of pain –

JACU *gets into her cage.*

HARRY. My God, she looks terrified. Do we have to use that one?

BERNIE. It's just in case she's getting into trouble. About to drink the bleach or tamper with an electrical cord or something. Jacu shouldn't need punishment, only protection. It's all right, Jacu. You can come out now. OK. You've read the literature, I take it, Helena? You'll know then that Jacu can get you drinks and sandwiches from the fridge, clear away empties, position a book on your reading stand, turn pages, put a cassette in the tape recorder or the video, clean up spills, reposition your arm on the armrest –

JACU. They made us work. They said they were taking us to school. But they made us work, to save the horses. They took us away from our mothers, and made us work. If we didn't do as we were told they beat us. They starved us.

BERNIE. And the verbal commands are all very simple. Watch this. Jacu. Music, Jacu!

Xingu flute music starts.

OK. Music off, Jacu.

Music does not stop.

Jacu?

Music still doesn't stop.

HARRY. She's listening to it.

BERNIE. Jacu, music off!

JACU. They say that in the forest – in the forest – forest song, forest music, in the trees – listen –

HARRY. She likes the music. Will you take a look at that?

Buzzer. Music suddenly very loud.

BERNIE. Jacu, music off! This is quite unexpected. She's never done this before.

HARRY. I tell you it's because she knows the music. It's authentic Xingu tribal music. She's heard it before, Bernie.

BERNIE. Jacu. You give me no choice.

Electric shock noise. Music abruptly off.

JACU. Out of pain. Out of pain. Out of pain. (*She whimpers.*)

BERNIE. Cage, Jacu. Well, I'm surprised, I can tell you. I'm really sorry, Helena, I'm sure it won't – Helena?

HELENA *crying.*

BERNIE. Well. I guess I'd better leave. I don't understand Jacu's behaviour. I don't understand it at all.

HARRY. Helena, you mustn't cry. It'll be all right.

JACU *child crying.*

BERNIE. D'you want me to take her away?

HELENA 1. No!

HARRY. No. I think we want to keep her. At least for the time being. Don't worry about it, Bernie, I'm sure it'll be OK another time. It was just that music. Come on. I'll see you to the door.

Their footsteps die away. Quietness; JACU and HELENA crying still.

JACU. Goodbye, Father. Goodbye, Father. No more green darkness. Out of pain. Never lose. Lose faith. Lose faith in the life of the forest. Never. Lose. Lose.

HELENA (*aloud*). Jacu.

JACU. Jacu?

HELENA. Jacu. Come here. Jacu. If I could move –

JACU. Jacu, lady, mother – out of pain – never lose faith – out of pain –

HELENA. I wish I could move my arms. Come and sit on my lap. Lap, Jacu. Do you know lap?

Sound effect to tell us JACU *sits on* HELENA's *lap.*

HELENA. If I could move my arms I could hold you. If I asked Harry, he could put my arms around you for me.

HARRY (*approach*). Ah, she's sitting on your lap.

HELENA 1. Put my arms around her, Harry.

HARRY. She looks as if she could do with a cuddle.

JACU. Mother. Where are all the other children? Where is the magic of the forest, the magic that turns old men young again, that changes bad things to good?

HARRY 1. Oh, Helena. It must be like a mother who can't hold her own child. (*Aloud.*) I'll cuddle her for you, shall I? I'll do it for both of us.

HELENA 1. Nobody touches, touches me now.

Fade.

Scene 27

HARRY 1. I watched them this morning. Helena looking out of one window. Jacu looking out of another. Looking out at the world through different windows.

HELENA 1. I see life through glass now, an onlooker, watching where I used to be. People walking on the pavement, the way I used to, they don't even notice their legs, they don't notice they're walking. I remember the way it was. I see how it is now.

JACU. There was a man called Tawapuh in our village who was ill, and a white man from another village far away, who was staying with us, said he knew a doctor in his own home who could cure him. Tawapuh, since he was going to the village of the white man, put on white man's clothes. He had not done this before. He flew away in a big silver bird. When he came back, he was not sick any more. But he said the white man's tribe were living in a strange world, where the air was unclean, the women afraid to be women and the food tasted unlike itself. The chiefs were not true chiefs because they had men with guns to guard them. A real chief needs no guarding. Our chief needed none. Tawapuh said he did wish we knew how to fly in a silver bird. He could see so much, so far. This was not a myth told to me by my mother. This was Tawapuh's real story. We do not need silver birds. (*Creep in music.*) We have our own birds, birds that sing in the dark green life of the forest, we have the magic of the forest, and the stories our mothers told us. I did not believe Tawapuh's story. I believed more in the stories my mother told me. I believed in the forest sky and the bird song in the evening and the morning, and in the heat of the day.

End music.

Scene 28

BERNIE. I'm sorry about yesterday.

HARRY. You mustn't worry, Bernie. We appreciate your help.

BERNIE. There is something special about Jacu.

HARRY. This morning they sat staring out of different windows for hours. But Jacu was sitting on Helena's lap when I came in here after you left yesterday.

BERNIE. I wish I could make her understand. The trouble is, now she'll associate me with all the aversion stimuli and with anyone who's ever hurt her in the past. I've never used a shock on her before. She'll never trust me again.

HARRY. You talk about her as if she's a human being, not a monkey.

JACU. Munducuru Indians say –

HARRY. In fact there's a myth, some of the tribes of the Alto-Xingu region of Brazil, the Munducuru – Helena – I haven't told you this –. (*A fractional pause: he's had enough.*) Why should I tell you things, when you never give me any feedback? I suppose I should give up thinking you might be interested in anything I might say. Jesus Christ. And just think, I told Laurette I wooed you with my stories. Stories of South America and the native Indians.

BERNIE. This myth of the Munducuru . . .

HARRY. They think that capuchin monkeys are children.

BERNIE. Human children?

HARRY. Children changed into monkeys. Of course Helena won't be able to have any children now. I won't be able to, either.

BERNIE. Harry –

HARRY. Oh, don't be embarrassed, Bernie, it's about time someone spoke their mind around here, in fact it's about time someone spoke, period. I haven't yelled at her so far yet. You had your turn at yelling yesterday. I forget the sound of my voice. You stop talking if no one talks back, if no one seems to be listening. You think you're going a bit nuts, talking when no one wants to hear.

BERNIE. Some of the people who already have a monkey at home tell us they feel about it as they would about a child if they had one.

HARRY. Do they really? What d'you think of that, then, Helena? Got yourself a brand new baby, have you?

BERNIE. I think it's time for me to show you some of the training in action. Perhaps Helena would like a drink.

HARRY. Perhaps Helena would like a drink, Jacu.

BERNIE. She won't understand if you speak to her like that.

HARRY. You mean it's OK for you to speak to Jacu like that, but not for me? Can I have a drink, Jacu? Or is it only Helena who gets drinks?

BERNIE. You say, in a normal voice, Drink, Jacu, and she'll go to the refrigerator, if you've shown her where it is, and get a prepared drink. You say Food, Jacu, and she'll get Helena a prepared snack. She'll give Helena her drink by tilting it into her mouth, and she'll fix the sandwich to a clamp and either let her bite it, or feed pieces to her. Of course this system isn't good for all kinds of food. You have to find your own way of making it work for you. D'you get the general picture?

HARRY. Yes. Speak to her nicely, and she'll perform nicely. Feed Helena sandwiches with tidy fillings, eh Helena, nice neat bites.

BERNIE. There's also a laser pointer. This is used in addition to the verbal commands to tell the monkey what you want. You can point to a book on the shelf with it, and say, Fetch, Jacu, and she'll get you your book. Or whatever you point at.

HARRY. Tell her to bring you the moon, Helena. That's what you've always wanted, isn't it? Well isn't it?

A short silence.

I'm going out. I need some air.

Door slams. Another short silence.

BERNIE. I wish there was a comfort command. Comfort, Jacu.

Scene 29

Abruptly, the sound of someone entering.

LAURETTE (*approaching*). Hi, honey, here's your favourite
visitor again. Got a present for you. It's not a monkey, I'm afraid,
but if she's your right arm, this here's going to be your left.

JACU. When my mother did not want to stop talking, my father
said she was like the guariba, the howler monkey, singing and
chattering in the branches all the day long. Go and climb trees
with the guaribas, he said, and she laughed. Her laughter was like
a clearing in the forest.

LAURETTE. Still not talking, then? How does the monkey like the
quiet life? How d'you get her to do her little chores around the
place? Got her on auto-pilot or something? My, my, the wonders
of science. Well, never mind, I can talk enough for two of us.
Three, I beg your pardon, Jacu.

JACU. The Warao tribe of Indians use the stomachs of dead guaribas
to make drums. Boom, boom, said my father, and my mother
would run laughing and shrieking like a monkey from the house.

LAURETTE. It's funny, Helena. Though you never say a word to
me, though you sit there and look at me quietly, yet you seem to
be listening to all my yattering on. I feel like I know you better
than I did before. Probably just an illusion. Probably it's only
you knowing me that makes me feel more comfortable.

JACU. My father said, the difference is that the guaribas howl at
sunrise and sunset. You, woman, you howl all the time. Then he
went too far. Then, my mother did howl at him and chase him
from the house, and it was his turn to run.

LAURETTE. Anyhow, you haven't opened your present. Oh, sorry.
Jacu, present. I've been thinking about your mother quite a lot. I
think she's lonely. I think you and Harry ought to have her to
stay. Hello?

JACU. Jacu, my father said, little forest bird, don't you grow up
like your mother. Learn how to be quiet, so you can listen to the
sounds of the forests, hear the sounds of the day and of the night.
(*Pause.*) The other lady is quiet. She must be listening.

HELENA 1. Mother, lonely?

LAURETTE. Jacu, present. Where's Harry? I keep asking you
questions. As if I expected you to answer. They say if you keep
talking to someone who's in a coma they might come round one
day. I know you're not in a coma, but sometimes I might be
forgiven for making the mistake. Jacu, present. Doesn't she know
present? OK then, I'll open it. I've got to tell you, this is fantastic.
I love opening presents. Harry says he's not surprised I like coming
round here so much, I get a free run at the talking, never had it

so good, he says. Smartass. Sorry. Don't swear at the dumb, they can't tell you if they object. Jeez, this is like practising in front of a mirror to be a stand-up comic. I don't know about your mother, I get pretty lonely too sometimes. You'd never have guessed if I hadn't told you.

HELENA 1. Laurette, lonely? Laurette?

LAURETTE. Here it is then. What d'you think? Anyone going to tell me what they think? And Harry must be lonely too. I used to – know him very well. You know that. But he never, not ever, not once, looked at me the way he still looks at you. No one's ever looked at me that way. Helena? Hello, anyone at home? D'you like your present? Do you know what it is? It's a mouth-stick. Yes, I know you've already got one but this one is gold-plated, God I feel like crying sometimes. I come round here because Christ's sake I care about you for I don't know what goddam reason since you clearly don't give a shit, sorry, about me, and I've brought you a gold-plated mouth-stick, your primary tool the doctor said, don't we all wish we could have a gold-plated primary tool? Helena? Tell me, Helena, do you give a damn anymore about anyone but yourself? (*Pause.*) Well actually, to be more accurate, it's only the mouthpiece that's gold-plated, but that's the important part, isn't it – the part you put in your mouth, and since you've scorned to use the one supplied I thought a little glamour might do the trick –

JACU *suddenly breaks into loud frantic chattering and screeching.*

LAURETTE (*after a pause*). Cut that out.

JACU *continues chattering and screeching. It goes on and on.*

LAURETTE. I said cut that out. Jacu. I'm talking.

JACU *still chattering and screeching.*

HELENA *starts laughing out loud.*

LAURETTE. And you needn't think it's OK – Helena? (*She listens to* HELENA *laughing.*) Helena, you're laughing. (HELENA *and* JACU *continue laughing and screeching, respectively.*) I don't believe it. I knew there had to be some good reason why I was born a fool. Jacu?

JACU. My mother, laughing because of what my father said. Laughter is like a clearing in the forest.

LAURETTE. Jacu. Have you got a kleenex somewhere? (*She's crying.*) Helena's laughing. Laurette's crying and Helena's laughing. Helena's laughing, for God's sake, give me a kleenex, Harry might come in.

JACU. My mother told my father he must not forget that when the howler monkey was heard in the hills, there would be rain in the forest. The noisy howler monkey was, for all its idle chatter, still the spirit of the gentle rain. Sweet rain, gentle rain, in the forest far away.

LAURETTE. Oh thanks. You took your time, didn't you, monkey face? (*Blows her nose.*) Still, she is a little wonder of science, isn't she? Whoever would guess she'd know the word for Kleenex and where to find them?

HARRY (*approaching*). Oh, Laurette, hello. How are you?

LAURETTE (*still sniffing*). Fine, thank you. Your wife has a surprise for you.

HARRY. Helena has?

LAURETTE. Well unless you have another wife in the closet.

HARRY. What's this then, Helena, what have you been up to?

LAURETTE. Oh, you mustn't expect miracles, she's not talking, but she's remembered how to laugh. I've got to go now.

HARRY. Have you been crying, Laurette?

LAURETTE (*going*). Me? I never cry. Never stop talking and never let them see you cry.

HARRY (*calling after her*). Well aren't you going to stay to tell me what was so funny?

LAURETTE (*off, calling*). 'Bye.

JACU. Goodbye, gentle rain.

HARRY. I don't suppose you'll tell me, will you, Helena? I'm sorry I blew up at you. I shouldn't have done that. I hope you've been OK. Not too lonely. Not much chance, with Laurette . . . I feel lonely most of the time these days.

HELENA 1. Harry. Lonely.

HARRY. I went shopping to cool off. Supermarket crowded to bursting. God, I hate shopping. I wouldn't hate it if you'd come. We could take Jacu. What d'you say? . . . What's that in Laurette's chair? (*Walking to it.*) Good God, it's another mouth-stick. She knows you don't – oh, I see. She's impossible, isn't she?

HELENA 1. Laurette. Lonely. Harry and Laurette.

HARRY. They don't make them like that in England, eh, Helena? Beautiful Helena? Still hiding behind the mask. A gold-plated mouth-stick. Nothing but the best. . . . It's like talking to an empty room. It's like being alone, only without the comforts of being alone. Why can't you talk, Jacu? Have you had a good day?

Do you like living here, or are we too sad for you? Does Helena talk to you while I'm out? Go stuff yourself, Harry, no one is listening. Save your breath, you might need it one day. Why don't you laugh for me?

JACU. When my father died, my mother was sad. She said it was like the sun going out. She did not talk so much after he died. Day and night, she did not care for a long time. Sun or moon, day or night, she did not care, she had no one to talk to and shout at any more.

HARRY. The fact is, Helena, I don't know how much more I can take. I can't go on like this. I know it's awful for you. Don't you think it's awful for me too? I do want to understand. I do still love you. I think about you all the time. You and Jacu, sitting looking out of different windows, God knows what the pair of you are thinking.

JACU. If I hurt myself, if I fell in the forest, my mother would hold me in her arms and say Jacu, listen to your pain, it offers you its wisdom. When you hear what your pain is telling you, it won't hurt you any more. She told me this so the forest could not hurt me. So that I would be free.

HARRY. I wanted to know. I wanted to understand. I lay down on the bed. I used to hold you and love you in that bed. I didn't move. I pretended there were weights on my body. I wanted to know what it's like for you. What it's like, being Helena, beautiful Helena, who doesn't move and doesn't speak. I lay for a long time, I didn't let myself move at all. I hardly let myself breathe. Why can you laugh for Laurette, but you can't tell me how you feel? What have I got to do? . . . I lay for an hour. Two hours. I told you I was going to have a nap, but I wasn't. The bed is comfortable, but lying absolutely still made it feel uncomfortable. There was nothing blocking my nose but it felt difficult to breathe.

JACU. Her soul could not go free. Her soul could not breathe. Her soul must be dying all the time.

HARRY. Difficult to breathe, as if something was weighing on me, crushing my lungs. Because I couldn't move to get air into them, I suppose. A feeling, not a physical reality. Do you have feelings these days, Helena, or just physical realities? I wanted to come and see you. I wanted to share it with you, but I had to do it alone. Like you've been doing it alone. I tried to think what it must have been like when you first knew. I lay still, and thought of that. I felt alone. I felt afraid. I wanted to push back the covers and sit up and shout no, it can't be true. But I couldn't sit up, could I? I wished I was dead. To be dead would be better than lying there knowing what I knew. And lying down there, there didn't seem much point in shouting either. People would run in and

look down at me. Like I was a specimen on a table. I began to
see how if you felt alone and afraid and you didn't shout about
it you'd find you had chosen silence without really meaning to.
I thought of all that gratitude I'd have in store. Always having to
have people do things for me. The most personal things. Having
them see parts of my body only mothers and lovers should see.
I make you a beautiful sandwich, but then why should you eat
beautiful food when you hate the body you're feeding? Or maybe
the sandwich needs a bit of salad. You can't get the salad. It's
second-rate food. Food prepared the way someone else thought
it should be, the way perhaps someone else had time to do it.
Brought to you by a monkey. I can get my own salad, Helena.
But I'm alone. I'm afraid. When I stopped being still, I was still
alone, afraid, suffocated. Cut off from you. Not knowing what to
do. Uncertain of the future. It seemed to me the worst thing maybe
was dependence. That's why I asked for Jacu. I thought maybe I
was helping with the worst thing. There's so little I can do. I'm
afraid to help, I know it's difficult to let me help. But the terrible
loneliness of such silence. I don't deserve that. You don't deserve
it. And Jacu doesn't deserve it. She's here for you, she should be
in the forest, and you ignore her. She must be as lonely and afraid
as the pair of us. She must wish she'd never been born. If I knew
what to do – if I knew what to do – if I knew (*Breaking down.*)
– if I knew –

Music holding back and building very slowly towards song.

MOTHER. If I knew what to do

BERNIE. If I knew

LAURETTE. If I knew

HARRY. If I knew

HELENA./HELENA 1. If they knew what to do

JACU. I know, far away, the forest still sings, still sings, in the green
darkness, still sings its forest song.

HELENA./HELENA 1. If they knew

JACU. Listen

HELENA./HELENA 1. Mother

JACU. Forest

HELENA./HELENA 1. Forest Mother

JACU. Earth child

HELENA./HELENA 1. Forest child

JACU. Earth mother

HELENA./HELENA 1. Child of the forest

JACU. Child of the earth

HELENA./HELENA 1. Mother of the child

JACU. Listen, in the forest, in the trees, listen, listen

HELENA./HELENA 1. The sounds of my childhood

JACU. The sounds of the forest, the forest song

HELENA./HELENA 1. Mother

JACU. Forest

HELENA./HELENA 1. You can cut the creeper

JACU. But never forget

HELENA./HELENA 1. The song of the forest

JACU. If you cut the creeper

HELENA./HELENA 1. Out of pain

JACU. She is still there

HELENA./HELENA 1. The creative fire

JACU. The phoenix rises

HELENA./HELENA 1. Listen, listen

JACU. The forest

HELENA./HELENA 1. The mother

JACU. To the earth

HELENA./HELENA 1. To the child

JACU. The song of the forest

HELENA./HELENA 1. Far away

JACU. The forest still sings

HELENA./HELENA 1. Far away . . . Mother, love

JACU. Listen! in the trees – listen!

HELENA./HELENA 1. Listen!

   Pause.

MOTHER. As mother to child

BERNIE. As mind to body

LAURETTE. As soul to sky

HARRY. As forest to earth

HELENA./HELENA 1. Mother

JACU. Child

HELENA./HELENA 1. Mother

JACU. Forest

MOTHER. As mother to child

BERNIE. As mind to body

LAURETTE. As soul to sky

HARRY. As forest to earth

HELENA./HELENA 1. As song of the forest

JACU. To man of the earth

HELENA./HELENA 1. As mother to child

JACU. The song

Music swells and ends.

Pause.

JACU. There has to be a clearing in the forest where men can live and build their village. There has to be a space where the forest gives way to men. There has to be day and night, sun and moon, man and woman, music and silence.

BERNIE. Where she comes from, man is changing the face of the earth.

HARRY. But the men still play the jakui while the women stay indoors.

HELENA. The little forest bird sings sadly now, as if she knew time had gone somewhere else.

JACU. Time. Time. Time and the forest, the sun and the moon, will always, always, always sing their song.

Jakui music. Bird call.

JACU. I was not born here. I was born where the sounds and the smells and the colour of the air are different, and the birds sing all the time in the green darkness of the forest. Never lose faith. Somewhere far away the forest still sings.

HELENA (*aloud*). Still, somewhere far away, the forest sings its song.

HARRY. Helena? Did you – speak?

HELENA. I'd like to call my mother tonight.

HARRY. What?

HELENA. And I'd like you to hold me tonight. (*Pause.*) I think we should ask her to stay. Lap, Jacu. (*Pause.*) Harry. Would you please put my arms around Jacu?

Flute music continues. Bird call.

JACU. Out of pain, the creative fire. Out of pain, the phoenix rises. And still, far away, the forest sings its song. Time and the forest, the sun and the moon, will always, always, sing their song.

Music continues under closing credits.

THE POPE'S BROTHER

(Il Fratello Del Papa)

by Steve Walker

Born in 1956, Steve Walker made his stage début four years later singing extracts from *The Threepenny Opera*, in a nightclub. There have been sixty-three one-man shows of his paintings and drawings since the first in his native Newcastle-upon-Tyne in 1977. His pictures hang in collections all over the world, including the Kremlin. Previous radio plays include *Him and It*, *Haunted by More Cake* and the six *Whoppers* plays. His screenplay, *The Companion*, will be broadcast in 1991; also, a new radio play, *Oates after His Fingers*. Walker's epic theological comedy, *The Pope's Brother*, was written in Rome in 1988 in the same room in which Ibsen wrote *Peer Gynt*. Any visitor to Rome may meet Tartufari in Scalini's in the Piazza Navona, or almost anywhere else. As this goes to press, Sidney Collyweston is believed to be in hiding in either Kuala Lumpur or Middlesbrough.

The Pope's Brother was first broadcast on 'Saturday Night Theatre', BBC Radio 4, on 28 July 1990. The cast was as follows:

SIDNEY COLLYWESTON	Dinsdale Landen
(the Pope's brother)	
GREGORY COLLYWESTON	Denys Hawthorne
(the Pope)	
TOMMASO TARTUFARI	Henry Goodman
(a high flying priest)	
CLAUDIA TARTUFARI	Jenny Howe
(his sister)	
CARDINAL NGOUPANDE	Ben Onwukwe
(to whom Sidney confesses)	
PYJAMAS	John Bull
(a betting man)	
Also:	
PUNTER	Vincent Brimble
SWISS GUARD	Vincent Brimble
MEDDLESOME PRIEST	Vincent Brimble
WILMA SPANGERHUFF	Jenny Howe
(an American tourist)	
SANDRO	Vincent Brimble
(a waiter)	
WOMAN IN THE CORSO	Jenny Howe
MAN IN THE CORSO	Vincent Brimble
JUNTA GENERAL SABATO	John Bull
GOD	David Bannerman
SISTER BRIDGET	Jenny Howe

Director: Peter Kavanagh
Running time, as broadcast: 72 minutes

Somewhere in Italy.

Acoustic of a cathedral.
Choir practising in background.
Sudden rush of clip-clopping footsteps.

SIDNEY (*breathless, worried*). You are Cardinal Ngoupande, are you not? THE Cardinal Ngoupande.

CARDINAL NGOUPANDE (*a deep, African voice*). I think so.

SIDNEY. I must talk to you.

CARDINAL NGOUPANDE. I am very busy just now. Perhaps another time.

SIDNEY (*increasingly agitated*). You don't understand. It's urgent, important. He's after me.

CARDINAL NGOUPANDE. Who?

SIDNEY. Him! Him! You know!

CARDINAL NGOUPANDE (*humouring a loony*). Ah, him! (*Calling.*) Sister, take this gentleman outside and give him a plate of spaghetti.

SIDNEY. Look! Look! This beard I'm wearing. (*Whispers.*) It's false.

CARDINAL NGOUPANDE. I would never have guessed.

SIDNEY. I'm Sidney Collyweston. See! THE Sidney Collyweston.

CARDINAL NGOUPANDE. Do I know you?

SIDNEY. We've not quite met, no. I'm the Pope's brother.

CARDINAL NGOUPANDE (*with sudden diplomatic largesse*). Quite all right, Sister. I'll deal with this matter, thank you. (*To* SIDNEY.) Come, I know a more private place.

They walk: their steps on cathedral stone.

SIDNEY (*breathlessly, trying to keep up*). My brother said, he said once that if there was a crisis, I should seek you out. Cardinal Ngoupande, he said, has a heart as big as the rest of him. (*More breathless.*) He said . . . he said . . . he said you were the most incorruptible man in the world.

CARDINAL NGOUPANDE (*a deep rolling laugh*).

SIDNEY. It's true though, isn't it?

CARDINAL NGOUPANDE. Here we are.

Plinking of a curtain being opened.

SIDNEY. In there? A confessing box? Not me, old darling.

CARDINAL NGOUPANDE. Do please hurry, man. That beard of yours isn't fooling anyone, you know.

SIDNEY. All right, all right.

Plinking of curtain being closed.
Woody clunks as SIDNEY settles himself.

Acoustic of the confessional.

CARDINAL NGOUPANDE. Yes.

SIDNEY. What?

CARDINAL NGOUPANDE. You have some things to tell me.

SIDNEY. Right . . . errrrrm. Bless me, Father, for I have sinned. It is errrrrrm . . . forty-seven years since my last confession. Sorry. (*In sudden agitated despair.*) Look – I've done terrible things, of course . . . I've been a scoundrel all my life. But I'm not here about that. I'm here about what's happened here. In Rome. I must fill you in.
   (*Increasingly agitated and loud.*) It's all Pyjamas' fault. They call him Pyjamas because he always wears pyjamas: he lives behind the betting shop where he works, you see, and never bothers to change. If he hadn't told me, about my brother, I would never have known. It's not that long ago I found out that the Duke of Edinburgh isn't a Scotsman. I mean, people were complaining about Margaret Thatcher for years and I thought she was a singer. I only read the racing pages, you see.

CARDINAL NGOUPANDE. Calm down now, there's a good fellow. And not so loud.

SIDNEY (*whispers*). Do you think he's out there, listening? (*Pause.*) I'll start at the betting shop, shall I? Or should I start with the chocolate? Or the murder – that was the worst? (*Becoming louder again, more confident.*) No, the betting shop, I think, give you a fuller picture that way or you'll not follow any of it. (*Fade up betting shop, race commentary, hum of punters.*) . . . I was waiting for the 2.30 from Uttoxeter when I popped a button. I'd put on a stone or two, you see: it just flew off, like a . . . what do they call those things? – a crosby! So I was looking for it on the floor when Pyjamas comes in and sticks a rolled newspaper up my bottom.

In the betting shop.

SIDNEY (*as the newspaper has been stuck up his bottom*). Oooooooo! Pyjamas, you idiot! Help me find my button, will you?

PYJAMAS. Here you are, Guv'nor!

SIDNEY. Since when have I been 'Governor' to you?

PYJAMAS. You lucky fat sod!

SIDNEY. Huh?

PYJAMAS. You got a result, best you ever had.

SIDNEY. The race hasn't started yet.

PYJAMAS. You don't look nothing like him!

SIDNEY. Who?

PYJAMAS. Who d'you think: Rubstic? Aldaniti? Shergar?

SIDNEY (*irritated*). What?

PYJAMAS. Your broffha. You's twins isn't yers?

SIDNEY (*with nostalgic awe*). My brother.

PYJAMAS. First English Pope in 468 years. Him! Your broffha. They made him Pope.

SIDNEY. Getaway!

PYJAMAS. Straight up! There's ees mugshot.

Rustle of newspaper as SIDNEY *snatches it.*

SIDNEY. Where's this, then?

PYJAMAS. Know yerh own broffha, don't yerh?

SIDNEY. Haven't set eyes on him in over thirty years. What, THAT . . . nothing like him – nothing like me anyway. Good God, it is him! It really is. Gregory Collyweston. (*Can't believe the good luck*.) I knew he'd joined up, but Pope. That's good going isn't it?

PYJAMAS. Leader of the world's 900 million Catholics, comprising 18.4 per cent of the world's population.

SIDNEY. No! Ha! Ha! Ha! (*Suddenly awestruck*.) Wait on, if he's Pope, what does that make me?

PYJAMAS. A jammy sod.

SIDNEY. What a stroke! I'll be an archbishop or something, do you think? If he's Holy I can't be far from it myself. We're almost the same man, for God's sake!

PYJAMAS. How come he's the Pope, then, and you're THAT?

SIDNEY. What?

PYJAMAS. That.

SIDNEY. Look here . . . I'm not such a nag. I'm a proper thoroughbred, you know – was, anyway, in my younger days.

PYJAMAS. No more worries now though. Yer can write yerh own cheque, Colly, mate. Yer've got something on him, haven't yer? Must have, from way back, yerh own broffha – must have.

SIDNEY. Well, yes, I don't know. But I'll bet he'll be pleased to see me if I turn up. Pope wouldn't be beastly to his own flesh-and-blood, despite my wasted life. Might even let me borrow a palace or something, full of nuns to do my bidding.

A huge dirty guffaw from them both.

SIDNEY (*with airy delight, on his way*). Jam on both sides for me from now on, old darling!

PYJAMAS (*calling after*). Here! Don't you want to see if your gee-gee's won?

SIDNEY (*calls back*). Couldn't care less!

PYJAMAS (*yells, a touch of earnestness*). Colly! Send me some silk pyjamas, will yer, Colly, eh? A yella pair!

SIDNEY (*hurrying back*). Ermm . . . Rome? . . . that's in Italy, isn't it?

PYJAMAS (*can't believe he's asking*). Yeah.

SIDNEY (*on his way again*). Just checking.

PYJAMAS (*after a private dirty laugh*). Here, see that geezer who just went out?

PUNTER (*angrily*). No.

PYJAMAS. Pope's brother. Straight up.

PUNTER (*in scornful disbelief*). Errrrrrrrrrrrrrrrrrrgh!

Acoustic of confessional.

SIDNEY (*suddenly close, in confessional*). I admit it – hadn't the foggiest where Italy was. But I can't know everything, can I? Never been abroad before, you see. Never been anywhere if a horse wasn't involved – though I did consider emigrating after what they did to Lester Piggott. Had a passport, though – you know, just in case. Especially after that doping business.

Tinkle of Italian music in background.

Italy! Ah! Took the train, of course. Wouldn't get me up in a Hairyplane, no fear! Ate a man's sandwich when he slipped out of the compartment for a widdle. Gave me a strange dream, that sandwich . . . I was being eaten by failed racehorses: they'd all escaped from the knackers yard and blamed me for their misfortunes: I'd bet on their noses you see, old darling, so they had to lose, just had to. Did you know they eat horse here? Of course you do. I expect that's what was in the sandwich. I'm telling you all this because I'm sure Greg would want me to tell you everything . . . I'm an idiot, you see, I don't know what's important.

CARDINAL NGOUPANDE (*calmly*). Keep going with it, please. You have arrived in Rome.

SIDNEY. Yes. Yes. Ah! I'm in Rome, then. I've arrived! (*Bring up sounds of Rome.*) I'm in the Vatican, looking up at Saint Peter's with my guidebook in my hand. So I somehow find my way to an official-looking bit but get myself collared by one of those funny-looking Swiss Guard chappies. Huge! Stood right in my way.

Exterior acoustic.
  Distant sound of traffic, of tourist guide yakking to his flock.

SIDNEY. Excuse me, I'd like to see the Pope, please.

SWISS GUARD. Mi scusi, signore?

SIDNEY. Tell him it's Sidney. He'll understand. Give him one helluva shock, mind!

SWISS GUARD. Mi dispiace ma non capisco.

SIDNEY. Go on, man. Don't just stand there. Get on with it. Look: Me – Sidney Collyweston. Yes? Pope: your Pope – he Gregory Collyweston. Mio Brothero. Comprenday?

SWISS GUARD. You go away please.

SIDNEY (*raising his voice*). I just want to see the Pope. It's not much to ask.

PRIEST (*approaching, thick Italian accent*). Perhaps I can be of some assistance.

SIDNEY. Hum? Ah, thankyou. I'm trying to explain to the General here: I'm Sidney Collyweston, the Pope's brother, you see.

PRIEST. Ah!

SIDNEY. I just heard he'd got the job on Wednesday and I came straight over. Frightfully hot, isn't it?

PRIEST (*to* SWISS GUARD). Questo signore e' americano. Lui sta cercando suo fratello che cucina spaghetti in un ristorante in Piazza Morgana ma si e' dimenticato il nome del ristorante.

SWISS GUARD. Si, la' c'e' un eccellente ristorante. Il Baccala' e' superbo. Non ho mai provato gli spaghetti.

SIDNEY (*losing confidence*). He'll be awfully pleased to see me. He'll make it worth your while.

PRIEST. I tell you where to go, please. I give directions, okay?

Acoustic of confessional.

SIDNEY (*in confessional*). Fobbed me off, didn't he! I ended up in a cake shop on the Via Veneto. Lovely cakes, mind you. (*In sudden despair.*) I hope you're following this. Should I tell you about the murder now and get it out of the way?

CARDINAL NGOUPANDE. Why don't you tell me how you met up with His Holiness.

SIDNEY (*enthusing again*). Ah! Yes! I can tell you that! They have these huge great audiences every now and then in the morning. To see the Pope. Thousands there, just like Derby Day. Every kind of nun, cripples, you name it. That's when I saw him. I was way at the back and he was coming to the front, blessing people with his fingers.

(*In audience hall, yelling.*) Greg! Greg! Gregory! It's me!

(*In confessional.*) They started dragging me off. Half a dozen bishops strangling me with my binoculars. But I gave them the slip, crawled about under everybody's legs like a jockey thrown off at Beecher's Brook. I popped up near the front.

(*In audience hall.*) Greg! I say, Greg!

(*In confessional, complains.*) They were hitting me with their Bibles. An evil-smelling Johnny in sunglasses had me in an armlock.

(*In audience hall.*) Oooh! Arrh! Look! Look at my face, man! I haven't changed that much. (*Desperate.*) Greggggggggggggggggggggg!!!!!!!! (*Partly muffled.*) 'I'm the King of the Castle and you're the dirty . . . mmmm . . . mmmm . . . mmmmmmm'

(*In confessional.*) They were bustling him away. Dozens of dark-suited bodies were between us. All I could see of him was one of his eyes, don't know which one. Then someone gave me a godalmighty wallop and at the same moment Greg's eye wrinkled up in pain, just as if they'd hit him and not me. He knew who I was then: I saw the moment. One word from him and they gave me my arms back, dusted me off and marched me into a smallish gold room full of crucifixions and men in silly hats . . .

Interior acoustic.

GREG (*highly emotional*). Sidney! Sidney! Heaven be praised!!!

SIDNEY. Hullo, big brother!

GREG (*laughing*). Only by five minutes!

SIDNEY. Looks like fifty years if you want the truth. What you been doing to yourself, boy!

GREG (*happily*). Nothing much.

SIDNEY. I mean to say, Greg old darling, I spend my life wallowing in every indulgence, up to my knees in damp racecourses every day and I couldn't be lovelier! You've been at best behaviour for forty years and you look like our Granny! Devil looks after his own, what? Ooops, sorry.

GREG (*chuckling*). You're just the same. (*In pride and delight announces to the throng.*) This is my brother, Sidney.

ROOMFUL OF CLERICS. Pleased to meet you.

SIDNEY. How d'you do.

GREG (*suddenly earnest, intimate*). Last night, Sidney, I prayed harder than I have ever prayed before. I prayed for guidance and the Blessed Lord has sent YOU, Sidney.

SIDNEY (*his first attempt to be truthful*). No. No. He doesn't know me, honestly.

GREG (*firmly*). You are wrong, Sidney.

SIDNEY. You should know! Ha! Ha! (*A sudden idea.*) Listen! Ha! Orange cake!

GREG. Orange cake?

SIDNEY. Yes, yes. In the taxi this morning. It stopped at some traffic lights and everything suddenly reeked of orange cake. I asked the driver where it was coming from but they only speak Latin around here. Don't you remember?

GREG. What?

SIDNEY. Our Mam's orange cake.

GREG. No.

SIDNEY. Yes you do. With the hundreds and thousands on the top.

GREG (*passionate*). Yes! Yes! I remember! (*Weeping.*) O, sweet Jesus! Sweet Jesus, thank you!!

SIDNEY (*with GREG snuffling behind him*). I nearly cried myself, I can tell you. Very devout our Mam, wasn't she? I expect that's where you get it from. And cruel, let's be fair, she was quite horridly cruel, but only to me and the family pets.

GREG. Shall we stand for a few moments in silent prayer?

SIDNEY. Er . . . all right.

A long prayerful silence, long enough to make people think their radios have broken. Then SIDNEY, clearing his throat, then others, in background. GREG murmurs an Amen. A hum of response.

GREG. You will stay, won't you, Sidney?

SIDNEY. Hum?

GREG. Here with me.

SIDNEY (*playing hard-to-get very badly*). Well, I don't know. I have business interests at home, you see, needing constant attention.

GREG (*crestfallen*). Oh.

SIDNEY. The turf, you know. I must keep up or I'll lose all idea of form. Where a horse is concerned you have to know everything, something's not enough.

GREG. I'm sure, yes. Oh, you know so much about the World, Sidney. I can see it in your eyes. (*To cardinals.*) You can, can't you, see it in his eyes?

A murmur of assent.

SIDNEY (*confused*). I'm no mug, if that's what you mean.

GREG (*with deep humility*). Please, Sidney, stay, and help me combat my unworthiness.

SIDNEY. Well, if you put it like that . . .

GREG *and* SIDNEY *laugh joyously,* SIDNEY *losing all restraint.*

GREG (*calling*). Tommaso!

TARTUFARI (*a soft, sinister voice.*) Holy Father.

GREG. Sidney, this is Father Tartufari, one of the brightest young men in our Curia. He will look after you.

SIDNEY. How's tricks?

TARTUFARI. I am much better, thankyou.

GREG (*quietly to* SIDNEY). Father Tartufari is recovering from an operation . . .

SIDNEY. Ooo!

GREG. . . . brain surgery. We rejoice that he has been spared. You won't wear him out, will you, Sidney?

SIDNEY. No. No. (*Transparently caddish.*) Oh, Greg. One thing. You don't have a bit spare cash, do you? A few zillion of that Lira stuff will suffice, just for pocket money. I came away in such a rush and the banks were closed.

GREG. Of course. Of course. Tartufari will look after you. Just ask him. He'll give you anything you need.

SIDNEY (*hopeful*). Anything?

GREG (*in joyful remembrance*). How much pocket money did we get?

SIDNEY. Oooooh, a threepenny bit a week . . . to share.

GREG. Yes! Yes!

SIDNEY. I had a moustache before it went up to sixpence.

They laugh together. Fade the laughter.

Fade up SIDNEY *and* TARTUFARI *entering room.*

TARTUFARI. This way, this way, please, here we are.

Door closes.

SIDNEY (*hugely impressed*). I say, this is rather plush! All mine, is it?

TARTUFARI. Yes, sir.

SIDNEY. Call me Colly, please. All the chaps do. (*Walking around the room.*) This furniture's rather super. Frightfully modern.

TARTUFARI. Made by our finest Italian designers. Do you like it? If it is not to your taste . . .

SIDNEY. Oh, erm . . . yes, it's the bee's knees, champion stuff. This a chair, is it?

TARTUFARI (*pleased*). I have supervised the selection during my convalescence. I am doing only light work.

SIDNEY. Who's the Sinatra fan?

TARTUFARI (*bashfully*). The Holy Father and myself. It is something we share from the old days.

SIDNEY. Ah.

TARTUFARI. You?

SIDNEY. What?

TARTUFARI. Frank Sinatra.

SIDNEY. Take him or leave him.

TARTUFARI. I have installed the hi-fi myself. Shall I play a record for us?

SIDNEY. Go on, then.

Sinatra sings 'Night and Day', loudly for a moment, then turned down.

SIDNEY. A tumour, was it?

TARTUFARI. Sorry?

SIDNEY. Your operation.

TARTUFARI. Two tumours, I regret to say. A purple-hot poker on each side of my head.

SIDNEY. Hard cheese. (*Boasts happily.*) I've never been ill, not even for a day, ever – what you think of that?

TARTUFARI. Most fortunate.

SIDNEY. Still, your hair's growing back nicely.

TARTUFARI. Thankyou, yes.

SIDNEY (*with a guffaw*). Wish mine would! Errrrm, is that the Leaning Tower of Pisa I can see?

TARTUFARI. It is in Pisa.

SIDNEY. Hum?

TARTUFARI. Pisa is far away, another city.

SIDNEY. That's not it then?

TARTUFARI. No.

SIDNEY. All those rooftops. Makes you wonder what's going on underneath, what? Wonderful to be able to see in. Greg and I had a castle when we were kiddies – toy one, you understand! – and you could lift the roof off and see our soldiers standing about inside. Of course God can, can't he?

TARTUFARI. I'm sorry?

SIDNEY. Can see through rooftops.

TARTUFARI. You have faith, Colly?

SIDNEY. Don't follow?

TARTUFARI. You believe in God?

SIDNEY. Silly question! I'm the Pope's brother, aren't I? Course I do. (*An afterthought.*) When I think about it.

TARTUFARI (*walking away*). There is an even better view from the bedroom. There is a balcony.

He opens the bedroom doors. Chimes tinkle lightly in the breeze. Sinatra sings more distantly.

SIDNEY (*following*). Corrrrrr . . . . a four-poster!!!! (*Jumps on to it – it squeaks as he bounces on it, laughing.*) Ha! Ha! Ha! Never slept in one of these before.

TARTUFARI. Twelve Popes have died in that bed.

SIDNEY (*stops bouncing, worried*). Errrrr! No ghosts, I hope?

TARTUFARI (*the slightest touch of amusement*). I don't think so. But then I have not slept there.

SIDNEY. Oh, don't, don't.

TARTUFARI. If you need me for any reason I am just down the corridor. The gold door next to the Botticelli.

SIDNEY. Botticelli. Got it! That's a painting, isn't it? Just checking.

TARTUFARI (*taking his leave*). You must be very tired.

SIDNEY. Wait, please. One thing. About Greg. The Holy thingummy. He's all right, is he? He said he'd been ill.

TARTUFARI. He is well, thankyou. Being Pope is proving a great strain upon his constitution, of course.

SIDNEY. Yes, yes, I'm sure. I wouldn't do it! I'll see him later, shall I?

TARTUFARI. Tomorrow. At breakfast. (*On his way.*) I don't eat. Sister Bridget will show you the way.

Doors close behind him.

SIDNEY (*calling after him*). Thanks, awfully!

Pause.
   Telephone being dialled.
   Sinatra in background.

SIDNEY (*hollering down phone*). Hello! Hello! Maxie! That you? Yes, yes, I'm in Rome, you know, staying with my brother. Erm, could you read out the card for Newmarket this afternoon? (*Distant hum of his bookmaker reading the card.*) Arh! Oooo! Yes. I'll have a monkey on that please. Yes. Yes. On account. That's all right, isn't it? – of course. What? Oh, that's Frank Sinatra. He has the room next to mine, you know. In the bath, yes. (*Hollers into room.*) Keep the noise down, Frank! (*Laughs hugely.*)

Fade up sounds of many people breakfasting in a large room.

SIDNEY (*approaching*). Good morning, one and all!!!

GREG. Good morning, Sidney. Sleep well?

SIDNEY. Like a dead horse, thankyou. (*Pulling out his chair and sitting down.*) I say, you don't do bad, do you. What a spread! Breakfast at home, I have two stale twiglets and a licorice allsort. (*Whispers.*) Don't they ever leave you alone, these decrepit Bishops?

GREG. It seems not.

SIDNEY (*to bishops*). Morning. Morning. (*Brightly, to* GREG.) Hey, look, I'm the only one here who isn't a Bishop! You couldn't, could you?

GREG. Pardon?

SIDNEY. Make me a Bishop!

GREG (*laughs*). Don't want to be like the Borgias, do we?

SIDNEY. Hmm? Oh. Ha! Ha! I should say not! Hmm?

GREG. I have thought of you every day, Sidney, all those years. I've often wanted to see you. But my life has been such a struggle with faith, and illness, and the great responsibilities the Lord has seen fit to bestow upon me. I did not wish to burden you.

SIDNEY (*tucking in, mouth full*). Oh, you should have, old darling!

GREG (*starkly*). Sidney, I have just told you a lie. It's unforgivable. I must tell you the truth. I hope this doesn't hurt you in any way, Sidney, but I must speak what is in my heart.

SIDNEY (*gulps his food, preparing for the worst*). Don't say it, Greg, please. I know, I'm a terrible lump . . . I must be dripping with sins . . .

GREG. You have been the great joy of my life.

SIDNEY (*amazed at being let off*). Have I?

GREG. We are joined at the soul, you and I. You must have guessed it.

SIDNEY (*eating again*). Don't go all soppy on me.

GREG (*his sentences trailing off slightly in an Anglican manner*). When I was in the monastery, quite a young man, it was a constant wonder to my superiors that I was so informed about the world and its ways, although I never stepped outside our walls except perhaps to banish a cat I'd found in our vegetable garden. I understood things that it was impossible for me to understand. Mere intuition couldn't account for it. No, it was your doing, Sidney. Everything you have felt in your wonderful busy life: the joy, pains and sorrows, I have felt also. Something in me has lived your every moment. It has been the making of me, the greatest enrichment of my life, a gift beyond measure. (*Pause.*) But you, Sidney?

SIDNEY (*mouth full*). Humm?

GREG. Have you really felt nothing of my struggle?

SIDNEY (*bluff, but a sudden sad truthfulness*). I'm an oaf, dear, I thought you knew.

GREG. You don't know yourself well enough, little brother. You are a most unique fellow.

SIDNEY (*unbelieving*). I am? (*Believing.*) Of course I am.

GREG. With a gift for happiness that the whole world has need of.

SIDNEY. Look, do you think you've been working too hard?

GREG. When you had your accident, I was so worried. I was unconscious myself, of course, but, strangest thing, I was praying for you . . . in my sleep.

SIDNEY. I've never had an accident.

GREG. Three years ago. September. You had a fall.

SIDNEY. Fall? Fall? Oh, you mean that night I was blind drunk and got run over by a milk cart. Not a scratch. Miracle, mind you, they all said.

GREG (*with import*). I was in hospital till Christmas. I have had a certain numbness in my back ever since.

SIDNEY. Lost me, sorry.

GREG. That time at Ampleforth, the term before you were expelled. You were beaten up, remember?

SIDNEY (*joyously*). When I put glue in that swot's desk!

GREG and SIDNEY (*together*). But it was the wrong desk!!!!!

GREG. It was that giant's desk. He dragged you into an empty classroom. Gave you what for.

SIDNEY (*boasts airily*). His best punches just bounced off me. I whacked him into submission with a stray cricket-stump.

GREG. They found me flat out in the locker-room, same afternoon.

SIDNEY. Sorry, doesn't ring a bell.

GREG (*irritated with* SIDNEY's *slowness*). Oh, Sidney! How could you not know!! We are like the Corsican Brothers, you and I. The twins in the Douglas Fairbanks picture. One's asleep in Corsica and the other is wounded in a duel in Paris. The sleeping one wakes up, screaming, feeling his brother's hurt. We are like that, at least I am with you. When you were struck by that milk cart, I received the injuries.

SIDNEY. Never!

GREG. Every time you catch a cold, I catch a cold.

SIDNEY. I've never had a cold.

GREG. Then I catch them for you.

SIDNEY. Straight up? Jolly decent of you. (*It sinks in.*) I'd have been more careful, if I'd known. Wrapped up in the cold and wotnot.

GREG. That's what I'm trying to say. It's the real reason I've kept out of contact with you. It would have ruined your life, if you'd known. It wouldn't have been your own life anymore. Do you understand, Sidney?

SIDNEY (*laughs*). You really mean, if I poke myself with my fork like this, you can feel it?

GREG. Ow! Yes.

SIDNEY. Ha! Ha! Isn't life a wonder!

GREG (*with the intonation of Chamberlain declaring war*). I felt I had to tell you now. God has brought you here to help me, Sidney. All our long entwined lives he has been preparing us. Now our time of testing has arrived. (*Pause.*) Sidney.

SIDNEY. I'm with you. Really. Yes.

GREG. Whatever goodness there is in me has flowed into you, Sidney, and made you the man you are. I'm sure of it! And your vitality, your *Lebensfunke*, has sparked in me and caused my bruised soul to rise. There must be no secrets between us. Our lives are one, Sidney.

SIDNEY (*slow-wittedly awestruck*). Yes . . . yes . . . we must be one, mustn't we, come to think of it. I mean, at my end I've had some rum moments in the past, almost did some truly dreadful things . . .

. . (*Suddenly bluff and cheery again.*) . . . . but something always held me back. I'll bet it was you, transmitting your big conscience into my little one, bobbing around in there like . . . a warm duck in a cold bath.

GREG (*utterly lost, as if he's never heard of ducks, warm or otherwise*). A warm duck, Sidney?

SIDNEY. Don't you have ducks here then? England's full of them these days.

GREG. Ah, Tommaso!

TARTUFARI. Good morning, Holy Father.

GREG. What have you got planned for my brother today?

TARTUFARI. A tour of the Eternal City, if he wishes.

SIDNEY. Spiffo!

Suddenly: zippy Italian music. . . . .

Fade music, fade up frantic Rome traffic. Acoustic of the car which TARTUFARI *is driving.*

TARTUFARI. This morning we see the Forum, the Colosseum, the Arch of Constantine. Then we have lunch in the Piazza Navona: very nice restaurant, I ate there with great pleasure before I was ill. Then we visit churches, many, many churches: Santa Maria Maggiore, Santa Maria del Popolo, San Giovani in Laterano, San Pietro in Vincoli . . . and we finish with a nice long walk around the Vatican Museum. I drive you around first, okay?

SIDNEY. I'm all yours.

TARTUFARI. On our right we have the Mausoleum of the Emperor Augustus.

SIDNEY (*profoundly uninterested*). Oh, yes.

Lots of horns peeping in traffic jam.

TARTUFARI (*under his breath*). Andiamo! Andiamo!

Their car starts off again.

TARTUFARI. This is the Piazza del Popolo. You see here we have the old gates of the city. In bygone times it is here that the pilgrims entered Rome from the North.

SIDNEY. All roads lead to Rome, eh?

TARTUFARI. That's right. We have here Santa Maria del Popolo and Santa Maria in Monte. Very beautiful. We shall see inside them another day.

Mad screech of brakes, angry peeping. TARTUFARI *winds down window, letting more noise in.*

TARTUFARI (*fast and furious*). Ehi! Oh burino! Ma che fai non ci vedi! Che ti credi di fare! Ehi! Ehi! Tu cerchi d'ammazzarmi! D'ammazzare il mio amico!!! Tu lo sai chi e'!!!! Ahhhhhhhhhhhh!!! Va all'inferno! Va all'inferno o ti ci mando io stesso! Idiota! Idiota! (*To* SIDNEY.) You see that! (*To his fellow motorist.*) Errrrrrrrrgh, you!

They drive off with a screech and a lurch and a yelp from SIDNEY, TARTUFARI *muttering under his breath.*

SIDNEY (*after another yelp*). Bit of Irish in you, what?

TARTUFARI (*snaps*). What you say?

SIDNEY (*calls over the noise of traffic*). I say, there's a demon in you when you're roused.

TARTUFARI (*couldn't be more contrite*). Please. I apologise. Forgive me. I am supposed to stay calm. My operation, you understand, I am not quite the same. (*Quickly returning to his travelogue voice.*) Here we are driving down the Corso. It is the main shopping street of Rome.

SIDNEY. Oooh!!! Do you think we could stop a minute. A present for a friend at home: a pair of yellow pyjamas, silk. Should be no trouble?

TARTUFARI. No trouble.

SIDNEY (*in his best caddish tone*). And a few oddments for myself. Nothing too expensive. You've a nice little wad on you, I suppose?

A snatch of Roman music.

Fade music, fade up sounds of restaurant.

SIDNEY (*with deep gastronomic satisfaction*). Arrrrrrrrrrrrrh! (*Sound of his knife and fork being laid down on plate, a mildish burp.*)

TARTUFARI. You enjoy?

SIDNEY. Exquisite, thankyou. You don't think I might have some more, do you? Just a ladleful. Or two.

TARTUFARI (*summoning waiter*). Mi scusi, per favore. Il mio amico ne vorrebbe ancora.

SIDNEY. Why don't you have something yourself? Go on! Just a nibble can't hurt! A bread roll! One of those green things! I feel dreadfully guilty.

TARTUFARI. No. Thankyou.

WAITER (*serving* SIDNEY). Signore. If you please.

SIDNEY. Ask him to give my compliments to the chef, will you? Best feed I've had in years. (*To* WAITER, *extra loud as if to an idiot*.) I say: best feed I've had in years.

WAITER. Thankyou, signore.

SIDNEY (*laughs*). Nice fella that. Reminds me of a bookmaker I know in Taunton. (*Suddenly serious*.) Look, Tommy. Could you do something for me?

TARTUFARI. Who is this Tommy?

SIDNEY. You, dear. Can't keep calling you Father, can I? People would talk. (*Struggling with embarrassment*.) Look, you couldn't dig me up a few books about God and things, hmm?

TARTUFARI. God . . . and things?

SIDNEY. Um-hum.

TARTUFARI. Perhaps . . . a Bible?

SIDNEY. Erm, yes, thankyou, a Bible, yes, a help, but it's not quite what I'm getting at. You see, I feel such a fool. I've nothing to talk to Greg about. He must think I'm a real plank. In England, you see, they have these irritating TV programmes, where they reunite brothers, sisters, aunts and things, people who haven't seen each other for a hundred years. One's an acrobat, the other's a shepherd. But what happens when the show's over and they're sitting alone, they've nothing to talk about but a few half-remembered days from their weeniehood, nothing in common, especially if one of them is Pope. I need something to gen me up on God, the angelic host, what it's all supposed to be about and why. You get my drift?

TARTUFARI. Yes, of course. You want some theological books.

SIDNEY. That's the ticket!!! Nothing too brainy, mind you: 'Theothingummy for Beginners', that sort of thing.

TARTUFARI. Yes, yes. This evening I shall bring you what you need. A little book of my own also, on this subject.

SIDNEY. You write books too!!!

TARTUFARI (*bashful*). It has been published in America. A very bad book. But it may be of some assistance.

WAITER. Signore?

SIDNEY. Ah, pudding!

Acoustic of the Sistine Chapel.
 Loud hum of tourists, clicking of cameras.

AMERICAN WOMAN (*in background*). Wilbur! Come and look here, Wilbur!

SIDNEY (*close*). Is this where Mussolini's buried, then?

TARTUFARI (*with only the slightest irritation, whispers*). This is the Sistine Chapel.

SIDNEY. Ah.

TARTUFARI (*whispers*). Built by Pope Sixtus IV at the end of the fifteenth century. It is 40 metres long, 21 metres wide, 13 metres high.

SIDNEY. Jolly impressive.

TARTUFARI. We have before us here 'The Last Judgement' of Michelangelo.

SIDNEY (*uninterested*). I see. Yes.

TARTUFARI. On the left we have the righteous rising up into Heaven, meanwhile on the right there are the damned souls descending into Hell. (*Suddenly personal.*) I never tire of gazing at it. Each figure, see, has gone to Hell in his own way. Look, please, him there, he must have done terrible things.

SIDNEY. Doesn't look very happy, does he?

TARTUFARI (*meaningfully*). No. Not happy.

SIDNEY. No tailors in Heaven, then? Or Hell?

TARTUFARI. Tailors?

SIDNEY. None of them are wearing any clothes. Just jockstraps.

TARTUFARI (*genuinely amused, perhaps over-amused*). Yes. Yes. Ha! Ha! Ha! Ha! (*Giggles loudly to himself.*)

SIDNEY (*with TARTUFARI still giggling, a touch worried*). I'll not go to Hell, will I? Not now. Before, yes. But now that I'm the Pope's Brother: must be worth a few points, eh?

TARTUFARI (*happily*). I hope I shall see you in Heaven. I shall show you around, just as I have shown you Rome today.

They both laugh.

Pause.

SIDNEY (*in confessional, thoughtful, blankly*). We had a lovely time. Saw everything – except the Mona Lisa, missed that one. Bit spooky, old Tommy, of course, at the best of times. Every ten minutes or so his head would twitch back on his neck and it would look like his eyes were going to twang out on their strings. Wouldn't eat! Never went to the toilet, either. I was always going. But I'll get on with anyone, me. I rather liked him.

Got back late after another feed, had a bit of supper with Greg. He told me what Pope had built what bit of Rome, then he remembered some old photos he had, tiny black-and-white things of Mam and Dad and us as kiddies and people we'd both forgotten. We both ended up just sitting back in our big gold chairs, looking at each other, tears in our eyes. Silly old buffers, what?

Still wasn't tired. Sat up in my four-poster thumbing through some vile theology books Tommy had lent me. Tiny type and millions of pages. Sent me straight off.

I distinctly remember I was having a dream about being at the seaside. I was with some of those people from the photographs, only in the dream I knew who they were. We were holding hands and jumping when the waves came. Then a voice called to me . . . . .

GOD (*close, a slow, soft voice coming from both sides at once, in good, precise English*). Sidney. Sidney.

SIDNEY (*in confessional, ominously*). I knew it wasn't a dream, because I came out of my dream to attend to it. I was in the four-poster. In the dark.

Pause.

GOD. Is it you, Sidney?

SIDNEY (*groggy*). Me? Me? Yes, this is me. Who are you?

GOD. This is Jesus, Sidney.

SIDNEY (*in a voice made small by awe*). Jesus? You mean . . . God?!

GOD. If you prefer.

SIDNEY (*a frightened moan*).

GOD. You are not drunken, Sidney. This really is God talking to you.

SIDNEY. Honest?

GOD (*laughs kindly*). Honest.

SIDNEY. Ooooh, er! You've made me wet the bed.

GOD. I am sorry if I frightened you, Sidney.

SIDNEY. No, it's quite all right. My fault, I'm sure.

GOD. I have been watching you, Sidney.

SIDNEY (*guiltily*). Oh? Just since I came here . . . or always?

GOD. Always, Sidney.

SIDNEY (*guilt-ridden*). Oh, dear.

GOD. You are one of my special people, Sidney.

SIDNEY. Me? Surely not.

GOD. This is why I have made your brother the Pope.

SIDNEY (*a weak worried moan*).

GOD. Someday a new Bible shall be written, with a Chapter in it all about you, Sidney. I have important plans for you. You won't disappoint me, will you, Sidney?

SIDNEY. No, sir.

GOD. But first I must be sure of you, Sidney. There are some simple tests I wish you to do for me.

SIDNEY. Anything, anything at all.

GOD (*a touch of Jehovah*). Until I inform you to cease you shall eat of nothing but chocolate.

SIDNEY. Chocolate?

GOD. Chocolate, Sidney.

SIDNEY. Errr . . . . . milk or plain?

GOD. Both, either, Sidney. I don't mind.

SIDNEY. All right, sir. You can rely on me.

GOD. One more thing, Sidney. This is our secret. No one, not even your brother, must know that I have spoken to you. Do you promise me this?

SIDNEY. It's going to be rather awkward . . .

GOD (*strictly*). Sidney!

SIDNEY. I . . . I . . I promise.

GOD (*fading away*). Goodnight, Sidney.

SIDNEY (*calling after*). Goodnight, Lord. (*Excited, to himself.*) I say! I say! Who'd have thought?

Acoustic of confessional.

SIDNEY (*in confessional*). It didn't seem too difficult at first. I went along to this luxurious sweetie shop, just outside the Vatican – best customer they ever had, me, over the next few weeks – and everything looked jolly tempting. I've always liked chocolate. Ask anyone: I'll eat anything. My first mistake was buying those big boxes. I didn't realise until I was back in my room, puzzling out what-was-inside-what-chocolate from one of those little paper guides with impossible drawings on it: only chocolate, he'd said, and these had marzipan, fudge, strawberry centres. So I passed out the boxes to nuns I found in the corridors – very grateful they were too – and stuck to bars from then on. Thirty, forty a day to start with.

CARDINAL NGOUPANDE (*highly vexed*). I have never heard such lies in a confessional!!!!

SIDNEY (*protests*). Eh?

CARDINAL NGOUPANDE. Breathe through the grille, please! Breathe through the grille!!!!

SIDNEY (*breathes*). Harrrrrrrrrrrrrrh. Harrrrrrrrrrrrrrrrrh.

CARDINAL NGOUPANDE. I thought so! You have been drinking!

SIDNEY (*small, hurt*). Only for courage.

CARDINAL NGOUPANDE. It is the liquor making up this preposterous story!!!

SIDNEY. No! No! Honest! On my Auntie Betty's grave!

CARDINAL NGOUPANDE. All my life I have prayed to God to show himself, to remove me from this jungle of confusion, this treacle-pot of unbearable uncertainty. I have had no sign!!! Nothing!!! (*Darkly*.) I do not believe you.

SIDNEY. Look, of course you don't believe me. Who would? But if I explain it all you'll come around, I know you will. Let me explain. Can I, please? Please?

Pause.

CARDINAL NGOUPANDE (*sighs*). Continue.

SIDNEY. Thankyou so much. (*Confused for a moment; has lost his place in the story*.) Errrrr . . . Ah! So, I did as I was told: I ate nothing but chocolate. But it's not the same in Italy as it is at home. It's always claggy from the heat. Dreadful stuff! I had to eat it, though, didn't I? I'd promised HIM. And those spreads in the Vatican! Those breakfasts! Ooooh – the hams, the strange delicious meaty cuttings, the queer tangy vegetables. Looking at them lying innocently in their silver dishes made me more and more unbearably hungry. All I could do was keep sneaking away from the table to scoff a few bars.

Acoustic of dining room.
  Hum of diners, clinks of eating.

GREG. Sidney?

SIDNEY. Humph?

GREG. Are you STILL not hungry?

SIDNEY (*brightly*). No, thankyou.

GREG. Dearie me! You've become as bad as Father Tartufari. (*Nervously.*) Perhaps Italian food does not agree with you?

SIDNEY. No, no. It's wonderful stuff. Not peckish, that's all.

GREG. I only say so because I've been feeling somewhat queasy myself just lately.

SIDNEY. Sorry to hear it, brother-of-mine. I'll go for a long walk this afternoon – that should make you feel better.

GREG (*touched*). Thankyou, Sidney. (*A sudden realisation.*) Sidney?

SIDNEY. Yes, Greg.

GREG. You haven't been eating chocolate, have you?

SIDNEY. Errrrrrrrrrrr – no.

GREG. What's that around your mouth, then? And on your shirt?

SIDNEY. Ah! . . . . You've caught me.

GREG (*deeply worried*). Sidney?

SIDNEY (*struggling*). Yes, you see, old darling, I looked at myself in the mirror last week and what did I see – a hippopotamus! I'm on a diet, a chocolate only diet. It's the latest thing in England.

GREG. No!

SIDNEY. I've lost two stones already. Here. . . . (*Sound of silver paper tearing and snap of chocolate, his mouth full.*) Go on, try some! Food of the Gods!

GREG (*weakly*). Thankyou. No.

SIDNEY. Go on.

GREG. I suddenly feel rather unwell.

SIDNEY. Oooo!

Acoustic of SIDNEY's *bedroom.*
   From the silence a sound like a needle playing at the beginning of a record.

GOD. Sidney.

SIDNEY (*startled awake, yells*). Arrrrhhh!

GOD. Sidney. It's Jesus, Sidney.

SIDNEY (*yawns*). Orrrrrrrrr. . . . Yes, hullo. I've been praying for you for days. I expect you were busy. This chocolate lark, it's just not on any more, you know. I'm a hundredweight fatter than I was and it's made Greg ill.

GOD. You have passed the test, Sidney.

SIDNEY. It's over, then?

GOD. It is over. I am very pleased with you, Sidney.

SIDNEY. Thankyou, Lord. Errrm: a favour, pretty-please?

GOD. Depends what it is, Sidney.

SIDNEY. I've always wanted to know what you look like. You couldn't appear for me, could you?

GOD (*strictly*). No, Sidney.

SIDNEY. You couldn't perhaps say who you look like? George Sanders? Scobie Breasley? One of the Beatles?

GOD (*very strictly indeed*). Sidney!!!

SIDNEY (*scared*). Sorry. Sorry.

GOD. I have another test for you, Sidney.

SIDNEY. Oh, no.

GOD. You will walk the length of the street known as the Corso. Do you know it?

SIDNEY. Yes. Yes. (*Sighs with relief.*) That's not a hard one.

GOD. You are to do it naked, Sidney.

SIDNEY. Eh? But it's over a mile that street and it's always jam-packed!

GOD (*a touch of Jehovah*). You heard me, Sidney.

SIDNEY. But . . . . . . but . . . . . I couldn't wear swimming-trunks, perhaps? I'm horrible when I'm stripped.

GOD. No, Sidney.

SIDNEY. But it's ridiculous! Why would you ask me to do such a stupid thing?

GOD. I move in a mysterious way, my wonders to perform, Sidney.

SIDNEY (*contrite*). Sorry, I was forgetting.

GOD. You know what you must do, Sidney?

SIDNEY (*miserably*). Yes.

GOD (*fading away*). Oh, Sidney . . .

SIDNEY. Humph?

GOD. Our secret, remember.

SIDNEY (*sighs*). You're the boss.

> *Exterior acoustic.*
>   *Sound of heavy rain on pavement.*
> *Unzipping, bundling up of clothes.*

SIDNEY. I hope you're watching this, God. Cos I'm not doing it
again whatever you do to me. Anyway, you'll be pleased to observe
that I've outsmarted you. It's 3 o'clock in the morning and there's
a rainstorm – not a soul about. I should make it to the other end,
no trouble.

> *Spank of SIDNEY's feet on the pavement. He hums snatches of
> 'Singing in the Rain' and occasionally chuckles with triumph as he
> hurries from doorway to doorway.*

> *He sneezes hugely, wetly.*

> *A car drives past. It peeps a tune.*

SIDNEY (*breathlessly, with sniffles*). They didn't see me, did they?
(*The car peeps again in the distance.*) No, I'm sure they didn't.
(*Anger breaking out.*) Why must all these shops leave their lights
blazing? (*Sneezes, then moans tearfully.*) I'm not even half way
yet.

WOMAN (*screams in horror*). Arrrrrrrrrrrrrhhhh!!!!

SIDNEY (*in a dither*). Don't worry, Madam, I'm not a pervert.

> *Sound of her feet running away. She screams again and blows a
> police-whistle.*

SIDNEY (*calls after, breezily*). I'm doing it for a bet, honest!

> *Sound of heavy feet approaching. Whistle still blowing.*

MAN (*in background*). Che cosa c'e'?

WOMAN (*in background*). Un uomo nudo!!! Un enorme uomo
nudo!!! Laggiu!!!

> *SIDNEY's feet spanking the pavement as he sprints away, wheezing
> heavily.*

MAN (*coming close, shouting*). Ehi, tu! Ehi! Ehi! Ippopotamo! (*A
wolf whistle, laughs hugely.*) Ippopotamo!

> *Fade laughter. Fade up interior acoustic.*

SIDNEY. Greg, old darling. They said I could stay for a few minutes.

GREG (*weakly*). Oh, Sidney, it's you. With the light behind you, you look just like Cardinal Ngoupande. If ever for any reason you need someone to rely on, go and see Cardinal Ngoupande. (*Sneezes.*)

SIDNEY. Bless you.

GREG. He's the most incorruptible man I know. He shall be the next Pope.

SIDNEY. Make him wait, eh?

GREG (*sneezes, blows his nose*). Come here, sit on the bed. I don't bite.

SIDNEY. What have you been doing to yourself, laddie?

GREG. Oh, oh, I don't know. I've caught a chill. (*Sniffs.*)

SIDNEY (*guilty*). I wonder how.

GREG. You all right?

SIDNEY. Yes. Yes.

GREG. I'd just got over that queasiness, and now this! Got to be careful, you see. There's a South American tour coming up. My first as Pontiff. Got to give them a good show. (*A huge wet sneeze.*) Well then, what shall we talk about?

SIDNEY (*with transparent clueless pretentiousness*). Errrrm . . . . . . how about the ontological argument.

GREG (*an excited, amazed sniff*). The ontological argument, Sidney?

SIDNEY (*pompously*). Yes. Yes. A special interest of mine.

GREG (*delighted and impressed*). I had no idea.

SIDNEY. Oh, I'm something of a theologian, in my own little way.

GREG (*bubbling over in Latin*). 'Aliquid quo nihil maius cogitari possit.'

SIDNEY. Uh?

GREG. Anselm. *The Proslogion.* Chapter two.

SIDNEY. Oh, that. Yes.

GREG (*bursting with excitement*). Do you find it a convincing proof? This is very interesting.

SIDNEY. A convincing proof? Well . . . to my mind – I was reading Farrar-Hockley on this subject just the other night – and I'd have to say, in all honesty . . . . . . yes . . . . . or rather: no.

GREG. Why's that, then?

SIDNEY (*desperate, drops his pomposity to reveal a more honest struggle*). Because. . . . I don't understand a word of it. (*Confused*.) If nothing can exist that is greater than the greatest thing that can possibly exist and God is the greatest thing that CAN possibly exist, then . . . . . errrrrrrm . . . . yes, well – (*Bluffs with a laugh*.) you're on to a winner, aren't you? (*Lost in confusion*.) I suppose.

GREG. So you are convinced?

SIDNEY. Hm? Ha! I should coco! (*Confused again*.) What? Well, He's there, anyway, isn't He, whatever they say?

GREG. You have a simple faith, Sidney.

SIDNEY (*worried*). Is that good or bad?

GREG (*tearfully*). It brings me great joy to see it, to feel it, little brother. (*Sneezes*.)

Pause.

SIDNEY. Greg?

GREG. Yes, Sidney.

SIDNEY. God does test us, doesn't He?

GREG. Yes. All the time.

SIDNEY. And if God asked me to do something, let's just say I thought He was asking me to do something for Him . . . . . I would have to do it, wouldn't I?

GREG. Yes.

SIDNEY. Even if I thought it was silly . . . . or wrong?

GREG. He knows best.

SIDNEY (*unsure*). I imagine so.

Plink-ploonk of bathroom.
   SIDNEY *splashing in the bath, singing and humming 'Jerusalem'. A tap drips slowly during the following scene.*

GOD (*suddenly, more hollow than previously, a faint echo*). Sidney!

SIDNEY (*calls*). Do you mind, I'm in the bath! Oh, it's you! I've had three hot baths today, trying to get rid of Greg's chill for him. He catches my colds, you know. Of course you do. (*Bravely*.) It's all your fault. I very nearly ended up in prison because of you!!!

GOD. Are you criticising me, Sidney?

SIDNEY. No, no. Didn't mean to come across impertinent. Sorry.

GOD. I forgive you, Sidney.

SIDNEY. Errrr, Lord. . . .

GOD. Yes, Sidney.

SIDNEY. I suppose you know your voice is coming out of the toilet.

GOD. Yes, Sidney.

SIDNEY (*mumbles*). None of my business.

GOD. I have a further test for you, Sidney.

SIDNEY. Not another one!

GOD. Yes, Sidney.

SIDNEY (*expecting the worst*). Go on, then – hit me.

GOD. You must have knowledge of the next woman you meet.

SIDNEY. Knowledge?

GOD. Do you understand me, Sidney?

SIDNEY (*tragic, terrified*). Yes, I think so. But I'm nearly sixty and I've never been much of a ladies' man. No one had seen me stripped in twenty years till the other night.

GOD. Will you obey me, Sidney?

SIDNEY (*muttering, helpless*). Yes, yes, if that's what you want, I'll try, I suppose. What if she won't?

GOD. She will be willing, Sidney.

SIDNEY. Cooo!

GOD. Goodbye, Sidney. (*Fading away.*) Our secret, remember.

SIDNEY (*in sudden panic, splashes as he stands up in the bath*). Wait! Wait! The next woman I see! That'll be Sister Bridget bringing me my morning cuppa! Not Sister Bridget! She's 300 years old! Her moustache is bushier than mineeeeeeeeeee! (*Huge splash as he falls back into the bath. A yelp.*)

The tinkle of the chimes at SIDNEY's *window.*
A knock.
No answer.
A more vigorous knock.

TARTUFARI. Colly! Are you locked in, Colly?

SIDNEY (*a rasping whisper, on the other side of the door*). I'm hiding.

TARTUFARI (*we have not heard him so cheerful*). Who from?

SIDNEY. Sister Bridget. She's not there, is she?

TARTUFARI. No.

SIDNEY. Sure?

TARTUFARI. I can't see her. Shall I fetch her for you?

SIDNEY. No! Tommy! No! No!

Click of door being unlocked, door eased open with a creak.

SIDNEY (*on our side of the door*). I've been hiding in here all night, just in case. I mustn't see Sister Bridget! I mustn't, you understand!!!

TARTUFARI (*jolly*). You and your games, Colly! Please, you must meet my sister. She has arrived from America today.

SIDNEY. Your sister? She's a woman, is she? Grown up and everything?

TARTUFARI. She is 23.

SIDNEY. But not a nun?

TARTUFARI (*finds this most amusing*). Noooooooooooo!

SIDNEY (*his voice quivering*). And very beautiful, am I right??

TARTUFARI. You hurry, get dressed, huh? and you shall see. We have coffee waiting for you in my room, okay?

SIDNEY (*horrified*). She's there now, is she?

TARTUFARI (*on his way*). She is waiting to meet you!

Dead quiet in the corridor, just SIDNEY's creaking footsteps.

SIDNEY (*whispers, to himself*). Next to the Botticelli, he said. Trouble is, I don't know a Botticelli from an egg sandwich. (*Sudden high anxiety.*) Ogh-O! Sister Bridget!!!

His creaking footsteps: fast.
Door opened and slammed in a hurry.
SIDNEY breathing heavily.

SIDNEY. Oh! Hello.

CLAUDIA (*trace of American in her good English*). Hello.

SIDNEY. Errrrr . . . . . Hello.

CLAUDIA (*amused*). Hello.

SIDNEY. Errrrr . . . . Good Morning.

CLAUDIA. Is something wrong?

SIDNEY. No. No. Just Sister Bridget. She was coming down the corridor. But I escaped.

CLAUDIA. Claudia Tartufari. Pleased to meet you.

SIDNEY. Charmed. (*Overexcited.*) Charmed!

CLAUDIA. I am sure we shall be great friends.

SIDNEY. I'm sure . . . . yes. (*A worried laugh.*)

CLAUDIA. Excuse me, but you are Mr Collyweston?

SIDNEY. Colly, please.

CLAUDIA. Tommaso said you were the Holy Father's TWIN brother.

SIDNEY. Yes, we are. I am.

CLAUDIA (*with the largesse of an experienced teaser*). But I was expecting an old man.

SIDNEY. Er . . . . aren't I?

CLAUDIA. You are teasing me, Mr Collyweston.

SIDNEY (*weakly*). Er . . . Colly.

CLAUDIA. I have coffee and biscuits, okay? Sit down, please.

SIDNEY. Thankyou, yes . . . . .

CLAUDIA. Comfortable?

SIDNEY (*said exactly as before*). Thankyou, yes . . . . . . Where's errrrrr . . . .

CLAUDIA. Tommaso was called away.

SIDNEY (*nervously, almost losing his voice*). Away?

CLAUDIA. A phone call. Just now. He sends his apologies. An important discovery in Spoleto. Some manuscripts.

SIDNEY. Oh?

CLAUDIA (*she pours coffee*). Proving one of his theories, he says.

SIDNEY (*accepting coffee*). Thankyou. (*In panic.*) He hasn't gone, has he?

CLAUDIA. To Spoleto. Yes. He'll be back in the morning.

SIDNEY (*despondently*). In the morning? Oh, dear.

CLAUDIA. I am to look after you.

SIDNEY (*more despondently*). Oh, dear.

CLAUDIA (*furious, puts down her coffee with an angry clatter*). Of course, if my company is so objectionable!!!

SIDNEY. No! No! You're lovely! Really! And very willing, I'm sure . . . . . or rather (*an embarrassed laugh*) you're nothing like a nun, are you?

CLAUDIA (*giggles*). What CAN you mean by that, Mr Collyweston?

SIDNEY (*loosening up a bit*). Actually, you are the first person who isn't a Pope or an Abbess or something that I've spoken to since I came here last month.

CLAUDIA. They are very stuffy, aren't they?

SIDNEY (*a sudden exuberance*). They don't know how to enjoy themselves!

CLAUDIA. But we do! Don't we?!

SIDNEY (*terrified*). What? Humph?

CLAUDIA. Know how to enjoy ourselves. Okay? Okay!!!

SIDNEY (*terrified, trying to be brave*). Yes. Yes! Ha! Ha! (*A miserable private groan.*)

Exterior acoustic: Borghese Gardens.
    They walk.

SIDNEY (*calmly, sincerely*). I can't remember when I've enjoyed a day so much. Thankyou, Claudia.

CLAUDIA. Are you teasing me again, Colly?

SIDNEY. No, no, I mean it. I feel young again. And I've a feeling that the best is yet to come. (*Bravely asking.*) Do you think so?

CLAUDIA. Sure. Why not? (*Laughs.*)

They continue walking in silence.

SIDNEY (*a big sniff of air*). It is very beautiful here.

CLAUDIA. The Borghese Gardens is my favourite place in all the World . . . . . .

SIDNEY. Did you come and play here as a child?

CLAUDIA (*curtly*). No! (*Suddenly serene again.*) Especially at this time of day, just as the sun is going down. Soon it will be dark. Do you love the night, Colly?

SIDNEY. You know, you are awfully like your brother. Same eyes, nose, everything. What you said just then: it could almost have been him! Now, Greg and I . . . . . .

CLAUDIA (*breaking away, stomping off ahead*). We are not at all alike!!!!

SIDNEY (*chasing*). Oh, but you are . . . . .

CLAUDIA (*stopping still, in a wild fury*). We are not alike! We are not!

SIDNEY. All right. So you're not. Who cares?

They set off walking again, in silence.

CLAUDIA (*a new, contemplative mood*). Tommaso, he is very changed since his operation. He is not the same man at all.

SIDNEY (*cautiously*). He seems much better, though, even in the short time I've known him.

CLAUDIA (*after a sob*). It is cruel!

SIDNEY. Cruel?

CLAUDIA. Colly. My brother cannot live much longer. Those tumours. They took some out, but his head is still full of them.

SIDNEY. Oh. No one said. He knows himself, does he?

CLAUDIA. Uh-huh.

SIDNEY. I'm very sorry, dear.

CLAUDIA (*tearfully*). Soon he will not be here for me to love.

SIDNEY. You never know. I'll speak to God about him – pray, I mean.

CLAUDIA (*sobbing*). I have so much love to give. I am bursting with love! (*Sniffing, getting control of herself.*) Colly?

They stop walking.

SIDNEY. Um?

CLAUDIA. Kiss me.

SIDNEY. I . . . . . um?

CLAUDIA. Please!

SIDNEY (*desperate for escape*). Don't you have any boyfriends your own age?

CLAUDIA. No.

SIDNEY. I'm terribly ugly, dear, you . . . . (*His mouth is blocked by her kiss.*)

A long kiss. Little grunts from SIDNEY.
When the kiss ends, breath bursts out of him as if he's been underwater for a week.

CLAUDIA (*covering his face with kisses*). Colly, Colly, Colly. I am so glad that you are here. You will never leave me, will you? Promise.

SIDNEY. Err . . . promise.

CLAUDIA (*joyful*). Does your heart beat faster?

SIDNEY (*delighted*). Yes. Oh, yes.

CLAUDIA. How much faster?

SIDNEY. As if I'd won the Derby. The horse, not the jockey.

They both laugh. Suddenly, a roller-skater zooms past, rattling heavily on the stone path.

SIDNEY. Yoooghhh! What was that?

CLAUDIA. It's just someone on his rolling-skates. I know what we can do!!!

SIDNEY (*worried*). What? What?

CLAUDIA (*runs away, calling as she goes*). I'll be right back! (*Calls in distance to skaters.*) Aspetta, per favore! Vorrei prendere in prestito i tuoi pattini a rotelle.

SIDNEY (*mutters to himself, while* CLAUDIA *is asking about the skates*). Oh, she's gorgeous! She's just too, too gorgeous. Oh, thankyou, Lord, thankyou for this one!

CLAUDIA (*running back, laughing*). Here we are, Colly! (*Spinning the wheels of a skate.*) Those men over there have kindly allowed us to borrow their skates.

SIDNEY. But I've never . . . what are you doing? (*Sound of skates being strapped on.*) Really, Claudia, sweetie, this isn't a good idea.

CLAUDIA. What big feet you have, Colly! (*Laughs with devilish wickedness.*) There! Just hold on to the lamp-post while I put mine on.

Sound of roller-skates uneasily keeping their balance.

SIDNEY (*losing his balance*). Oooooohh!

CLAUDIA (*loving it*). All ready!

SIDNEY. I'm not moving! I'm staying right here!

CLAUDIA. Give me your hands, Colly. You want to be my hero, don't you?

SIDNEY. You'll not let go of me?

They skate slowly: she perfectly, he dangerously.

CLAUDIA. Okay?

SIDNEY (*triumphant*). Ha! Ha! Wonderful! It's like flying! Ha! Ha! (*Suddenly worried, further away.*) I said don't let go. (*Further away, his skates get faster.*) Claudia! (*Faster still, further and further away.*) Claudiaaaaa!

CLAUDIA (*closer to us, in hysterics as* SIDNEY *sails away, applauding.*)

SIDNEY (*in distance*). Helpppppppppppp!

A huge crashing clatter.
A cry from SIDNEY.

SIDNEY's *bedroom.*
Sinatra sings 'Heaven, I'm in Heaven!' in the background.

SIDNEY (*close*). Good job that ice-cream cart was in the way. I'd have gone right down those steps.

CLAUDIA (*kissing him, close*). My hero.

SIDNEY. Do you know, 400 Popes have died in this bed.

CLAUDIA. And what else, I wonder? (*Giggles.*)

SIDNEY. Little minx! (*They kiss,* SIDNEY *comes up breathless.*) Oooooooo! Didn't do badly, did I?

CLAUDIA. Wanna try again?

SIDNEY. Don't think I could, dear. (*She changes his opinion.*) Cor! Ooooooo!

CLAUDIA. Colly?

SIDNEY (*concentrating on his kissing*). Um?

CLAUDIA. Do you know why people hate the Jews?

SIDNEY (*can't believe he's heard right*). Um?

CLAUDIA. Because God is a Jew.

SIDNEY (*absently, while nuzzling*). God's English. I happen to know.

CLAUDIA. We are right to hate the Jews because we all of us hate God our Heavenly Father. Everyone hates their father, earthly, Heavenly . . . .It's all in Freud if you look . . . .

SIDNEY. I say, this is hardly the time . . . . . OH, I see! I can talk about the ontological argument if you like, if that's what gets you going?

CLAUDIA (*laughs wildly*).

SIDNEY (*suddenly anxious*). Shhhhhhhhhhhhhh! Shhhhhhhhh! (*Holds her mouth. She giggles gagged. He whispers.*) There's someone in the living room.

CLAUDIA *continues to giggle gagged.*
SIDNEY *listens. Just Sinatra.*
Then the needle is lifted off the record.

GREG (*after a moment, from living room*). Sidney. Sidney.

SIDNEY (*whispers*). Oh, God! It's my brother! Please be quiet, girl!

She giggles more, kicks the blankets.

SIDNEY. Shhhhh!

Door opens.

GREG (*approaching, innocently*). Sidney! There you are! We missed you at dinner tonight. You're in bed very early. Are you feeling well? You must be! I've never felt better in my whole life! It's having you here, I'm sure. Some palpitations earlier . . . but now I feel all alive and tingly! (*One of CLAUDIA's giggles escapes. GREG is perturbed, unbelieving.*) Sidney?!

SIDNEY. Look, old darling, why don't you go and pour yourself a lemonade. I'll just get dressed. (*A rasping whisper to the giggling, kicking CLAUDIA.*) Shhhh, girl! Lie still!

CLAUDIA (*all her giggles escape, she pummels the bed with her kicks*). Wheeeeeeeeeeeeeeeee! Whooooooooooooooooooooo!

GREG (*in profoundest disappointment*). Oh, Sidney. Sidney. This is an evil thing you have done. Who is the girl?

SIDNEY (*introduces as if at a fête*). Claudia – cover yourself up, will you! – this is my brother Gregory . . . the sixteenth.

GREG. Seventeenth.

SIDNEY. Greg, this is Claudia . . . (*With reddest shame.*) . . . Father Tartufari's sister.

GREG (*the wind knocked out of him*). Ohhhhhhhhhh! (*In tears.*) I can see I have been mistaken about you, Sidney. . . . (*On his way.*) . . . about everything. (*Slams door.*)

SIDNEY (*chasing after, opens door*). Greg! Greg! (*In despair.*) Oh, Greg! (*Calls after angrily.*) I never vowed to be celibate, did

I? If you'd had the decency to make me a Bishop it might've been different! (*Stomping back*.) Damn! Damn-damn-damn!

CLAUDIA (*in background, still laughing*). Meeeeeeeeeeeeeow! Meeeeeeeeeeeeeeow!

SIDNEY (*furious*). For God's sake, *SHUT UP!*

Fade up SIDNEY *snoring*.

SIDNEY (*in his sleep, between snores*). Claudia! Claudia!

GOD. Sidney. Sidney.

SIDNEY (*his snores phutter out like a dying motor-boat*). Ufhg?

GOD. Sidney.

SIDNEY. I shouldn't talk to you at all.

GOD. Come, come, Sidney.

SIDNEY. Fiddling with a chap's feelings! They've sent her back to America.

GOD. I am sorry, Sidney.

SIDNEY. I'll bet! A proper old fool I've made of myself . . . . with your Holy help. Greg's gone all Catholic on me – wouldn't speak to me for three days, now he's nicer than ever but with that hurt look in his eyes. And he's ill! My broken heart is making him ill. And Sister Bridget is behaving very oddly! I'm sure she's putting stuff in my morning coffee, that stuff they gave us in the army, to stop us thinking of women. And Tommy . . . . poor Tommy. – Look, about Father Tartufari. May I ask a favour . . . . I mean, I've done plenty for you, old darling. You couldn't magic away his tumours, could you? His head's full of them, I'm told.

GOD. Very well, Sidney. They are gone.

SIDNEY. What! Just like that! Gone!

GOD. Gone, Sidney.

SIDNEY. I say, you are a marvel!

GOD. I am what I am, Sidney.

SIDNEY (*in delight*). Ha! Haaaaaaaaaa!

GOD. There is a final test, Sidney. One more test.

SIDNEY. All right. Fire away. I'm game!

GOD. If you are successful in this, Sidney, then everything shall be yours, all that I have planned for you in my Great Design.

SIDNEY. Go on. Go on.

GOD. I wish you to kill Father Tartufari.

SIDNEY. Ugh?

GOD. You heard me, Sidney.

SIDNEY (*hopeful*). No, I heard it wrong.

GOD. I said that I wish you to kill Father Tartufari.

SIDNEY. But how can you ask me such a thing!!! I mean, you saved his life just a moment ago and now . . . . it's too horrible. No. I won't do it!

GOD. The whole world shall be yours, Sidney, if you will do this for me. You will never die. Constant joy shall be yours.

SIDNEY. No. No.

GOD. Everything a man could want, Sidney. A great house on the Berkshire Downs, stables full of the fleetest horses . . .

SIDNEY. Claudia?

GOD. Claudia, Sidney. (*Pause.*) Well, Sidney?

SIDNEY (*anxious, frightened*). I don't know.

GOD (*losing his usual calm*). My plans for everyone depend on this, Sidney. A world without pain! Without illness! A world without malice or trickery! (*Rasps.*) It will be certain eternal happiness for everyone in the world if you will only kill Tartufari. (*Pause.*) Sidney?

SIDNEY (*weakly*). All right, then. You know best.

GOD (*fading away*). Thankyou, thank you, Sidney. Goodnight, Sidney.

Sudden acoustic of a restaurant. Buzz of diners. SIDNEY *and* TARTUFARI *celebrating: loud drunken laughter.*

SIDNEY. Sandro! Another bottle, laddie! (*Close.*) You sure he's never been a bookmaker in Taunton?

WAITER. I have never.

Pop of cork, wine being poured.

TARTUFARI (*whoozy*). I can't drink any more, Colly. Please, okay.

SIDNEY. But we must celebrate, Tommy lad. (*Conspiratorially.*) Sandro! Come here! Tell Sandro, go on.

TARTUFARI (*shyly, to* SANDRO). I was ill, now I am well. (*Hugely, to whole restaurant.*) I was dying, now I am cured!!! I was lost, but now I am found!!!

Scattered applause from diners.

SIDNEY (*by himself, sings*). 'For he's a jolly good fellow . . . la . . . la . . . lala . . . la . . . laar . . . la.'

TARTUFARI (*taking a bow*). Thankyou. Thankyou. Thankyou one and all.

TARTUFARI *flops back in his seat, rattling everything. He laughs with delight, then hiccups.*

SIDNEY. To miracles!

Clink of glasses.

TARTUFARI (*awestruck*). It really is a miracle, Colly. The doctors, they X-ray me twice. They cannot believe what they see. One was disappointed – an atheist, I think.

SIDNEY. Serves him right!

TARTUFARI (*with deep affection*). You know, somehow, my fat English friend, I think I am owing it all to you.

SIDNEY. Tosh! . . . . . Have another green thing! I've had twelve already! Unless it was the same one twelve times.

Quick fade on hilarious laughter.

The late-night streets of Rome.
   The approach of staggering footsteps.

SIDNEY (*in distance, approaching, sings*). 'Just one Cornetto . . . save it for meeeeeee . . . delicious ice-cream . . . from Italeeeeeeeeeeeeeeeeeeeeeee.'

TARTUFARI (*running towards us and away again. To the Heavens*). God he is in his Heaven – everything it is right with the world!!!! (*Laughs, falls over, close.*) Oooops! (*Laughs.*)

SIDNEY. Steady on, old lad. (*A drunken giggle, a raspberry, more laughter, sudden alcoholic seriousness.*) Your sister – lovely woman.

TARTUFARI. Beautiful!

SIDNEY (*weepy*). I miss her so much.

TARTUFARI (*staggering away*). I go get her for you.

SIDNEY (*staggering after*). No, no, lad. She's in America. At University. She went back. Remember.

TARTUFARI (*in massive disappointment*). Oooooooooooooooooooh! (*A sudden idea.*) We go! Now! To America! You carry me, okay?

SIDNEY. Climb onboard!

Grunts of effort as SIDNEY *gives* TARTUFARI *a piggyback.*

TARTUFARI. I shall be handsome again. My hair will grow long and black. I will be fat, just like you – monstrously fat I shall be! Okay?

SIDNEY. Okay!

Immediately as SIDNEY *says 'Okay', he trips; sound of whump on to pavement and into bushes.*

TARTUFARI (*comes up laughing, suddenly anxious*). Colly! Colly!

Pause.
       Moan of SIDNEY.
       Rustle of bushes as TARTUFARI *goes to find him.*

TARTUFARI. Hello, old darling! What you doing down there?

SIDNEY (*close, distraught*). You're my friend, aren't you, Tommy? I wouldn't hurt you – you know that. You'll understand. Eh, sweetie?

       Corridor in Vatican.
       SIDNEY *and* TARTUFARI *giggling.*

SIDNEY. Shhhhhhhhhhhhhhh! We'll wake up Sister Bridget!

TARTUFARI (*yells*). Sister Bridget!!!! Yoooooo-hoooooooo!

SIDNEY. Shhhhhhhhhhh!

They fumblingly open a door.

TARTUFARI (*desperately anxious*). Colly! One of my feet has come off.

SIDNEY. That's a shoe. There's no foot in it.

TARTUFARI. Must have been all those X-rays. That doctor, he hated me, I could tell.

SIDNEY. Up we come, little fella. Uncle Colly will carry you to beddy-byes.

Giggles from TARTUFARI *as he is lifted.*
       Things knocked off the furniture.
       Whump of TARTUFARI *being flung on to bed, moan of bedsprings.*

SIDNEY (*in confessional, close, cold, slow*). I don't know how I did it. Except to say that I thought it might be like in the Bible, where whatsisname is told to kill his kiddie and he's about to do for him when God suddenly says don't bother. My heart was banging in my ears, sobering me up, bang after bang. I put the pillow over his face . . . and sat on it. I didn't think he'd move at all, he was so sloshed.

TARTUFARI *resisting, screaming under the pillow.*

SIDNEY (*in bedroom, weeping*). Don't worry, dearest old darling. It'll be all over soon. They'll be waiting for you – the Popes and Saint Francis and all that crowd. They'll explain. You'll not hate old Colly, not then, not then.

TARTUFARI's *screams are weaker and weaker, they stop.*

SIDNEY (*in confessional*). When I took the pillow off him it was the most hateful expression I'd ever seen on a man's face – far worse than Dickie Pymlott's when he lost all his dosh on the Oaks and waddled off to the bog with a razor-blade. I couldn't look. I found myself staring at the record-rack beside his lovely hi-fi and thinking . . . he'll never hear Frank Sinatra again, poor dear.
     Then I dashed back to my own room to be sick.

Sound of aeroplane on runway. Engines starting.

SIDNEY (*approaching down aisle*). Buon giorno. Buona sera. Buon giorno. Buona sera. (*Nervously.*) Hiya, Greg! Still invited, am I?

GREG (*vexed*). Sidney! Where have you been?

SIDNEY (*plomps in his seat, worried*). Look, Greg – I've never actually, as such, been up in one of these things before. I'm awfully scared.

GREG. So that's what it is! I spent all night hanging over my sink. I thought you'd been on a binge, Sidney, but it seems I have misjudged you.

SIDNEY. Sorry?

GREG. No, it's not your fault. I can see you are frightened. You have been very brave coming here today. Come now, strap yourself in.

SIDNEY (*struggling with seatbelt*). It doesn't reach.

GREG (*whispers*). My heart too – they would have made me cancel the trip if I'd told them – it was beating in my ears all night.

Engine noise intensifies.

SIDNEY (*in panic*). It moved!

GREG. Calm yourself, Sidney! You'll soon get used to it. In South America we'll be doing heaps of flying.

SIDNEY. Heaps?!

GREG (*shuffling papers*). Will you read one of my speeches for me and tell me what you think? We're not going to be sick again, are we?

SIDNEY. No. I've been silly. Nothing can happen to me. He promised.

GREG. A barley-sugar, Sidney, for the takeoff. Your ears.

SIDNEY. What?

GREG. Who promised?

SIDNEY (*sweet in mouth*). He'll not mind if I tell you. Not now.

GREG. Who's this, Sidney?

SIDNEY (*through sweet*) God. Jesus. Him. He's been speaking to me.

GREG (*hopeful*). Sidney?

SIDNEY. He has plans for me, important plans: a chapter in the Bible, all to myself. I've been undergoing a series of tests, you understand. That's why I had that nookie with . . . (*Voice lowered in shame.*) . . . Father Tartufari's sister. HE told me to.

GREG (*between suspicion and anger*). HE told you to.

SIDNEY. God did. As a test.

GREG (*angry*). I see.

SIDNEY. Other things, too. That chocolate business and . . .

GREG. Your sense of humour defeats me, Sidney. I had hoped that Father Tartufari's company might have brought some gravity to your behaviour. (*Calling over the seat.*) Where is Father Tartufari? Oh, look, there he is. He's missed the plane.

SIDNEY. Um? No, that's not him.

GREG. Yes it is.

SIDNEY. No.

GREG. Look. That's Sister Bridget with him. Wave, Sidney, wave.

SIDNEY (*in absolute utter horror*). Ugh! Ugh! (*On his feet, scrambling.*) We must stop the plane!!!!

GREG. It's too late, Sidney. Sit down.

SIDNEY. We must! We must!

GREG. The Father will get another plane.

SIDNEY (*mad*). You don't understand! Let me off this thing! Help!!!!!!!

Whooooosh of aeroplane taking off, leading straight into 'La Cucaracha'.

Fade music into multitudes hailing the Pope.

JUNTA GENERAL (*voice raised over noise of cheering*). Is wonderful, no?

SIDNEY (*voice raised*). Sorry?

JUNTA GENERAL. Our Pope. He makes the people so happy. Look at all the big smiles. I am most happy of all. Today, everyone he is here: the revolutionaries they come down from the mountains, my men they catch them.

SIDNEY. Which General are you? Are you the one who hangs people upside-down over hot coals? Or are you the one who buries them in a bag full of mongeese?

JUNTA GENERAL. No, that's not me! Hot coals is this General here.

SIDNEY. Er . . . how-do-you-do.

JUNTA GENERAL. Mongeese: that's him standing next to the Pope.

SIDNEY. They look such gentle souls.

JUNTA GENERAL. Ha! Ha! I joke you! Big joke, huh? We have nothing bad like that here. Everyone happy here, all the time. Hey, where you Bishop of?

SIDNEY. Aintree.

JUNTA GENERAL. Where that?

SIDNEY. It's on the moon. (*In dithering panic.*) Excuse me, I've just seen someone I know.

Huge cheers from multitude while SIDNEY *pushes his way through the throng.*

SIDNEY (*calling*). Tommy! Tommy, it's me!

TARTUFARI (*close*). Hello, Colly.

SIDNEY (*voice raised over the noise, blankly*). Tommy, old lad. All right, are you?

TARTUFARI. Marvellous, isn't it? I've never seen so many people. Not even in Saint Peter's Square.

SIDNEY (*trying to be his old self*). It's like coming home with a National winner.

TARTUFARI. I can't hear you!

A huge cheer.

TARTUFARI. That was quite a celebration we had!

SIDNEY. I don't remember a thing! Sorry!

TARTUFARI. Me neither. We weren't too naughty I hope?

SIDNEY. Don't fret yourself – I rubbed the moustaches off the Botticelli.

TARTUFARI (*doesn't hear, then suddenly gets the joke*). Sorry? Oh! Ha! Ha!

Pause.

SIDNEY. What did Claudia say?

TARTUFARI. Who?

SIDNEY. Claudia.

TARTUFARI. Sorry?

SIDNEY. Your sister, you nit, when you told her the good news . . . about you being better.

TARTUFARI. Oh! She was pleased.

SIDNEY. She loves you very much. You are very lucky.

A gigantic cheer.

Fade cheering under SIDNEY's *speech:*

SIDNEY (*in confessional*). He gave me a conceited little wink. Something about that wink shocked me – I don't know if Claudia had winked like that, or maybe it suggested that they were more than just brother and sister, that he'd done to her what I did with her. I hated him for that wink . . . . and hated him because he had the impertinence to be alive when I'd gone to all the pain and trouble of killing him. But he wasn't going to get away with it! I decided there and then, under that statue of Simon Bolivar, that I'd finish my job on him the next chance I got.

Interior acoustic.
    Drifting in from outside: sounds of festivities. Music, shouting and fire crackers.

We were staying in the Presidential Palace, full of pictures of the dreadful man . . . . and everywhere those vicious little soldiers, armed to the teeth. Tartufari and myself had rooms on the same floor. With a soldier on guard every few yards, sitting in a chair. Greg was feeling off, so he wouldn't let me eat any of the feast in case I made him ill, you see. And I can't abide speeches, especially in Spanish. So I went upstairs with a bottle and a coconut to watch the festivities from my balcony. Now, all the titchy soldiers, in all the titchy chairs, were fast asleep.

Snoring of soldiers in background.

I went up to the one who was snoring the loudest, unbuttoned his holster, took the gun out and went up to Tartufari's door. I put my bottle and my coconut down and went in.

Acoustic of TARTUFARI's *room. Pause.* SIDNEY *is awestruck.*

There was a breeze. The white curtain filled the room like a sail. Tartufari was suffering from the jet-lag – he'd been there since 5, was all scrunched up, with the pillow over his head to keep out the noise of the festivities. I was quite cold. My heart was hardly beating at all.

Pause. Raise sound of festivities.

I waited for some particularly loud firecrackers to pop. Then I shot him.

Loud firecrackers with six louder gunshots.

I put the gun back in its place and spent half an hour in my room trying to open the coconut. I was rather pleased with myself: I'd been James Bondish . . . and I'd done God's will. Then the telephone rang. It was Cardinal Wozzywinski saying that Greg was feeling poorly and wanted to speak to me. So I went down. I stole a soldier's hat on the way – I thought it might amuse Greg. Our dad had beaten hell out of him when he wouldn't join the army, you know.

I knocked on the door and they were a long time in answering it. I was about to naff off when it opened. It was Tartufari.

TARTUFARI. Colly, at last! The Holy Father has had a heart attack. A mild one. He is okay now.

SIDNEY *screams.*

SIDNEY (*over the end of the scream*). I bolted the gate, old darling! I ran like five Red Rums sewn together. Don't know where I got the energy from! I was halfway down a massive stairway when I ran into El Presidente and all his Generals coming up. Skittled the lot. So then I hightailed it back to my room, sucked my bottle for a bit and took things out on the coconut. But of course there was Tartufari's room – I'd forgotten all about that. And it was HIS room, I knew, definitely HIS room. I went back in.

Acoustic of TARTUFARI's *room.*
  Small sounds of festivities from outside.

The breeze had died down. It was very hot. I turned on the bedside light and all the lights in the room came on. My old mate Pyjamas was in the bed, full of holes, bloodified, wearing the yellow silk pyjamas I'd bought him in Rome.

SIDNEY (*in room*). Pyjamas?

PYJAMAS (*weakly*). Thanks for the jarmas, Colly. Handsome.

SIDNEY. But . . . . but . . . how'd you get here, you silly thing. This is South America, you know?

PYJAMAS (*more weakly*). I'll be late for the dogs. (*Expires with a sigh.*)

SIDNEY (*lost, frantic*). Pyjamas! Pyjamas! No! This makes no sense at all! Pyjamas! Pyjamas!

Fade with SIDNEY *shouting.*

SIDNEY (*in confessional, sadly*). The shock went straight through me into Greg. It made his mild heart attack into a massive one. They had to call off the rest of the tour, as you know. We came home. They wouldn't let me see him. I was in a daze. I found some chocky bars in a drawer: scoffed the lot. Then I fell asleep. It was dark when I woke up.

GOD. Sidney. Sidney.

SIDNEY (*in confessional*). But I didn't answer that time. I'd been having thoughts. I got up and walked into the living-room. Little green lights suddenly went up and down on the hi-fi.

GOD (*hollow-sounding, from bedroom in background*). Sidney. Sidney?

SIDNEY. I walked down the corridor, past the Botticelli, and like a mad horse I kicked open the door. Tartufari was sitting in front of his hi-fi, headphones over his fluffy hair, microphone in his hand.

TARTUFARI (GOD'*s voice, with us and echoing through the hi-fi*). Good evening, Sidney. Any requests? (*Sings.*) 'I did it my way . . .'

SIDNEY. YOU!!! (*Slaps microphone out of* TARTUFARI'*s hands. It plonks and fizzes. In an unbelieving, confused fury.*) You mean there's no God? Never has been!

TARTUFARI (*his own voice mixed with* GOD'*s*). No, Sidney.

SIDNEY. You little bastard! You filthy, slimy cheat. It was you all the time.

TARTUFARI. That's right, Sidney. (*Laughs.*)

SIDNEY. The chocolate, the streak, the sex with Claudia, killing you. It was all to get at Greg through me.

TARTUFARI. The penny, it has dropped.

SIDNEY. I worked it out in South America, actually. But I couldn't get myself to admit I'd been such a fool . . . and it didn't quite add up. Still doesn't. About Pyjamas . . . how did you? . . .

TARTUFARI. I thought you said you had worked it all out, Sidney.

SIDNEY (*furious*). How can you hate Greg so much? He's the finest man who ever breathed! What can he have done to make you hate him so much?!!

TARTUFARI (*extra calm*). I want to be Pope, Sidney.

SIDNEY. You've as much chance of being elected Pope as I have!

TARTUFARI. That's where you are wrong, Sidney.

SIDNEY. You're not even a Cardinal.

TARTUFARI (*chuckles*).

SIDNEY. You're mad. It was those brain tumours you had, they made you do it. No, I'm forgetting, you've still got them, haven't you? (*In triumph.*) Good! Good! Hah! (*In sudden panic.*) Oh . . . look, there's not the remotest chance that Claudia was in on this. She wasn't, was she?

TARTUFARI. Who's Claudia?

SIDNEY. Your sister, damn you!!!

TARTUFARI. But I have no sister, Sidney.

SIDNEY. Uh?

CLAUDIA (*a wicked, teasing voice*). I am so glad that you are here, Colly. Promise me you will never leave me.

SIDNEY (*in confessional*). You won't believe this, but he changed . . . right in front of my eyes, into Claudia . . . stark naked, flowers in her hair, so beautiful, blowing kisses. I wanted to hold her . . . before it dawned. I never ever did see them together, in one place. I should have guessed something was dodgy.

CLAUDIA. Pity about that ice-cream cart, old darling. Or you would have gone bumpity-bumpity-bumpity, all the way down those steps!

SIDNEY (*in confessional*). Then he was Pyjamas, drenched in blood, dancing with . . . what are those things . . . castanets . . .

PYJAMAS (*dancing, maracas on the go*). Hiya, Colly, mate! Wanna sure thing? I'll tell you a sure thing! Next Pope! Come here and I'll whisper . . . (*Laughs.*)

SIDNEY. You're not Pyjamas, you devil! Pyjamas is dead! Or is he? I don't know. Is he?

TARTUFARI (*a high cackling laughter*).

SIDNEY (*low, determined, fierce*). I'll kill you properly this time.

A Manichaean struggle.
    SIDNEY *has* TARTUFARI *by the throat.* TARTUFARI *rasps and hisses, occasionally guffaws horribly. The hi-fi is set going. Sinatra sings 'Fly Me to the Moon', echoing down the corridors, but it is shoved and the needle bounces on to another song. It is shoved again, bounces to the end where it rests and crackles.*

SIDNEY (*in confessional,* TARTUFARI'*s mania in background, rising all the time, with* SIDNEY *shouting over it*). I had him by the neck, was pulling his new hair out in great greasy lumps. But suddenly he wasn't there. He was hanging off a picture on the other side of the room. I'm not sure, but he may even have been in the picture, running through classical ruins like a diabolical Charlie Chaplin. Then he burst out and was all over the room, running over everything, through everything, squeaking and yelling, like a bat, like a clockwork bat. (*Bring up* TARTUFARI'*s mania.*) Around and around. I was dizzy. My mouth was full of chocolate. He was on all sides at once. I swiped and swiped, hit him and hit him, knockout punches they were, but the room was full of him, dozens of him, and Claudia, striking disgusting poses, and then horses, everywhere horses, coming around bends and jumping over me, boxing my ears with their hooves. And Tartufari was riding them all with a huge mad face and purple-hot horns all over his head. He scooped me up, I was drenched in chocolate, and flung me over the horse, like a body that a Sheriff brings into town, and the horse rose up and dived through the window.

Huge crash of glass.
    Mad neigh of horse.

SIDNEY (*on horse, yells, going far away fast*). Sister Bridgettttttt!!!!!!

Silence . . . .

SIDNEY (*in confessional, calmly now*). Next thing, I was falling. High in the sky with all of Rome below me. I could see Tartufari, on his horse, on the top of Saint Peter's, laughing his head off, waving like an old friend. I landed on the Palatine Hill, just behind the Colosseum, in a big pool of runny chocolate. Not a scratch on me, just chocolate. (*Pause.*) Since then I've been wandering about . . . and looking for you. (*Suddenly overcome.*) It's been Hell, really it has. Cars keep veering off at me. I keep finding scorpions in my pockets. That's a horrible thing now, isn't it? He's determined to get me. Absolutely determined, he is. But you'll help, won't you, Cardinal Ngoupande. You'll tell me what to do. Exorcise Tartufari. Can we do that?

CARDINAL NGOUPANDE. You are a very foolish man, Sidney.

SIDNEY. I know. I know.

CARDINAL NGOUPANDE. A question?

SIDNEY. Anything.

CARDINAL NGOUPANDE. Is there some common denominator to his disguises. I mean, would you recognise him?

SIDNEY (*boasts largely*). Oh, yes. Now I'm wise to it. He's tried dozens of disguises these past few days. No, he'll not fool me again.

CARDINAL NGOUPANDE (*a slow satisfied sinister chuckle*).

Choir singing in background.

SIDNEY (*exhausted, tearful*). That ontological-theological argument thing. I can't stop myself thinking about it. I mean, if God's so great how can he allow Tartufari to do this to me? I've been good, lately, a saint. I did everything I was told . . . . . I shouldn't have, should I, that's the heart of it, not when there's only evil in the world. Of course, Cardinal Ngoupande, you'll say that if there's Paradise to come . . . . a little toothache now, who can complain? But I'm a little plastic duck in a boiling ocean and it's never going to be any different, is it? And when I persuade myself that I haven't actually been talking to God Himself these past weeks, I feel so empty that I call out to Him in such a big prayer . . . . but . . . . . well . . . . of course.

   Is there somewhere I can rest? I feel suddenly light. As if I'm not myself anymore. I feel awful. My nose is stuffed up. I've never had a cold before! Ooh, and my joints.

CARDINAL NGOUPANDE. I know what it is, Sidney.

SIDNEY. New strain going around, is there?

CARDINAL NGOUPANDE. Your brother has just died, Sidney.

SIDNEY. Died?

CARDINAL NGOUPANDE. Moments ago. It will be announced soon.

SIDNEY. His heart, I suppose.

CARDINAL NGOUPANDE. Actually, the result of a fall some days previously, from a great height, although it seems he never left his apartments. All his bones broken, every last one, and dying slowly . . . until moments ago.

SIDNEY (*with hope and dread*). Hold on . . . moments ago? You said moments ago. How can you know he died moments ago? You've been in here with me.

TARTUFARI (*close*). Here, there, everywhere, Sidney.

SIDNEY (*while bolting from confessional*). Oh, God!

> TARTUFARI *laughs, hugely, filling the cathedral. His laugh becomes* CARDINAL NGOUPANDE's *laugh. Then* CLAUDIA's *laugh. Then all at once.*

> *Fade down laughter, fade up* SIDNEY's *footsteps in the crypt of the cathedral. He is breathless.* TARTUFARI's *laughter is heard faintly in distance.* SIDNEY *stops, wheezing, getting his breath back. Suddenly, a faint angelic hum.*

GREG (*a brighter, younger* GREG). Sid! Sid!

SIDNEY (*hushed*). Greg? That really you? No tricks.

GREG. It's me, Sid!

SIDNEY. I can't see you. Where are you?

GREG. Gone, Sid.

SIDNEY. Gone?

GREG. Gone. Do you remember that tree-house we had, little brother?

SIDNEY. Look – he's after me. What shall I do?

GREG. That's where I am, the tree-house. All our comics are still here. Come on up, Sidney!

SIDNEY. No! No! I don't want to be dead.

GREG. I can see for miles. Dad and Mam are in the garden. Auntie Betty is at the kitchen window. She's baking, Sid – we can have some later.

SIDNEY (*in overblown righteous fury*). You sent me to Cardinal Ngoupande, you great nit!!! But he's Tartufari! Everybody might be Tartufari for all I know!!! You know what he did to us, don't you? You know what's happened here!?!

GREG. It doesn't matter, Sidney. (*Fondly.*) Hurry along, lad. Hurry along.

> *A lake, somewhere in Northern Italy.*
> *Gulls shrieking near and far.*
> *Sound of oars in water: three slow strokes.*

SIDNEY (*tired from rowing*). This nunnery of yours, Sister Bridget. They'll take me in, will they? . . . . . They will! Even though I'm not a woman? They'll not snip anything off? . . . . . Good! And we'll be safe? Really safe?

Three more pulls of the oars.

(*Wistfully.*) Will I ever see another outsider romp home, d'yer think? Hm? Hm? You must have been to at least one of the Irish courses when you were a girl. Eh? Eh? (*Fed up.*) I say, this would have been a lot easier if you hadn't taken that vow of silence.

SISTER BRIDGET (*very Irish, snaps*). Shut your blather and put your back into it!

Rowing slightly quicker, grunts from SIDNEY.
  Cries of the gulls, near and far.
  A bell tolls in the distance.
  Huge cry of a gull, close.

The bell tolls.

Amen.